ON THE O
SUPERH

T0119786

ON THE ORIGIN OF
SUPERHEROES

FROM THE BIG BANG TO
ACTION COMICS NO. 1

CHRIS GAVALER

UNIVERSITY OF IOWA PRESS ⚡ IOWA CITY

University of Iowa Press, Iowa City 52242

Copyright © 2015 by the University of Iowa Press

www.uiowapress.org

Printed in the United States of America

Design by April Leidig

No part of this book may be reproduced or used in any form or by any
means without permission in writing from the publisher. All reasonable
steps have been taken to contact copyright holders of material
used in this book. The publisher would be pleased to make suitable
arrangements with any whom it has not been possible to reach.

The University of Iowa Press is a member of Green Press Initiative
and is committed to preserving natural resources.

Printed on acid-free paper

Library of Congress Cataloging-in-Publication Data

Gavaler, Chris.

On the origin of superheroes : from the big bang

to Action Comics no. 1 / Chris Gavaler.

pages cm

Includes bibliographical references and index.

ISBN 978-1-60938-381-7 (pbk)

ISBN 978-1-60938-382-4 (ebk)

1. Heroes in literature. 2. Superheroes in literature. 3. Heroic virtue.

4. Heroes—History. 5. Heroes—Mythology. I. Title.

PN56.5.H45G38   2015

809'.93352—dc23   2015008647

To John Gavaler

CONTENTS

Bill's a highbrow with a lot of college degrees.
I reckon he's smart in some ways; but his being too
snooty to read the comic strips is just plain silly. How can
he teach history like it was important if he feels above
the history we're makin'? Folks that dig up our
civilization are going to learn more about us
from our comic strips than by looking at ruins.

✦ ✦ ✦

Aunt Het, a single-panel comic strip
written by Robert Quillen, c. 1930s

Cameron and Madeleine Gavaler, 2002.

ORIGIN STORY

What do you want to be when you grow up?

My daughter has been fielding that question since she was two. She's headed to college now, so the question has morphed into "What do you want to major in?" But she told me that her answer, her secret answer, the heart of hearts answer she'll never write on any application form, hasn't changed since she wore pull-ups:

"Batman."

That's still the first word that pops into her head. "Astronaut" is second. But "Batman" is better. "He doesn't have X-ray vision or any other crazy powers," she says, "but he still spends his life and money helping people." He's a bad-ass altruist. Also the Batmobile is really cool. And his ears. My daughter has always thought the bat ears on his hood were cute. She used to chew on them. The dolls in our attic are gouged with her teeth marks.

A field of graduate and undergraduate classes in comics studies has popped up since she stopped hosting tea parties with action figures, but to the best of my knowledge, no school offers a major in Batman — not even mine. We live a five-minute stroll from the campus where I teach, so my daughter would rather blast off to an alien planet than stay in our Virginia smallville for college. Her brother is finishing middle school and still peruses the occasional comic book from my childhood trove. He's gnawed on his fair share of attic superheroes, but I'm sure he'll be feeling the warmth of alien suns soon too.

Which means neither will get to take my course. It spawned in 2008 when a group of honors students were scouring campus for a professor willing to design and teach a seminar on superheroes. They'd suffered a few rounds of blank stares and grinning rejections when they wandered into my wife's office. She was chairing our English department at the time, and you'll never guess whose office she sent them to next. I said yes. Of course I said yes. I'd always enjoyed comics as a kid and then with our own kids. Now I'd just augment that with a bit of research.

My wife says she doesn't regret her choice, but neither of us predicted the black hole–sized obsession the topic would open in me. Conference panels, print symposiums, international journals, radio interviews, cybercasts, newspaper op-eds, lit mags, one-act play festivals — my appetite for cape-and-mask forums keeps expanding. When my wife and another good friend spurred me to start a blog, neither had superheroes in mind then either. I could blame those meddling honors students, but that first class of sidekicks flew off to solo adventures years ago. I'm the one who keeps offering revised versions of the course every spring term while posting my weekly blog links on campus notices.

The first day of ENGL 255 usually begins with some polite but bemused variation on "Why superheroes, Professor?" Colleagues ask me the same question, only with the preface, "Don't take this the wrong way, but." The short answer is easy. Superheroes, like most any pop culture production, reflect a lot about us. And since superheroes have been flying for decades, they document our evolution too. On the surface of their unitards, they're just pleasantly absurd wish fulfillments. But our nation's history of obsessions flexes just under those tights: sexuality, violence, prejudice, politics, our most nightmarish fears, our most utopian aspirations — it's all churning in there. But you have to get up close. You have to be willing to wrestle a bit, to pull on Superman's cape. We all need to sink our teeth into Batman's head.

But before we bite open any skulls, let's identify the patient.

What is a superhero?

I can cite a half-dozen scholars with superhero criteria ranging from leotards to dead parents to celibacy. But even the most hair-splitting definitions leave some nonconsensus gray area. Bruce Wayne, for instance, possesses no superhuman abilities, so can Batman technically be a "super" hero? And does the Punisher's homicidal vigilantism bar him from the "hero" half of the term? Hollywood's Thor is thoroughly super-powered, but without a human side, isn't he just a low-flying god? Buffy the Vampire Slayer has the superpowers and the duality, but no nifty costume — so does that count? What about Harry Potter? Or Nick Fury? Or Mary Poppins? Or the volunteers who unload and sort my clothes donations at our local Goodwill? Is any extraordinary do-gooder a superhero?

I begin the first day of class by writing down every superhero trope my students can brainstorm; it only takes ten minutes before we run out of chalkboard. Think of it as a census bureau questionnaire of possible traits. The list is long and mutating, but if you slash Xs through enough boxes, I say you're in — even if your boxes aren't the same boxes as the masked detectives, altruistic monsters, supernatural vigilantes, and sci-fi Robin Hoods sitting around you. Superheroes are the ultimate amalgams, all-swallowing über-characters that consume other genres like black holes. They defy conventional definitions because they contain too many conventions. If that nondefinition sounds cowardly, philosopher Ludwig Wittgenstein plays the same game with "game" (what traits do marathons, chess, and solitaire share?). The no-common-denominator approach puts me at odds with must-have definitions (superpowered Mary and superhero-commanding Nick are out because they don't have aliases) and those that conjure circular genre logic to exclude trait-bearers who don't reside in official superhero territory (bye-bye Harry and Buffy). These are good arguments, but they're also why superhero prehistory is so invisible. Definitions work like erasers. I prefer the pointy end of my pencil.

I'm also at odds with the U.S. patent office. A "superhero" (or "super-hero" or "super hero") is a trademarked term that Marvel and DC have owned jointly since 1979. The two corporations argued that consumers associate the word with their products, and so any other company marketing a character as a superhero would be exploiting them. That might have been true at the time. Charlton Comics dropped out of the comic book market in the late 70s, but they had been calling their superpowered do-gooders "Action Heroes" (later converted to DC's *Watchmen* by Alan Moore and Dave Gibbons). It's considerably less true after the emergence of other publishers, Dark Horse in 1986, Image in 1992, Dynamite in 2005. Only in a legalistic sense are Spawn, Hellboy, and Michael Chabon's the Escapist (Dark Horse published the comic book adaptation) not superheroes.

Chevron and Gulf wouldn't have much luck barring other oil companies from using "gas station" on the grounds that Chevron and Gulf were the first to open ones. The term is used too generically now. Of course Marvel and DC can't control the generic use of "superhero" either. Other companies can call their characters "superheroes" within a text, just not in a title or an advertisement. So then is Nostalgia Ventures following or breaking trademark law with the phrase "THE FIRST SUPERHERO" on the cover of their Doc Savage reprints?

Some dictionaries trace "superhero" to the early 60s, fueling Marvel and DC's claim since their Silver Age characters reinvented the genre then. But the word goes back much farther. Michael Chabon says June 1938. The Pulitzer Prize–winning author of *The Adventures of Kavalier and Clay* dubs *Action Comics* No. 1 "Minute Zero of the superhero idea." I'd already read his comic book–based historical novel, but made sure I knew how to pronounce his name ("Cha" as in Shea Stadium, "bon" as in Jovi) before having dinner with him and about ten other faculty members and university students before his lecture on campus. He sat opposite me, as a way of avoiding the more central seat he should have taken. He's a little shy, but less soft-spoken behind a podium. My seminar was still gestating, or my Superhero students would have attended too.

I asked Mr. Chabon about his script for *Spider-Man 2* (in my defense, *McSweeney's* had recently posted it), but he said, and then repeated twice, that his only interest in screenwriting was the family health benefits he received through the writer's guild. I didn't ask him about his article "Secret Skin: An Essay in Unitard Theory," a handout I have since shared a half-dozen times with my classes. I was, thankfully, not yet drafting this prehistory of the genre, so his smile did not tighten the way my wife's used to before she imposed a five-minute limit on any conversational gambit involving muscle-stretched spandex.

Mr. Chabon will forgive me if I sometimes imagine I'm still leaning over our bread basket in conversation. He tells me in the *New Yorker*: "There were costumed crime-fighters before Superman (the Phantom, Zorro), but only as there were pop quartets before the Beatles. Superman invented and exhausted his genre in a single bound."

It's a pithy summary of conventional wisdom, one I took on faith when I sketched my first timeline. Aside from the Shadow and a few other pulp heroes of the 30s, there was just Zorro a decade earlier, and the Scarlet Pimpernel a decade and half before that. My imaginary Michael didn't answer when I asked about the gaps. I assumed I'd never heard of any Roaring Twenties superheroes because the Roaring Twenties were busy roaring through other genres. Same for the fifteen-year gap between Baroness Orczy's flowery Pimpernel and Johnston McCulley's Z-slashing imitation.

I was wrong. The first three decades of the century are awash with masked and superpowered do-gooders. My latest rough count: forty. The number doubles with the horde of "mystery men" who crawl from under the Shadow's 1930 cloak, plus the Scarlet Pimpernel's garden of pre-1903 predecessors, some known, others lost in the mulch of crumbled penny dreadfuls. A century before Krypton exploded, the Grey Champion was confronting redcoats in the streets of colonial New England, while the demonic Jibbenainosay scourged the Kentucky frontier. Meanwhile across the Atlantic, Spring-Heeled Jack was leaping Victorian stage-coaches in single bounds as Dr. Hesselius administered to the victims of vampire attacks. Add to the Victorian Justice League the superdetective Nick Carter, a man with the strength of three, surpassed only by Tarzan's jungle-perfected physique and the Night Wind's preternatural speed and crowbar-knotting muscles. While the Scarlet Pimpernel was assuming his thousand disguises, the reformed Grey Seal and Jimmy Valentine were turning their criminal prowess to good as urban Robin Hoods.

That Kryptonian rocket didn't just drop out of the sky. By 1914—the year both of Superman's creators, Joe Shuster and Jerry Siegel, were born —the superhero's most defining characteristics were well-rehearsed standards: secret identities, aliases, disguises, signature symbols, traumatic origins, extraordinary powers, self-sacrificing altruism. Some of these very earliest incarnations are startlingly full-blown, some are fragmentary foreshadowings, but superheroes have a sprawling, action-packed history that predates the Man of Tomorrow by decades and even centuries.

You could still claim that at least the word "superhero" originated after 1938 as imitators capitalized on Superman's popularity. Except that Shuster used the term himself while sketching pre-1936 drafts, labeling Superman "THE GREATEST SUPER-HERO OF ALL TIME!" Pulp publishers Street and Smith advertised Doc Savage as a "SUPERMAN!" while also referring to him and the Shadow as "superheroes" as early as 1932. Future DC publisher Harry Donenfeld launched *Super-Detective* magazine in the early 30s too, but the prefix had been popular for at least a decade. Bruce Graeme opens his 1925 novel *Blackshirt* with a complaint: "A super-criminal — bah! It is all tommy-rot, this 'super' business." When World War I pilot Alan Bott used "super-hero" in his 1917 memoir *An Airman's Outings*, it was a complaint then too. Bott was objecting that members of Parliament were exaggerating the powers of British fighter pilots by calling them "the super-heroes of the war."

The prefix's spread was übermensch-related. Alexander Tille, the first English translator of Nietzsche's *Thus Spoke Zarathustra*, preferred "beyond-man," but the second went with "Superman" after George Bernard Shaw's play *Man and Superman* popularized the word in 1903. Shaw didn't coin it though. New York's *Forum* magazine mentioned "the 'cosmic, super-man' of the future" in 1894, early evidence of the flow of "übers" across the English Channel, including even "superhero," how Tille rendered Nietzsche's "Über-Held" in 1896 and the designation London's *Daily Mail* thought Alfred Dreyfus's brother, Mathieu Dreyfus, deserved in 1899. If you prefer adjectives, Philadelphia's *Evening Telegraph* described the "superheroic action" of the war in Cuba in 1869, but no one complained of "supermania" before 1904, when Shaw was spreading the gospel of superman eugenics.

By the time Siegel attached the name Superman to his hero, supermen were everywhere. Type the term into the *New York Times* archives, and you'll view hundreds of hits. He appeared most regularly on sports pages. While Jack Dempsey insisted that "it will take a superman to beat" boxer Tom Heeney, football stars Red Grange and Frank Johavac were both declared "Superman." Babe Ruth was a "Baseball Superman," as was Giants pitcher Red Ruffing, and golfer Cecil Leitch was a "superwoman of the links." Other supermen leaped from the arts pages: dancer Michel Fokine was a "Superman of the toe," actor Robert Loraine a "Superman of the Stage," Stravinsky a "Superman of Jazz," Schoenberg another musical "Superman," and singer Enrico Caruso had the "lungs . . . of a superman."

According to the book review section, any man worthy of a biography was by definition a superman: Napoleon, Charles II, Garibaldi, Genghis Khan, Cromwell. Ben Franklin was honored as a "Super-man" on his 217th birthday. Among living politicians, Woodrow Wilson, Franklin Roosevelt, and Benito Mussolini were repeatedly called or compared to supermen. By 1938, the word was generic for any kind of excellence. Siegel wasn't even the first writer to apply it to a pulp hero. That honor goes to Edgar Rice Burroughs; Tarzan is a "superman" in his 1912 debut. Using the word for a name was the equivalent of calling a character "Genius" or "Epitome." Or, better yet, "Super-hero."

And that's just the term, not the character type. If we ignore the Sports and Arts & Leisure pages and stick to lowbrow publications starting in the mid-nineteenth century, all those pulps and penny dreadfuls, I count at least eighty pre-Superman supermen. About the number of folks who attended Chabon's lecture — the best my wife says she's ever attended at our university. Not a stadium crowd, but the Beatles didn't fill the equivalent of Shea when they started. Comics' Lennon and McCartney are probably Stan Lee and Jack Kirby, making Siegel and Shuster's Superman closer to Elvis — not rock 'n' roll's originator, but the guy who exploded it into the mainstream. Presley looked so good on stage because his burgeoning genre was already poised to applaud him.

And those gyrating hips are still rocking the genre. Picture superhero history as an hourglass body. Add a buxom bosom and willowy waist and it's the inhuman shape of a cartoon superheroine. When Tim Burton zippered Michelle Pfeiffer into a Catwoman bodysuit, they could only shoot a few seconds before she passed out. I dressed as a Playboy Bunny for Halloween once. I was a scrawny high school boy and, needless to say, did not fill the expectations of that genre. But I understand the shape now. The thin middle space where the glass almost touches, that's 1938.

That's Superman — the frontier line dividing superheroes into pre and post comic book order.

That's why Chabon says the character "invented" the genre. It's like saying Sherlock Holmes invented the detective story — untrue since Conan Doyle built upon Poe, Dickens, and Collins, and yet without Holmes I doubt all those paperbacks in the supermarket aisle would exist. After reading *Uncle Tom's Cabin*, George Eliot said Harriet Beecher Stowe "*invented* the Negro novel.*" The statement is equal nonsense since novels by and about African Americans preceded it (including Frederick Douglass's *The Heroic Slave*, also published in 1852), but Stowe's popularized the preexisting genre so massively that no novel that followed it could be read without placing it in relation to *Uncle Tom's Cabin*. It's *as if* Stowe invented the genre, even though she was participating in a range of already defined genre tropes.

That's Superman's relationship to superheroes. After him, the hourglass widens into a spacious ball of imitation and evolution. Every speck of superhero sand after 1938 dribbled into existence though the opening of *Action Comics* No. 1. The top half, all that wide-open sand crowding down to spill through that one tiny opening, that's prehistory, the superheroes who were superheroes before superheroes were a thing. The dozens and dozens of stories that developed all the tropes and clichés that tumbled together to form Superman, the generic superhero that exponentially popularized the genre.

That's the time travel story I'm writing. That's my multiverse. Not a tight little screenplay, but a sprawling crossover maxi-series with a dozen subplots and a cast of thousands. If there's a superhero writer's guild, I want the family health benefits too.

So by the time we get to *Actions Comics*, the superhero story is basically over. The comic book incarnations are epilogues, fossilized echoes. They're also the boot prints that track our cultural history. Comic book readers like to divide superheroes into Ages, the Golden of the 40s, the Silver of the 60s, the Bronze of the 70s, and so forth. That's not the kind of history you'll find here. When I say the Bronze Age, I mean the actual

Bronze Age, c. 1200 B.C.E. You know from the title, this book begins with the Big Bang, so that leaves fourteen billion years to cover. We're going to need a sturdy time machine.

My family and I have a soft spot for a certain blue police box (*Doctor Who* fans call it Time and Relative Dimension in Space), but I'm going with Doctor Doom's. For his first and oddly circuitous plan for world mastery, Victor Von Doom flung the Fantastic Four centuries into the past to retrieve Merlin's gems from Blackbeard's treasure chest. His time machine looks like a door dropped flat on the floor. You don't open it. You stand on it, and it rises through you. So for an evil genius, Doom really does understand a thing or two about time. When the going gets rocky, you grip it like a door ripped from the *Titanic* as its waves try to pull you down.

That's also as close as I get to a methodology. My time machine is a whirlpool, mixing history, biography, and multimedia analysis. I apologize to fellow scholars who find the absence of footnotes and internal citations frustrating—though do please flip to the back and check out my list of companion essays published in academic journals and their combined works cited. I honestly love writing that kind of specialized scholarship, but the book currently in your hands is more omnivorous. You don't need a degree or even a classroom before jumping in. It's also personal. I learned about superheroes as a kid, and then learned more while my kids were kids, so my control panel is thumbtacked with family snapshots. And because I think temporal links reveal some of the most important qualities of the character type, you should expect frequent, neck-snapping leaps between the twirling past and the swirling present as we track superheroes to their dozens of origin points at once. If it helps, here's a map:

1. After a brief detour through celestial mechanics, turn left at the Big Bang and merge into multilaned World Mythology. Take the Neolithic cave painting bypass and exit for the Book of Genesis. Circle Judah and Roman-occupied Israel until you pass the Crucifixion. Are demigods and messiahs superheroes? You tell me.

2. Superheroes are revolutionists. They overthrow the natural order and establish themselves as our benevolent protectors. So we'll need to trace those anarchist impulses from England's Guy Fawkes

and Cromwell to the American and French Revolutions. The egalitarian age of democracy demands a new aristocracy of superhuman Napoleons.

3. Take a walk on the dark side. These Napoleonic Fausts open the gates of hell and mingle with the stuff of nightmares. The Gothic nineteenth century swarms with sinister fairies, charming vampires, walking corpses, and ectoplasmic ghosts — all of the dark forces pulsing in the heart of the superhero.

4. The Western's frontier is a time-travel paradox. It came into existence after it vanished. We'll tour both sides of the divide, Indian and cowboy, as these all-American figures struggle through the cultural consciousness that shapes superheroism. There will be a detour to Mars, so dress accordingly.

5. Darwin is both the superhero's God and Devil. Evolution terrified humanity, so humanity fought back with the superman of eugenics. That means Adolf Hitler and the House of Slytherin. But it also means some of the genre's most beloved heroes are well-born aristocrats fighting to preserve their own privilege against the degenerate masses.

6. And with great privilege comes questionable morality. Does the clan of superheroes have the right to kill? What ultimately is the difference between a supervillain thwarting humanity for his own pleasure and a superman pursuing his coincidentally prosocial self-interest? This is an extended stop inside the Jokeresque heart of Batman.

7. The Superhero Guide to Love & Sex strips the genre down to its erotic roots. Unmasking is a hero's greatest desire, but once he removes his fetish costume, he's a stay-at-home dad trapped in domesticated retirement. That double fear and lust drives superheroes from their Don Juan origins to their twentieth-century foreplay.

8. The last decade before the beginning. The two-world superhero formula swallows up time-travelers, pirates, Martians, detectives, and Hobbits — until Krypton explodes them all into the familiar comic book pulp of the superhero universe.

Which will conclude our tour. Please stop by the bibliographic gift shop to plan your own time-travel itinerary.

⚡⚡⚡

I'll issue one more Reader Advisory before departure, a final SPOILER ALERT!

If you're a fan of unexamined American exceptionalism and hyper-masculinity, this could be a bumpy ride. When I streamed the recent PBS documentary *Superheroes: A Never-Ending Battle* with my class, we were told superheroes were an "innocent mythology" that "uplifted us" and showed "us how to be a better version of ourselves." I'm going to have to disagree. I grew up on comics. Superheroes literally taught me to read. But setting my childhood nostalgia aside, the character type is not all about truth and justice. The genre, like any genre, boils our world down into something digestible. Good guys fighting bad guys is simple and so often comforting. It's both wonderfully and horribly childish. All simplifications are distortions, and our justice system swears to tell the whole truth. So this is my tell-all unmasking, an inside scoop of the superhero brain, both its best and ugliest bits smeared on my operating table for all to examine.

I love superheroes. But I hate them too.

Now here's why.

Gustave Dore, "Satan descends upon Earth," *Paradise Lost*, 1866.

CHAPTER 1

IN THE BEGINNING

Action Comics No. 1 was the Big Bang of the Golden Age of Comics, the start point for superhero histories. Except this one. We won't open the first page of *Action Comics* till closing the last page of this book. We could start in 1883, the year Friedrich Nietzsche discovered God's body in Crime Alley and declared him dead, but we'd miss fourteen billion years that way. Stan Lee says God isn't dead, just sleeping (more on that deistic conundrum near the end of this chapter), but either way, God exploded the universe into existence before losing consciousness. Or universes. To explain the metaphysical underpinnings of superheroes' two-dimensional morality, I wanted to begin this tour of the multiverse in mythological times — but that first requires a Silver Age detour, plus a further definition of terminology.

"Thinkers who entertain the possibility that there are lots of universes," explains Jim Holt, "use the term 'multiverse' (or sometimes 'megaverse') for the entire ensemble of them." Holt writes about science for the *New Yorker* and is the author of *Why Does the World Exist?*, so by "thinkers" he means theologians, physicists, philosophers, and mathematicians. He does not mean comic book writers. Though he should.

The multiverse was created in 1957, not by God but by the physicist Hugh Everett. He called it MWI, the "many-worlds interpretation" of quantum physics. Because things get weird and literally unmeasurable at the subatomic level, the multiverse offers a way of explaining paradoxes like Erwin Schrödinger's 1935 thought experiment in which a cat can somehow be both dead and alive. Everett made that impossibility possible by splitting the cat into two universes.

But, unknown to Everett and Holt, DC editor Julie (stands for Julius) Schwartz had produced the same model a year earlier. Only instead of a cat, he used a superhero. DC's *Showcase* No. 4, cover dated October 1956, introduced the Flash — the Big Bang event of the Silver Age of Comics. The Golden Age Flash had dropped out of circulation in 1949, and though this new Flash resembled him (same name, same symbol, same superpower), he was not the same character (different costume, different secret identity, different origin). Schwartz followed up his experiment with a new Green Lantern in 1959 and split the old Justice Society into the new Justice League in 1960. That's also the year Andy Nimmo, vice-chair of the British Interplanetary Society, first used "multiverse" to describe Everett's clunkier-sounding many-worlds theory. (American philosopher William James actually coined "multiverse" in the 1890s, but that's a very different animal.)

So how can there be two Flashes? Or two Green Lanterns? Or two anythings? Because, Schwartz theorized, the new characters lived on Earth-1, and the 40s characters on Earth-2. Schwartz provided empirical evidence when, in 1961, the Earth-1 Flash vibrated his way into the Earth-2 Flash's universe. It turned out that events on Earth-2 had entered Earth-1 through the dreams of Golden Age comic book creators. Which weirdly matches Holt's description: "quantum field forbids these parallel worlds from interacting in any but the ghostliest of ways."

Schwartz's research was soon duplicated by physicist Richard Feynman, who used it to win a 1965 Nobel Prize. Feynman, like Schwartz, argued for the existence of not just multiple worlds but multiple histories. Apparently new universes pop into existence at every fork in time. When, for instance, Schrödinger's cat both did and did not die. Or when the Flash both did and did not vibrate into a neighboring dimension. Feynman used the less catchy phrases "path integral formulation" and "sum over histories," but DC didn't adopt the actual word "multiverse" until 1976. Writers needed a term for the ensemble of universes they'd spent the last two decades spinning into existence.

Earth-3 (where everything is an evil mirror of Earth-1) bubbled up in

1964. The next year a supervillain created Earth-A (stands for Alternate) in order to eliminate the Justice League. In 1966, after buying Quality Comics, DC decided that subset of superheroes' Golden Age adventures took place on Earth-X where World War II still rages. They gave Captain Marvel his own universe too; starting in 1973, he and all of the 1940s Fawcett Comics characters (DC swallowed up competitors like a black hole) moved to Earth-S (stands for Shazam). Since they couldn't buy Marvel, DC had to create Crossover Earth for team-ups (Superman and Spider-Man were the first in 1976), and they even designated an Earth for the rest of us (Earth Prime).

The list goes on (Charlton Comics eventually ended up on Earth-4, Jack Kirby's New Gods on 17), and I'm not counting all the "Imaginary Stories" that took place in universes left unlabeled because they never came into contact with Earth-1 characters. On Earth-Whatever, for instance, Clark and Lois marry and raise superbabies. And on Earth-Whatchamacallit, the infant Superman is adopted by the Waynes, so Clark and Bruce grow up as brothers. Basically any "what if" can spawn a parallel world.

Marvel literalized that "what if" theory in 1977 with *What If?* The first issue (my eleven-year-old self bought it from a rotating 7-Eleven rack) asked: "What If Spider-Man Had Joined the Fantastic Four?" Instead of killing cats, the omniscient Watcher used a hit-and-run example to illustrate how any single event leads to multiple realities. The accident bystander:

(A) does nothing, and the victim is killed,
(B) pushes the victim to safety but is struck himself, or
(C) gets both himself and the victim to safety.

Or D. All three. Which is what Feynman said happens. Our reality, Earth-1218 in the Marvel multiverse, is somehow the averaged sum of all events. Or maybe that's Earth-616, where most of Marvel's comic book characters live. Or Earth-199999 and their movie incarnations. Marvel has a lot of hit-and-run worlds to average out.

But What Ifs and Imaginary Tales are not the same. In fact, they reveal how deep the DC/Marvel cosmological divide runs. Marvel's multiverse looks like a quantum theory multiverse, while DC's fits the inflationary model because Earth-S and Earth-4 and Earth-X were not created at points of divergence. Those worlds were floating out there all along. Which, oddly, is the more impressive theory because it has actual data to back it up. Holt explains:

> measurements of the cosmic background radiation — the echo left over from the Big Bang — indicate that the space we live in is infinite, and that matter is spread randomly throughout it. Therefore, all possible arrangements of matter must exist out there somewhere — including exact and inexact replicas of our own world and the beings in it.

A variation on the inflationary theory goes even farther and posits isolated pocket universes, each born from its own Big Bang. Eventually each universe (ours too) will collapse in its own Big Crunch or, preferably, a Big Bounce, causing a new universe to be rebooted in its place.

At least that's the theory. Except in comic books where it's verifiable fact. It happened in 1985. The twelve-issue series *Crisis on Infinite Earths* ended with all the surviving worlds of the DC multiverse imploding and reforming as "New Earth." Only this time there were no additional pocket universes connected to it, so no more multiverse. Sure, DC couldn't resist a few Imaginary Tales (newly termed "Elseworlds"), but superheroes from Earth-1 — or I guess it would just be "Earth" now — never (okay, almost never) interacted with their counterparts from parallel Earths. Which is why DC cleaned out its multiverse in the first place. All those JLA and JSA team-ups were getting tedious. DC prefers "reboot" over "Big Bounce," which is fair since physicists didn't start using the second term till 1987, after DC's new universe had stabilized.

Meanwhile, Marvel has been drifting into the inflationary model with its larger Megaverse and the crunching of its own alternate Earths. It's hit the refresh button a few times, but not as impressively as DC restarting all titles at No. 1. So now there are two *Action Comics* No. 1, one dated 1938, one 2011, both the products of the many-markets interpretation of quantum publishing. That last reboot even popped the multiverse (now called the Multiversity) back into existence, including Earth-2. Or, rather, a rebounced Earth-2 in an infinite range of Earth-2 variations, all of which DC will eventually publish, though not necessarily here on Earth Prime.

In March 2014, astronomer John M. Kovac, of the Harvard-Smithsonian Center for Astrophysics, thought his team spotted evidence of the Big Bang. Telescopes positioned on the South Pole detected gravitational waves, wrinkles in the space-time fabric made in the universe's first moments of existence. It turns out they were only interstellar dust. But comic book astronomers are way ahead of Kovac. Krona, a rogue scientist from the planet Oa at the center of the DC universe, witnessed the hand of God forming creation before his observation machine fragmented into the multiverse. Galen, of a pre–Big Bang civilization, steered his ship into the convergence point of the Big Crunch before emerging as the planet-eating Galactus, sole survivor of Marvel's Big Bang.

Dave Sims's Judge was there too. I was a fan of the independent Canadian comic *Cerebus*, until Sims mailed my wife insults to her reader comment letter and used his editorial page for misogynist rants. For *Cerebus* No. 109, Sims draws a Big Bang creation myth in which the Void unthinkingly rapes the Light, exploding her into a multiverse of bastard stars. The Sumerians' god of wind has sex with a mountain with similar results. Hesoid's void, Chaos, somehow gives birth to the elements all by itself. The Egyptians called that empty sea Nu. Genesis 1:2 opens with a black hole too: "the earth was formless and empty, darkness was over the surface of the deep," followed by God's "Let there be light," the biblical Big Bang.

Most mythologies start with the formless horror a blank page, until an artist draws the universe in human terms. Marvel personifies the Big Bang's offspring as Eternity, an aspect of the four-faced Living Tribunal, who oversees the larger multiverse while working under the One-Above-All and delegating assignments to Magistrati. It's only slightly more complicated than Gnostic Christianity's team of Demiurgos, Aeons, and Archons. Comics are only the latest mythology to anthropomorphize the workings of the universe. We've always preferred our gods in human form.

"All mythology," writes Ralph Waldo Emerson in *Representative Men*, "opens with demigods," the human-yet-divine offspring of flighty imagination and earthbound necessity. The adventures of Gilgamesh were Mesopotamia's first big superhero saga. Fans of Nanabush freely traded his stories across the future U.S.-Canadian border. The tales of Maui island-hopped the Pacific for centuries. Even the Egyptian god Horus roamed Europe before settling in the Nile Valley. He, or some other equally bird-headed godman, debuted in France during the Stone Age. He was a minor character though, relegated to the back of *Lascaux*, the first comic book in human history. Comics would later become synonymous with superheroes, providing the character type its most enduring home, but the first visual representation of a superhuman is chiseled into prehistory. Humans have been thinking about superheroes for over seventeen millennia.

It would be thematically convenient to report that the first comic book was *Big Bang Comics* No. 1, but that Golden Age retro-reboot didn't appear till 1994. *Lascaux* No. 1 has been around since 15,000 B.C.E. It was a single edition, printed on limestone, and arranged in a pair of strips over 128 feet long. The title refers to the medium ("*lascaux*" is French for "limestone"), but it is also the genre (cave drawings) as well as the specific work of art. Similarly, "pulp fiction" refers to magazines printed on paper made from wood pulp but later came to mean the tales themselves, eventually inspiring Quentin Tarantino to adopt the term as the title of his 1994 *Pulp Fiction*. The film is about criminals because the magazines were about criminals, the same way comics would come to mean superheroes.

Most scholars refer to the *Lascaux* creators as "Cro-Magnons," a generic designation which in this case is accurate. The bones of the first so-called Cro-Magnons were found in a hole ("*creux*" in French) on property owned by a farmer named Magnon in a nearby town. Cro-Magnons are the People of Magnon's Hole. More specifically, the creators of *Lascaux* were a loose collective of artists of the Neolithic Age who signed their work with a symbol resembling the head of a four-pronged pitchfork. This signature resembles a superhero emblem, but since it also appears in other caves of the region it must denote a clan or congregation and so is closer to a corporate logo — like the globe Atlas Comics used before evolving into Marvel in the 1960s. It may also be an umbrella logo like the circled "DC" icon that linked National Allied Publications with its affiliate branches All-American Comics and Detective Comics in the 1940s.

Since *Lascaux* appeared before France passed its first law protecting authors' rights in 1793, the artists' heirs retain no proprietary claim. A legal challenge could argue that the 1940 rediscovery of the cave signifies a new "first" publication, but even that copyright would likely lapse while the case was held up in court. Dozens of 1940s superheroes are public domain now too, their publishers extinct. Four Prong went out of business millennia ago and so collects no royalties on the postcards, T-shirts, refrigerator magnets, and other gift shop memorabilia that appropriate *Lascaux* artwork.

Legal issues aside, the work has influenced comic books for centuries. Curators liken it to Michelangelo's most acclaimed graphic novel, the Sistine Chapel. The comparison is apt, as the *Lascaux* artists also painted religious imagery on the ceilings of a temple while lying on their backs suspended by wooden platforms. The scope is also similar, with the largest bull drawing spanning seventeen feet. Michelangelo, however, worked in distinct panels depicting the superhuman adventures of an anthropomorphic God. *Lascaux* includes no formal frames or gutter, prefiguring Will Eisner's use of open-page space. The absence of captions and word balloons is also apparent in later works by Jim Steranko and Alan Moore.

Walt Disney and Max Fleischer duplicated animation techniques from Four Prong too. Many of the horses and bulls in *Lascaux* are drawn at angled perspectives, with the closest front leg straight and the second front leg bent and slightly detached from the body to suggest motion. A single animal may be drawn multiple times in an overlapping row, with head or back end incomplete, to evoke forward progression — a technique repeated by numerous artists to suggest the movements of such speedsters as Flash and Quicksilver. When viewed with Four Prong candle technology (a hollowed rock filled with reindeer fat and a juniper wick), the moving figures flicker like nickelodeon frames.

The artists also innovated crushed minerals for their palette, even for black, avoiding the charcoals favored by their contemporaries. Curators comment on the flawlessness of the artists as revealed by the lack of a single false or erased line in all *Lascaux*. This impression, however, may be due to the now invisible lines produced by one or more pencilers that later inkers obscured as they finalized the art. Credit is also due to the nuanced style of the colorists, whose muted amber bulls prefigure Lynn Varley's award-winning work in *The Dark Knight Returns*.

Sadly, after its republication in 1940, *Lascaux* was no longer preserved in its clay-sealed microclimate — the geological equivalent of an acid-free Mylar bag — and so it has been significantly downgraded from its former near-mint condition. As a result, reprints are flooding the market. *Lascaux II* — a painstakingly reproduced concrete tunnel located near the original — opened in 1983, *Lascaux III* is currently on tour, and *Lascaux IV* is in production.

While *Lascaux* has thrilled equine, bovine, and cervine enthusiasts for thousands of years, newcomers may be disappointed to find that Four Prong wasn't big on superheroes. Though introducing the first superhuman character, that debut figure is featured only on the cave's most inaccessible panel, and while many of the representational bulls and horses possess only a slight Cubist quality of abstraction, that lone humanoid is essentially a stick-figure with a bird's head and penis. Because of his semirecumbent posture, scholars have dubbed him Wounded Man, though he bears no relation to the *Wounded Man* manga published in Japan in the 1980s. Wounded Man may also be the earliest representation of the falcon-headed Horus, a supersavior rebooted in Christian mythology. Fans of bird-headed godmen should also check out Wounded Man's adventures in the comic books of ancient Egypt.

I won't attempt to compile a complete index of early comics — the murals of Teotihuacan, the silk tapestries of the Tang dynasty, the illustrated epic *Shahnemah* by the Persian poet Ferdowsi — let alone the rosters of all their superhuman characters. But I think we can agree that super-powered humanoids debuted long long long before *Action Comics* No. 1.

So then are superheroes just antiquity in spandex? That's the we-used-to-call-them-gods argument M. Night Shyamalan makes in his 2000 film *Unbreakable* and Peter Berg repeats in his 2008 *Hancock*. I don't agree, but it is a decent argument. As mentioned, "superhero" comes from Shaw's "superman," which comes from Nietzsche's "übermensch," which comes from Goethe's "übermenschen," which is regularly translated "superhuman" or "demigod." Though only in a mathematical sense can "greater-than-human" equal "less-than-god." The difference is significant, because the superheroic impulse moves in only one of those two directions.

Superheroes aren't just gods drawn down to human form. Superheroes raise humans up to the miraculous. A magic word, a blast of radiation, even a bullet through a loved one, and some earthly nobody is transcending earthly limitations. That's way more heroic than some all-powerful being dropping down to slum with his mud-born worshippers. Gods may look or act human, but superheroes bridge the divine-mundane chasm with their own both/neither category as mortal deities. By combining heaven and earth, they create a third sphere that flips the hierarchy. They're fundamentally divided, but they prefer their "mensch" over their "über." They are humans who become gods but then choose to be human.

That's why I don't like ancients cavorting with my hard-earned-spandex-wearers. Except maybe Chris Hemsworth. He plays a comically hunky Thor, and I suppose Hercules had a respectable stint as an Avenger too. I didn't even object when he went on to anchor the now forgotten Bronze Age team, the Champions. But I prefer Eric Shanower's *The Age of Bronze*. The meticulously researched, multivolume interpretation of the Trojan War is a trove of source materials, archaeological to Shakespearean, all compiled, sifted, rewoven, and painstakingly etched into a literal epic of graphic storytelling. Yet from the dozens and dozens of Trojan tales, Shanower omits one detail:

The gods.

"No supernatural intervention," he told an auditorium of Washington and Lee University students. My Superheroes class attended, but would you believe it was Professor Laughy of our Classics department who invited a comic book artist to campus? When another professor asked why "suppressing the supernatural" was the impetus behind the project, Shanower said he wanted to "bring the story down to human level." He was tired of blaming the gods for our bad behavior.

For Cassandra's "origin story," that meant replacing Apollo — the source of both her prophetic visions and her inability to convince anyone they're true — with a priestly pedophile. The curse "no one will believe you" takes on a horrifically human meaning. Shanower's take on Herakles (yes, same guy as Hercules) is less disturbing. While the mass of *Age of Bronze* is rendered in near photo-realism (down to the authentically rounded crenellations in Troy's walls and the embroidered hems of King Priam's robes), Shanower reduces that most famous demigod to a "cartoony buffoon." He's basically Popeye's nemesis, Bluto. The visual effect, explained Shanower, suggests that the king's memory (Priam retells a story from his childhood) is unreliably exaggerated, the lines literally warped.

And that's another reason to dispense with gods. Comic books' childhood was spent in superhero tights, with the medium and the character type coming-of-age hand-in-glove. If you want to create a literary work of artistic force and erudition (and, wow, does that describe *Age of Bronze*), it helps to give the kid stuff the boot. Not that Shanower has anything against kid stuff. He admitted at dinner (Classics let me tag along) that he was a big *X-Men* fan growing up and was there for the Claremont-Byrne Dark Phoenix Saga, Marvel's Greek Tragedy, and climax of the Bronze Age. But how can you draw a naturalistic Herakles without also drawing a line pointing back to Jack Kirby's 1965 Hercules? Any god, even in an authoritative rendering of the Trojan War, might as well scribble "It's clobberin' time!" in his talk bubble.

Look at Robert Sullivan and Chris Slane's *Maui: Legends of the Outcast*. They published their graphic novel in 1996, two years before Image Comics started *Age of Bronze*, but it originates at least a thousand years earlier, when the first Maori rowed to Aotearoa (aka New Zealand). They carried tales of Maui, one of the most ubiquitous heroes of Polynesian mythology. When Sullivan visited my Superheroes class (a side trip between my wife's poetry course and his evening reading), he said he didn't intend any superhero allusions when adapting the Maui legends — and yet my students were ready to list them.

They'd identified "outcast" as a superhero trait on the first day of class, and there it is on the cover. An origin story follows, with the hero suffering a character-defining wrong that both motivates him and imbues him with special abilities. After Maui's mother tosses him stillborn into the ocean, a prayer to the gods transforms him: "Revive the child. Let destiny take him to great deeds. Grant him unnatural powers." Those include shape-shifting, so soon Maui is fluttering around as a bird and buzzing in ears and flapping his fins underwater. He even appears in a half-human state, his body covered in green scales. He gets a costume too, a special battle suit able to withstand the fire of the sun. He wears no cape or symbol on his chest, but Slane colors his eyes blue and red — an iconic image that separates him from his fellow Maori. He also sports a Tony Stark–size ego, though technically all his adventures benefit humankind, securing his people food, land, and fire.

I'm not trying to draft Maui for the Justice League (though, actually, yeah, that'd be cool), but like it or not, when you draw a legendary godman inside a comic book panel, it's going to flip the switch marked "superhero" in your reader's brain. I think Shanower recognizes that. He spent the early 80s inking Silver Age legend Curt Swan's Superman — and redrawing all of the elder artist's perspective errors. *Age of Bronze* makes Swan's drawings look as quaint as Popeye. Sullivan looks back at *Maui* with misgivings too. He wishes he'd made the goddess of death (she chews up Maui in her rocky vagina) less monstrously godlike and a little more, well, human.

Even Thomas Carlyle, the guy who wrote the book on hero worship (his 1840 collection of "Great Men" lectures is redundantly titled *On Heroes, Hero-Worship, and Heroes in History*), drags the gods down to Earth. Odin, Carlyle conjectures, was just a warrior who became "tenfold greater when dead":

the man Odin, speaking with a Hero's voice and heart, as with an impressiveness out of Heaven, told his People the infinite importance of Valor, how man thereby became a god; and that his People, feeling a response to it in their own hearts, believed this message of his, and thought it a message out of Heaven, and him a Divinity for telling it them.

Remember that Alan Bott, one of the first writers to put the word "superhero" into print, feared the same process was happening to World War I fighter pilots; the public was raising them to godly heights and therefore missing their most heroic quality, their humanity.

Not that everyone has given up on the gods. Julie Taymor spun her Broadway Spider-Man back to Mt. Olympus. Peter Parker sings about Icarus and gives class presentations on the goddess Arachne. A random universe didn't transform Peter into a web-slinging mutant. It was a divine plan. Arachne was watching and waiting all along. "The fates have delivered you," she sings — an echo of Stan Lee's description of that radioactive spider "whom fate has given a starring, if brief, role to play in the drama we call life!" Bono wasn't convinced. When he ended the Broadway team-up and cut Ms. Taymor loose, her mythology went with her. One reviewer estimated actress T. V. Carpio's Arachne role was snipped by more than half. But that wasn't enough to rescue the show. *Spider-Man: Turn on the Dark* closed after three years, at a loss of $60 million.

Gods just aren't as interesting as their superhero half-brothers. Hercules knew that. He made his dad send him to Earth even though it meant turning mortal. That's *The Mighty Hercules* version, a second-rate TV cartoon in production as Marvel was casting *The Mighty Thor* down to earthly newsstands in the early 60s. The crown princes of both Olympus and Asgard would rather be humans.

My favorite demigod, that mightily dorky Hercules, died the year I was born. Those were reruns I was watching Sunday mornings before church on Pittsburgh's UHF channel 53. Like Priam's memory, mine is staticky, but I think Zeus molds Hercules's godly powers into a magic ring to slip on while battling cartoon villainy. Odin pulls the same trick with a walking stick, transforming his son into a limping amnesiac. Anything to bring a god down to our level. That's what comics do so well. As much as they recycle old mythologies, superheroes are more than new tales of ancient gods. They are earthly adventures. A superhero is nothing if not human.

⚡ ⚡ ⚡

The Norse had a Big Bang too. They named their void Ginnungagap, the shapeless chaos dividing the realms of fire and ice. Things started booming when the two accidentally touched and gave birth to the first being, a giant named Ymir, whom Odin later killed and chopped into Earth. That's not the Odin of Marvel or Carlyle, but the *Poetic Edda* compiled in the thirteenth century from oral traditions.

The Bible started as oral traditions too, before later poets came along and fancied them up. John Milton wrote his poetic compendium on ancient Christian mythology in the sixteenth century. Odin and his brothers overthrew Ymir so Odin could rule heaven—which is also Satan's plot when he and his brothers try to overthrow God in *Paradise Lost*. Milton adds a page to Big Bang mythology as well. His God created the Earth just after booting the rebel angels out of heaven:

> There is a place
> (If ancient and prophetic fame in Heav'n
> Err not) another World, the happy seat
> Of some new Race call'd *Man*, about this time
> To be created like to us, though less
> In power and excellence, but favour'd more
> Of him who rules above;

That's Beelzebub, one of Satan's lieutenants, talking. He thinks attacking Earth is a better military strategy than storming heaven. When Satan flaps across the void to check out God's latest handiwork, Milton likens it to the wonder of looking upon "some renown'd Metropolis / With glistering Spires and Pinnacles adorn'd."

Milton, like Joe Shuster after crafting the skyscrapers of his comic book Metropolis, was blind when he wrote *Paradise Lost*, so the un-illustrated text is a comic book in only the thematic sense. Its slugfest between Lucifer's League of Fallen Angels and Archangel Michael's Righteous Avengers is Christianity's first superheroes vs. supervillains battle scene. My father remembers hearing the tale from the nuns in his parochial school. He emailed me about that recently:

> Have you ever commented in your writings on what I consider the archetypal superhero plot, one that has its origin in the Bible? I'm referring to the story of archangel Michael being called on to save heaven from being taken over by Lucifer by having a violent confrontation with Lucifer and vanquishing him. This story is so embedded in the Western religious psyche that to this day Catholics still pray to St. Michael to "defend us in battle" with Lucifer.

Not a question you might expect from a retired research chemist, but my father only entered the field because he had the textbooks after his older brother dropped them to become a priest. My father's colleagues were physicists, but he preferred working alone in his lab. He said his job was a version of Twenty Questions with God: "Does it have something to do with . . ." But out of the lab, he prefers questions like: "Why is there a powerful subconscious longing in the Western world for a superhero to save us from evil?" He blames the Michael vs. Lucifer story for injecting the need for an übermensch — rather than a collective effort — into the human psyche, turning humanity into a damsel-in-distress waiting to be rescued. "Ever since," he says, "people are continually looking for such a person, most of the time to their eventual detriment when they believe they have found one."

"That's pretty good, Dad. I hadn't thought of Michael as the original superhero. I may have to flagrantly steal your insight."

"I would be delighted," he wrote, and went on about how little of the Michael vs. Lucifer myth is actually included in the Bible, mostly snippets in Revelation, and certainly no big battle scenes. In the version he learned from the nuns, Lucifer is the greatest and most brilliant of the angels who rebelled against God. So God dispatches Michael who defeats Lucifer and sends him down to hell. ("Why an all-powerful God didn't take on the job himself was never explained.") The long version is an oral tradition, told and retold for about 2,000 years, proof of the imaginative grip it still has on the Judeo-Christian brain. The same brain that invented superheroes.

When I looked up Revelation 12 in my King James, I couldn't help imagining how Jack Kirby or Steve Ditko would illustrate the passages. The New Testament author even divides his script into panels. You just need caption boxes:

[7] And there was war in heaven: Michael and his angels fought against the dragon; and the dragon fought and his angels, [8] And prevailed not; neither was their place found any more in heaven. [9] And the great dragon was cast out, that old serpent, called the Devil, and Satan, which deceiveth the whole world: he was cast out into the earth, and his angels were cast out with him.

I'd assign Revelation 20 to Neal Adams or Bill Sienkiewicz:

[1] And I saw an angel come down from heaven, having the key of the bottomless pit and a great chain in his hand. [2] And he laid hold on the dragon, that old serpent, which is the Devil, and Satan, and bound him a thousand years, [3] And cast him into the bottomless pit, and shut him up, and set a seal upon him, that he should deceive the nations no more, till the thousand years should be fulfilled: and after that he must be loosed a little season.

Daniel 12:1 makes Michael sounds like a superhero too: "At that time, Michael, the great heavenly prince, the grand defender and guardian of your people, will arise." And, according to Milton, those chains he uses on Satan are adamantine, like Wolverine's adamantium claws. No wonder God made him team leader:

> Go *Michael* of Celestial Armies Prince,
> And thou in Military prowess next
> *Gabriel*, lead forth to Battel these my Sons
> Invincible, lead forth my armed Saints
> By Thousands and by Millions rang'd for fight;
> Equal in number to that Godless crew
> Rebellious, them with Fire and hostile Arms
> Fearless assault, and to the brow of Heav'n
> Pursuing drive them out from God and bliss,

> Into thir place of punishment, the Gulf
> Of *Tartarus*, which ready opens wide
> His fiery *Chaos* to receave thir fall.

Ultimately though, Michael doesn't make my first Justice League roster. He's a couple of pegs down from Supreme Creator on the "super" scale, but still nowhere near enough to Homo sapiens. Archangels are too godly to bridge that gulf. To be a superhero, Michael would need to trade in his immortality for a magic ring or a walking cane like those other mythological Sons Invincible, Thor and Hercules.

But Michael's ur-battle with Satan is still central to superhero metaphysics. As if obeying a thermodynamic law of creativity, a superhero's dichotomy-breaking superhumanness is coupled with a corresponding widening of the Good-Evil divide. For all its surface absurdity, a comic book universe is rigidly logical. Humans can rise into half-gods (or descend into half-demons if you're a supervillain) in terms of physical power, but they also have to sacrifice their human complexity to become vessels of moral absolutism.

So *Paradise Lost* is close, but for a fully superheroic version of the Bible, we need an evangelist. Fundamentalist pastor Michael Pearl understands the metaphysics of comic books so well, he titles his Bible adaptation *Good and Evil* and advertises it as "The Ultimate Superhero Graphic Novel!" Instead of settling for "typical religious art," he hired former Marvel and DC artist Danny Bulanadi to sketch his scripts. I know Bulanadi because his 1979 Man-Thing is in my attic box of childhood comics. His 80s and 90s credits also include Conan, Captain America, Blue Beetle, Hulk, Indiana Jones, Fantastic Four, and the Micronauts. After transforming into a born-again Christian, Bulanadi "was not comfortable with the work he was doing and so quit." I'm not sure what exactly that means, since *Good and Evil* encapsulates the same comic book values as most other superhero tales.

Pearl says it's "impossible to cover the entire Bible," so he selects "just that Old Testament background that is pertinent"— which apparently requires inserting a few supervillain scenes too. "The Bible," according to Pearl, "tells us God created numerous kinds of angelic beings to offer praise around his throne, but one called Lucifer led a third of them in rebellion." Though tales of rebellious angels don't appear in the Bible till the book of Isaiah, Pearl needs us to know about them on page one.

"But," he adds, "this is not their story."

Except it is. We haven't gotten through the first week of creation before Bulanadi is sketching evil eyes peering from the blackness of his panels. "On the sixth day," Pearl declares, "with the evil ones watching, God formed a new creature from the dust of the ground." They're there again a page later as God is forming Eve: "Satan, the Evil One, watched." Two more panels and Bulanadi is drawing a bipedal lizard monster that would look at home in *Tales to Astonish*: "Satan hated God and wanted to destroy what God was doing, but he needed a way to communicate with Eve, so he entered the body of a beautiful creature and spoke through its mouth."

Pearl and Bulanadi disagree about the adjective "beautiful," but, more important, Pearl disagrees with God. In Genesis 3:1, "the serpent was more crafty than any other beast of the field that the Lord God had made." So Satan isn't a "beast of the field," and there's nothing suggesting he "entered" it. Because Revelation calls its dragon "that old serpent," theologians like to retcon him into the Garden of Eden. Professor Gertz, who teaches The Bible as Literature in my department, assures me this is the standard interpretation — which is my point. It's an interpretation. It actually takes a good deal of theological cutting and pasting to turn all these supervillains into a single arch-nemesis. The Devil just means the Enemy, and he doesn't enter till the book of Job. Lucifer is the Morning Star, aka the planet Venus; the passage Revelation borrows from Isaiah 14 is a description of the planet's light sinking below the horizon. But keeping with tradition, Pearl plays up God's arch-nemesis. "Here is promise of a future battle," he tells us, as Bulanadi's lizard monster morphs into a snake. Pearl, like any good comic book writer, needs more fight scenes.

If you're looking for a more faithful Bible adaptation, I suggest Robert Crumb's *The Book of Genesis Illustrated*. If you're also familiar with Crumb's *Bible of Filth* (it includes the outrageously incestuous "A Family that LAYS Together STAYS Together"), you'll assume he's out to lampoon Christianity again. The prominent cover warning, "Adult Supervision Recommended for Minors," doesn't help. But you'd be wrong. Crumb's drawings are respectful. Yes, he, unlike Bulanadi, forgoes conveniently angled vegetation, so there are plenty of full-frontals of Adam and Eve in the Garden, but no sex, just a little cuddling, all of it in God's benevolent presence.

The long beard and robe are intentional clichés, but they bring out the odd thing about Bulanadi's God. His main superpower is invisibility. The tails of his squiggly talk bubbles point at nothing. When he "formed a new creature from the dust of the ground," Bulanadi draws the dust forming itself. When "God breathed his own life into the body of clay," Bulanadi's glowing cyclone of holy oxygen swirls from off-panel. Crumb, meanwhile, places God front and center, getting his hands dirty and embracing Adam as he exhales into his nostrils.

Crumb also includes all of God's words. "Every other comic book version of the Bible I've seen," he writes, "contains passages of completely made-up narratives and dialogue, in an attempt to streamline and 'modernize' the old scriptures, and still, these various comic book Bibles all claim to adhere to the belief that the Bible is 'the Word of God,' or 'Inspired by God,' whereas I, ironically, do NOT." Go to Pearl's No Great Joy website and you'll learn that "the sixty-six books of the King James Version, nothing added or deleted, constitute the whole of Scripture 'given by inspiration of God' to English speaking people." Crumb uses King James too, but unlike Pearl, he includes "every word of the original text."

Selectiveness always privileges some ideas over others. Pearl's bowdlerized Genesis is heavy on "obey" and "rebellion," the same words he emphasizes in his self-published parenting manual, *To Train Up a Child*. His comic book God demands absolute obedience, and so the obedient Pearl demands absolute obedience from children too. Part of a child's training "is to come submissively. However, if you are just beginning to institute training on an already rebellious child . . . then use whatever force is necessary to bring him to bay." So far Pearl's comic book understanding of Christianity has resulted in the deaths of three children and the convictions of six parents for unlawful corporal punishment, felony child abuse, torture, voluntary manslaughter, and second- and first-degree murder.

Pearl calls these folks good Christian parents. Frank Miller might call them Batman.

Miller and artist Jim Lee's *All Star Batman and Robin* features a Pearl-style Bruce Wayne abusing his new ward, Dick Grayson. According to a sheriff's report, a pair of Pearl-followers deprived their adoptive daughter "of food for days at a time and had made her sleep in a cold barn." Miller's Batman keeps Robin in a cave and tells him to catch rats if he's hungry. If he cries, he gets slapped. Pearl recommends using a plumbing tube.

"It has come to my attention," writes the evangelist, "that a vocal few are decrying our sensible application of the Biblical rod in training up our children. I laugh at my caustic critics, for our properly spanked and trained children grow to maturity in great peace and love." And sure enough, Batman's tough love program transforms little Dick from a whimpering orphan to a power-punching Batman Jr. Apparently a diet of beatings and cave vermin can do that. Alfred may disagree, but Robin gets with the righteous program. When you live in a comic book world of Good and Evil, choices are easy.

The D.A. who prosecuted two of Pearl's followers called his parenting manual "truly an evil book." I'm not a big Miller fan, but I wouldn't call his work evil. I wouldn't call anything evil. That moral simplification belongs only in comic books and Bibles. But Miller, like Pearl, is an evangelist. His God is the same Manichaean kind of absolute good vs. evil, the one little Bruce prayed to when he swore "by the spirits of my dead parents to avenge their deaths by spending the rest of my life warring on all criminals." Miller's Batman and Pearl follow that holy vow to its brutal end, but the same infernal engine fuels the entire Michael vs. Lucifer genre. Superheroes are divinely pledged instruments of absolutism.

Add that to the superhero census bureau checklist.

⚡⚡⚡

According to Genesis, the biblical Big Bang hit about 6,000 years ago —and so about 11,000 years after the People of Magnon's Hole painted *Lascaux*. That's a serious timeline glitch, but comic book writers face this sort of quandary every day (how, for example, can Peter Parker enter college in 1965 and graduate in 1978 without aging thirteen years?). But instead of detouring down another quantum physics rabbit hole, let's keep this biblical part of the tour simple.

Tradition credits Moses for recording Genesis around 1400 B.C.E. Troy fell about two hundred years later. Wait another two hundred years and King David is writing the next comic book ur-script:

> Dogs surround me.
> A pack of villains encircles me.
> Lord, how many are my foes!
> Do all these evildoers know nothing?
> Though they plot evil
> And devise wicked schemes,
> They cannot succeed.
>
> It is God who arms me with strength
> And keeps my way secure.
> He will sharpen his sword.
> He will bend and string his bow.
> He has prepared his deadly weapons.
> He makes ready his flaming arrows.
> Though an army besiege me,
> My heart will not fear.
> He makes my feet like the feet of a deer.
> He causes me to stand on the heights.
> He trains my hands for battle.
> My arms can bend a bow of bronze.
>
> You, Lord, hear the desire of the afflicted,
> Defending the fatherless and the oppressed.
> Strike all my enemies on the jaw.
> Break the teeth of the wicked.
> Strike them with terror, Lord.
> Break the arm of the wicked man.

> The Lord mighty in battle,
> He made darkness his covering, his canopy around him —
> The dark rain clouds of the sky.
> On the wicked he will rain.

Call it "The Batman Psalms," and I would love to see Jim Lee draw it. I edited it on a dare from my daughter's high school Latin teacher after he misread a group email calling our drinking cohorts to meet for beers at our local bar, The Palms, at 8:30. Psalms has no book 8, chapter 30, so for homework Pat suggested we compose one: "Let's start an ex post facto apocryphal and/or gnostic psalm tradition."

No one obeyed — myself included, since I didn't write a word. The above is a collage of Psalms 1–25, which tradition attributes to David, composed after sundry battles with Goliath, the Philistines, the Amale-kites, and other of Judah's neighboring supervillain teams. Supposedly, the Manichees of third-century Iran injected the concept of absolute good vs. evil into the Judeo-Christian tradition, but Israel c. 1000 B.C. looks a lot like Gotham to me.

Crime Alley is an urban Valley of the Shadow of Death, with warrior-king Bruce Wayne to patrol it. Unlike Michael, who was already super-powered before God sent him into battle, David is calling God's power down to the human realm. He's raising his merely human self to super-heroic heights by praying to God for superpowered intervention. The Psalms is a long, poetic way of shouting "Shazam!"

David's Psalms are popular with other warrior-kings too. When Oliver Cromwell led his army of Puritans against the English Crown, his men marched into battle singing David's songs of Zion. They were God's army fighting God's war against God's enemies. America's ultimate war pres-ident, Abraham Lincoln, was a fan too, quoting Psalm 3 during his Civil War prayers. Even George W. Bush talked like David. Less than a week after 9/11, he announced, "there are evil people in this world. And we'll be alert. . . . My administration has a job to do and we're going to do it. We will rid the world of the evildoers." In 2002, he asked the nation to "stand squarely in the face of the evildoers that hate America," repeating his call "to fight evil" a month later: "the American people stand squarely in the face of the evil doers."

His speechwriters included David, since "evil people" and "evil doers" entered the English language via the first book of Psalms. That's what Glenn Greenwald labels "a dualistic worldview" in his 2007 *A Tragic Legacy: How a Good vs. Evil Mentality Destroyed the Bush Presidency.* When Bob Woodward asked Bush whether he consulted with his father before invading Iraq, Bush said he had appealed to a "higher Father" instead.

Frank Miller's Batman was a top adviser too. While the United States was storming Iraq, Miller wanted to pit Batman against Al-Qaeda in *Holy Terror, Batman!* In the aftermath of 9/11, writes political journalist Jonathan Schell, it was as if "history was being authored by a third-rate writer . . . to follow the plot of a bad comic book." Not only was Osama bin Laden "a comic-book, caricature villain," but Bush accepted his "invitation to enter into the world of an apocalyptic comic book," turning "himself into a sort of real life action figure . . . on the deck of the USS *Abraham Lincoln.*"

Cromwell will join my list of revolutionary heroes in chapter two, but Lincoln and Bush will not. Although they use Psalms to transform themselves into war presidents, their real superpower is transforming the universe into the one Danny Bulanadi drew for Michael Pearl. Schell calls it a bad comic book because it's black and white. It obeys the superhero metaphysics of moral absolutism, a serial form that perpetuates conflict. Batman's war on criminals, like any Manichaean struggle, is never ending.

King David's plotline, however, eventually closed, and his throne passed to successors. But once you cut the world in two, it's hard to put back together. Lincoln's successor, Andrew Johnson, was impeached for not exacting sufficient vengeance on the former Confederacy. Obama declared the War on Terror over in 2013, but his drone and surveillance policies continued to argue otherwise.

Judah was luckier. The kingdom had David's son Solomon to take office. The only thing he tried to chop in half was a baby. Solomon provides the first letter of the acronym "Shazam," the wizard who gave little Billy Batson the power to turn into Captain Marvel. His war cabinet includes the wisdom of Solomon, the strength of Hercules, the stamina of Atlas, Zeus's power, Achillean courage, and a dash of Mercury's speed. But he's still just a kid at heart. Fawcett Comics introduced him in 1939, months after the fatherless Batman started defending Gotham's oppressed. Soon Captain Marvel was surpassing even Superman to become the reigning superhero of Golden Age sales.

He was a kinder, gentler ruler. Batman's utility belt holstered a pistol in those days, but after he started machine-gunning bad guys from his batplane in 1940, the Lord of DC judged him too violent. He could still strike his enemies on the jaw, but no more deadly weapons. Meanwhile, Shazam was all about family values, sharing his Marvelous powers with Captain Marvel Jr. and Mary Marvel, and then Uncle Marvel and his niece Freckles joined the tribe, and even Hoppy the Marvel Bunny — then war president Franklin Roosevelt led the United States into World War II. Despite all that non-Manichaean wisdom, even Captain Marvel had to battle Captain Nazi.

A warrior king is easier to rally behind. American comic books, like the Psalms of any nation, keep things simple. Who doesn't want to live in a world of pure Good and Evil when the national narrative promises God is on your side? Comics continue that biblical tradition, soothing readers with the righteous victories of heroes drawn by a divine hand.

After Solomon, Judah and Israel suffered new waves of supervillains: Assyria, Babylon, Persia, Greece, Rome. Various Caesars — Julius, Augustus, Tiberius, Caligula — reigned while the most famous Mediterranean godman adventured in occupied Israel. The gospels are fuzzy and/or contradictory regarding exact dates and places, making it hard to say much about the historical Jesus. Recent studies have razored the verifiable facts down to a skeleton so thin I made the mistake of suggesting at a dinner party that there's not enough evidence to prove a historical Jesus existed. Isn't it a question of faith?

This did not make me popular with the religion professor sitting across the table. She cited the usual witnesses, Josephus, Tactus, Pliny, all nice guys but flimsy on cross-examination. It's tricky when you know how many Christs (it's not a name but a title, "the messiah") were wandering Roman-controlled Israel during the first century. Add the even longer tradition of pagan godmen born of virgins who die and are reborn, and Jesus is the most rebooted superhero in history.

But if Jesus wasn't the first self-sacrificing demigod to save the world, he's by far the most influential. It doesn't take a biblical scholar to recognize family resemblances: a Jew found by Egyptians, a Kryptonian by humans; humans reared by apes, fairies, elves; a wizard by muggles; a king by backwater nobles; the Son of God by humans. The boy is fated to grow up extraordinary: prophet, Man of Steel, Lord of the Jungle, Peter Pan, Santa Claus, Voldemort-slayer, king of England, Messiah. Directors also love to shoot their spandex godmen in crucifix-evoking poses, Superman especially (*Smallville*, *Superman Returns*, *Man of Steel*), and a *Last Temptation* motif runs through the screen genre too (*Superman II*, *Blade*, *Spider-Man 2*, *The Fantastic Four*, *The Dark Knight Rises*, *The Wolverine*, *X-Men: Days of Future Past*). From his first *Action Comics* appearance, Superman, "Champion of the Oppressed," echoed prophecy: "They will cry to the Lord because of oppressors, and He will send them a Savior and a Champion" (Isaiah 19:20).

Siegel and Shuster drew their supersavior from layers of Judeo-Christian inspirations, the same way Gnostic gospel writers plumbed traditions to craft their tales of Jesus Christ. If comic books really were gospels, the Complete Testament of Superman would fill a library and include hundreds if not thousands of creators. The actual New Testament includes only twenty-seven books, with Paul doing most of the work, while Matthew, Mark, Luke, and John hog most of the credit. Similarly, a Best of Superman might feature Alan Moore, Mark Waid, and Grant Morrison, while leaving out Otto Binder, Dan Cameron, and William Woolfork.

The original editors of the Bible had to whittle down their best-of compilation from a range of available texts too. "Bible" means "books." It's a multiauthor omnibus of thematically related genre stories, same as *Action Comics*. And, like the sprawling continuities of Marvel and DC, it doesn't always cohere. New writers revised old stories that already overlapped, repeated, and contradicted. It would take a hell of an editor to assemble it into a harmonious whole. The original gospels numbered in the dozens, until the Council of Laodicea razored them down in A.D. 363.

Marvel and DC editors do that all the time, tossing out old tales to usher in the latest reboot, while also retaining a scrambled assortment of the past for new writers to weave into the new Continuity.

Michael Pearl's *Good and Evil* is that kind of weaving. So is *The Children's Bible* my parents gave me when I was two. According to the 1968 inscription, "from Mommy & Daddy," it was a Christmas present, one marketed for broad appeal. Since the four Gospels "contain one message," its editors declare, "they are combined as a single story." The Golden Press advisory board even included a rabbi, though I doubt he really agreed that "the New Testament completes the Old." The "beautifully illustrated in full color" artwork is uncredited, so I don't know who decided Jesus was blond. A dark-skinned, turbaned man walks in front of a camel on the cover spine — an image my perspective-challenged imagination merged into a camel-headed man. I didn't realize he didn't exist until I was boxing the book with my early 80s *Rolling Stones* to join the comics in my attic.

My childhood imagination was more at home with Marvel. Back then they were still being edited by Stanley Lieber, aka Stan Lee. His uncle, Martin Goodman, sold Marvel in 1968 but stayed on as publisher until 1972, when Lee took over, handing the editor in chief plaque to a string of apostles. Though Lee's Jewish parents immigrated from Romania, he told *The Times of Israel* that he "always tried to write stuff that would be for everybody. I never wanted to proselytize." When asked about all the Jewish artists and writers he worked with, he'd rather tick off Italian names instead. He swore he had nothing to do with the Thing's retconned Judaism. He's proud of Izzy Cohen though, the Jewish soldier he created for Sgt. Fury's Howling Commandos, but only because Izzy was part of "the first fully ethnic platoon in comics," which included a black soldier, an Italian, an Englishman, and an American Indian — "everything I could think of! A full international platoon of all religions and people."

Though "not a particularly religious person," Lee told several interviewers that he "read the Bible" and loved "the rhythm of the words," all those "Thous and Doths and Begets," and tried "to get that flavor in stories like Thor." I'm not sure if refried Norse mythology counts as holy scripture, but more than just biblical "phraseology" crept into

Spider-Man. When Peter Parker's Uncle Ben tells him "with great power there must also come great responsibility," he's merging Luke 12:48 ("From everyone who has been given much, much will be demanded") and Acts 4:33 ("And with great power gave the apostles witness of the resurrection of the Lord Jesus: and great grace was upon them all"). And the whole tragic twist of Marvel's Silver Age heroes — that superpowers are both a blessing and a curse — comes down to one word, "barak," from Job 1:5. It means both "bless" and "curse."

Marvel Comics existed only because its predecessor, Timely Comics, published its founding texts. Marvel's Silver Age is built on Timely's Golden Age the way the New Testament built on the Hebrew Bible. Martin Goodman remained the company's publishing deity, but Lee's bullpen was its Council of Laodicea, crafting not just stand-alone tales but an interlocking bible of adventures. Lee was the Holy Roman Emperor, imposing order on disparate realms through the unprecedented use of panel footnotes that referenced not only previous issues of a given title ("See Fantastic Four #3 March") but cross-referenced separate titles ("For the details of that memorable battle, see Spider-Man #14 — Editor") into a single, harmonious Continuity.

The Marvel universe even includes a version of Jesus Christ. After all those miraculous godmen who self-sacrificingly save humanity once a month, Lee and Jack Kirby crafted the "perfect human" in 1967. Known as "Him," the God-like superbeing destroys the evil scientists who created him and abandons Earth. That is until Lee abandoned his editor post and first apostle Roy Thomas resurrected "Him" as a Counter-Earth Jesus rechristened Adam Warlock. The blond supersavior battles the Antichrist-like Man-Beast and his animal-headed minions, while beseeching Counter-Earth creator High Evolutionary to spare the flawed world from his disappointed wrath.

Comic book writers usually bury the Bible deeper in the subtext, but I still missed all those allusions as a kid. I also missed the fundamental contradiction. Adam Warlock, like any superhero, chooses the human half of his split-identity when he accepts his job as savior, fighting the good fight with his fists. Like the mighty Michael and all the angelic superheroes continuing his absolute mission, Adam Warlock hurls himself into battle against his demon foes. On the first day of class, none of my students have ever called out the word "violent" when brainstorming superhero traits, so I always add it myself. And then circle it. Twice. I won't declare it a must-have on a superhero census bureau checklist, but it's pretty damn close.

But the demigod Jesus Christ is a very different kind of superman. When it comes to defeating Absolute Evil, Christian mythology reverses genre expectations and has its ultimate hero win by losing. The super-heroic Jesus could pummel Herod and Pilate and their Roman minions, but he submits to torture and execution instead. He is radically nonviolent, a suicidally self-sacrificing über-pacifist, and so perhaps the most un-superhero of them all. As much as superheroes look like saviors, their parables are Christianity's antithesis.

⚡ ⚡ ⚡

I doubt even the Council of Laodicea could edit *The Testament of Adam Warlock* into coherence, because, like most superhero comics, the biblically jumbled plotlines and ad hoc revisions are the never-ending work of dozens of incompatible prophets and successive bishops. No all-powerful hand guides the decades-long creative process. When Stephen Thompson asked a roster of celebrities whether there's a God, Stan Lee answered: "I really don't know. I just don't know."

Our nation's third president was more diplomatic. Thomas Jefferson names "Nature's God" in the first sentence of the Declaration of Independence, "Creator" in the second, and "divine Providence" in the last. Still, the United States's third commander in chief and Marvel's fourth publisher have a lot in common. Like Lee, Jefferson kept religion out of his workplace, building the "wall of separation between church and state." The atheist president sat at his Oval Office desk with a razor, slicing gospels down to his own coherent but non-"superstitious" storyline, same as Shanower did with Troy. The miracles, the resurrection, any mention of Christ's divinity, they're all cuttings in his tax-financed wastebasket.

I would demand Congress begin impeachment proceedings, but God struck the sinner down in 1826. Technically, Jefferson was a deist, and the Oval Office wasn't built yet — but he was called a "howling atheist" even before he was elected ("Should the infidel Jefferson be elected to the Presidency, the seal of death is that moment set on our holy religion") and began editing *The Jefferson Bible*. The founding father believed God, like a clockmaker, manufactured human beings, wound them up, and watched them go.

Stan's God says the same:

> I gave them minds as I recall
> It was all so long ago.
> I gave them minds that they might use
> To choose, to think, to know.
> For the hapless weak must need be wise
> If they would prove their worth.
> And then I gave them paradise
> The fertile, verdant Earth.
>
> At first I found the plan was sound
> And somewhat entertaining.
> But once begun, the deed now done,
> My interest started waning.
>
> The seed thus sown
> The twig now grown
> I left them there
> Alone.

Those are stanzas from Lee's 1970 poem "God Woke" (unpublished till Jeff McLaughlin included it in a collection of interviews in 2007). Lee never assigned the eight-page text to any of his artists, so *The Lee Bible*, unlike my *Children's Bible*, isn't illustrated. It describes our Creator waking up from a cosmic nap with a nagging half-memory of Earth and so returning to see how humanity is fairing without Him. He doesn't much like "the man sounds everywhere," but the one that sends him into despair is "The haunting, hollow sound of Prayer." As Thomas Jefferson or any other good deist would tell you, God doesn't answer them. Lee's God laughs at all the "ranting" and then frowns and sighs with boredom. He doesn't like all the hypocrisy either, but it's people's yearning for Him that's most baffling. Finally, the "carnage, the slaughter" in His name brings Him to tears as "He looked His last at man," once again leaving us on our own.

Lee isn't as skilled a poet as Milton, but he is a deistic creator. Like Jefferson's Grand Architect, Lee and his artistic co-Gods set the Marvel pantheon into motion, then stepped back and watched the bullpen spin the wheels of the multiverse. Their bible is probably no more heretical than *The Jefferson Bible*, though Jefferson would object to all the superstitious miracle-working. Jefferson is a kind of superhero too. A mere mortal who had the godly audacity to declare all men — even divinely appointed kings — equal (lots more on that revolutionary breakthrough next chapter). Like Lee, Jefferson lived in a deistic universe. All superhero universes are deistic. Dead, sleeping, or just annoyingly silent, God has to be absent. Otherwise there's no void to fill, no divinely empty space for humans to rise into. A Supreme Finger has to press the Big Bang button, and then as that Hand of God retracts, a few mighty mortals are sucked into the power vacuum.

But God isn't really absent. That would be too Chaotic, a return to Nu and Ginnungagap. Instead, superheroes exist in a highly ordered universe, one in which the secret One-Above-All silently divides the complexities of human behavior into the simplest binaries, Good and Evil, Right and Wrong, Us and Them. Comic books aren't reassuring just because they depict godmen dedicated to our protection. The fabric of their time-space is warped for happy endings. Bulanadi isn't the only comic book artist drawing God just outside the frame. Despite the cosmological differences between Marvel and DC, the same God of superhero reality makes sure his more-than-human good guys always win.

After defining the multiverse's moral metaphysics, the Judeo-Christian tradition also provides a few superhero character blueprints. Archangel Michael, King David, and Jesus Christ never joined the Justice League, but other biblical descendants have.

The Golem, a superpowered and literal mudblood, is strong, impervious to pain, and, when mixed from clay, can shape-shift a bit. The word "golem" debuts in Psalms 139:16 ("my substance, yet being unperfect") when David praises God for creating him. The Talmud (c. 200 C.E.) uses the term to describe Adam's creation: "In the first hour, his dust was gathered; in the second, it was kneaded into a shapeless mass." That's pretty much the description of Ben Grimm that Stan Lee typed for Jack Kirby in 1960: "He's sort of shapeless — he's become a THING." I don't know if either had the Golem in mind, but Karl Kesel did in 2002 when he decided Ben's full name was Benjamin Jacob Grimm.

Another Talmud passage documents the first golem: "Rabbah created a man, and sent him to Rabbi Zera. Rabbi Zera spoke to him, but received no answer. Thereupon he said unto him: 'Thou art a creature of the magicians. Return to thy dust.'" That's the Golem Marvel reconstituted in 1974 — though he'd been adventuring in Prague since the 1800s. Benjamin Kuras, author of *As Golems Go*, says he's still patrolling there: "After living through the Austro-Hungarian Empire, Nazism and decades of communism, the Czechs are drawn to a character with supernatural powers that will help liberate them from oppression."

If you're not up on your Kabbalistic techniques, *Sefer Yetzirah* (*The Book of Formation*) gives a how-to for Golem animating. Since a statue can't shout "Shazam!" you have to place the magic word in its mouth on a slip of paper. Shazam's wizard forefather, Merlin, received his magic straight from God. Merlin is a bit of a golem too, clumped together by the fact-challenged historian Geoffrey of Monmouth from several stray wizards wandering the early Arthurian highlands, c. 1136. Geoffrey christened him Merlinus because he thought his Welsh name, Myrddin, sounded like shit, *merde* in French. He doesn't wander into comics till 1936, two years ahead of Superman. His descendant at Quality Comics had an annoying habit of talking backward when spell casting: "RALOP RAEB, ESAHC YAWA EHT SIZAN!"

I thought BBC Wales was cheating when they made their 2008 Merlin so young, but then I read Merlin's debut appearance in *Histories of the Kings of Britain*. Geoffrey introduces him as one of two "youths," traveling with his nonelderly mom. Next thing the kid is stumping the king's second-rate wizards and revealing the napping place of dragons under the castle: "All they that stood by were no less astonished at such wisdom being found in him, deeming that he was possessed of some spirit of God."

I expected him to stick around to aid Uther's son, but the magical youth vanishes before another God-inspired superhero predecessor, Arthur, takes the throne. My introduction to Camelot came in the twelfth grade, with the standard A. P. English syllabus selection "Sir Gawain and the Green Knight." By the fourteenth century, King Arthur and his Knights of the Round Table were English folklore's mightiest superteam: "But of all that here built, of Britain the kings, / ever was Arthur highest, as I have heard tell." Merlin receives only a cameo, so when the supervillainess Morgan la Faye sends a supernatural thug (his superhuman healing powers include the ability to reattach his severed head) to Camelot's Christmas feast, Sir Gawain accepts the challenge, resulting in a 2,525-line maxi-series spin-off.

Gawain's romance involves secret identities (the Green Knight is really Bertilak de Hautdesert!) and mighty challenges chivalrously performed in service to a noble and God-fearing nation. The Justice Society of America, the first superhero team in comics, began as individual adventures too. The *All Star Comics* cover features the team of Golden Age heroes sitting around a literal round table, with the Spectre and Dr. Fate assuming Merlin's magical duties.

The Arthur-influenced author Edmund Spenser spun his roundtable of Christian knight-errants in the 1590s, even soldering the first Iron Man: "His name was *Talus*, made of yron mould, / Immoueable, resistlesse, without end." If you're rusty on Renaissance English, that's "iron mold," "immovable," and "resistless," all Tony Stark synonyms. Talus's other superpowers include speed ("him pursew'd so light, / As that it seem'd aboue the ground he went"); invulnerability (though a bad guy "streight at him with all his force did go," Talus was "mou'd no more therewith, then when a rocke / Is lightly stricken with some stones throw"); and strength ("But to him leaping, lent him such a knocke, / That on the ground he layd him like a senseless blocke"). And that's just from his first adventure.

The executive branch of *The Faerie Queene*'s dynamic duo is Sir Artegall, Knight of Justice. The sidekick yron man worked for his mentor guru,
the heavenly Astraea, before she "willed him with *Artegall* to wend, / And
doe what euer thing he did intend." She also gives Artegall a nifty sword
"Tempered with Adamant," like Michael's chains and Wolverine's claws.
Together, "They two enough t'encounter an whole Regiment."

Art is more diplomat than warrior, but his word-mincing is made possible by his trusty page's "yron flale," the big stick of his foreign policy. A
Page of Justice is handy for castle storming ("at the length he has yrent
the door"), mob dispersal ("hid themselves in holes and bushes from his
view"), and executions ("And down the rock him throwing, in the sea
he drouned"). He has no qualms dispatching women either ("Over the
Castle wall adowne her cast, / And there her drowned in the durty mud").
In fact, Talus has no qualms of any kind. It doesn't matter if his target
offers prayers, cash, or sex, "he was nothing mou'd, nor tempted" and
"Withouten pitty of her goodly hew."

The guy is a drone. Commander in chief Artegall gives the lethal nod,
and his War Machine, "swift as swallow" and "strong as Lyon," descends.
Ed Craun, my department's emeritus sci-fi and Spenser expert, likens one
adventure to a search-and-destroy mission in the caves of Afghanistan.
Talus, he tells me, represents the Law of Retaliation, lex Talonis, the biblical eye-for-an-eye. He's Tony Stark's shrapnel-pierced heart still beating
at the moral center of the superhero multiverse.

We could continue touring superheroically Christian soldiers, but
having established the multiverse's Godly underpinnings, it's time to
overthrow it. Superheroes, for all their simplified morality, also share
a long lineage with the heaven-storming Odin and Lucifer. Talus's least
superheroic trait is his obedience. Lucifer was once God's sidekick too,
before deciding he'd rather rule in hell. Superheroes preserve a lot of pre–
Big Bang chaos in their DNA, and that rebellious impulse to explode old
hierarchies gives rise to chapter two's revolutionary supermen.

FNSB13, "Napoleon Batman," 2014.

CHAPTER 2

REVOLUTION

Superman looks like a model citizen, a superpowered Boy Scout championing his democratic nation's bourgeois establishment. You could say he embodies the 1954 Comics Code mandate that "policemen, judges, government officials, and respected institutions shall never be presented in such a way as to create disrespect for established authority."

But that's more a suggestion than a founding principle — like the Federation's Prime Directive (thou shalt not interfere with developing civilizations) that every week's *Star Trek* plot requires Kirk to boldly violate. In comics, government exists to be disrespected. James Frank Vlamos, a Paul Revere of superhero criticism, shouted his warning in 1941: "the lawful processes of police and courts have" been replaced by the "methods . . . of a bully" who "flouts every accepted law of man and morals."

If you don't believe him, open *Action Comics* No. 12. Superman bursts through the wall of a radio station and shoves an announcer in the face: "Beat it! And tell that control engineer that if he shuts me off the air, I'll make a bee-line for his gizzard!" The superbully then declares "war on reckless drivers" and, while dodging police bullets, demolishes a car pound (the owners are traffic violators), a used car lot (the cars are unsafe), and a manufacturing plant (the owners use cheap materials). He even kidnaps the mayor and frightens him into obeying his orders. This guy is a tyrant and his own army-of-one.

When Umberto Eco sat down with a stack of 40s and 50s comics in 1963, not much had changed: "Each of these heroes is gifted with such powers that he could actually take over the government, defeat the army, or alter the equilibrium of planetary politics." Jump another twenty years and Hal Blythe and Charlie Sweet see the same threat, ignored only because the "reader does not care how often the superhero transgresses man's petty laws, for the hero operates under a higher law that always has the ultimate good of society at its center."

It's an old idea. Emerson offered the same basic fanboy argument a hundred years before Vlamos: "Mankind have in all ages attached themselves to a few persons who either by the quality of that idea they embodied or by the largeness of their reception were entitled to the position of leaders and law-givers." Lucky for democracy, superheroes' higher laws usually coincide with the actual laws passed by elected Houses of Commons and Representatives. But it's one person, not Parliament or Congress, defining what ultimately is and isn't good for society. Vlamos calls that nihilism. We used to call it monarchy.

Before the dawn of election ballots, kings represented God and so ruled by divine right. When God retired from politics, supermen claimed the empty throne. Even when they allow some petty president or prime minister to sit on it, superheroes — even the upstanding Clark Kent — pledge allegiance to no government. They may act alongside law enforcement, even accepting deputy status if it makes officials feel better, but they're free agents. Even while the star-spangled warriors of World War II fought for democracy, they never represented it. Peel back Captain America's flag costume and you find Guy Fawkes and Oliver Cromwell, revolutionary radicals championing their own self-defined liberty. Today we'd call them terrorists.

That antigovernment urge penned the legends of Robin Hood before spreading into the coups of seventeenth-century England and leaping to the American colonies where neither king nor Parliament stood above the convictions of a superheroic individual. The egalitarianism of the American Revolution washed back across the Atlantic to remove the aristocratic heads of the French government, but the age still demanded a reinvented form of elitism. When Napoleon conceived of himself as a superior being, he revolutionized the hero genre too. The Gray Champion, Jean Valjean, the Count of Monte Cristo, the Scarlet Pimpernel,

Zorro, V, they are their own parliament of supermen ruling above all others — citizens, monarchs, and God.

Robin Hood, founding father of noble outlaws, has no secret origin. He may be a literary mutation of the more historically verifiable Fulk fitz Warins, a twelfth-century nobleman who led a team of rebel bandits against the king after the king handed his inheritance to a rival. After three years of marauding, Fulk got his castle back, and superheroes got their first blast of semiennobling rebel radiation.

William Langland knew some "rymes of Robyn hood" when he penned *Piers Plowman* in the late 1300s, but no one can hum those tunes now. "Robert Hude the Waythman" appears in Andrew of Wyntoun's *Orygynale Chronicle*, c. 1420, and twenty years later, Walter Bower condemns "foolish people" who "are so inordinately fond of celebrating" that "*famous assassin*." Richard Grafton's 1569 Robert Hood "was for his manhoode and chivalry advaunced to the noble dignité of an Erle" but "so prodigally exceeded in charges and expences, that he fell into great debt, by reason wherof, so many actions and sutes were commenced against him, wherunto he aunswered not, that by order of lawe he was outlawed." Not a very admirable start to a do-gooding career, but by 1609 Robert Jones was singing what "A noble thiefe was Robin Hoode."

That antinoble nobility is one of superheroes' founding paradoxes. They're born to disrespect authority. Emerson says it's their mission: "The great, or such as hold of nature and transcend fashions by their fidelity to universal ideas, are saviors from these federal errors, and defend us from our contemporaries." Thomas Carlyle worships hero-saviors even more: "the History of the world is but the Biography of great men."

Tom and Waldo founded the Great Man Fan Club, comic books inherited it, and today's Hollywood worships superheroes more than ever. Maybe that's why Alan Moore — arguably the most acclaimed writer in comic books' eight decades — hates them so much. "I don't think the superhero stands for anything good," he told the *Guardian*'s Stuart Kelly. "They were originally in the hands of writers who would actively expand the imagination of their nine-to-13-year-old audience." But since all they do nowadays is entertain thirty-to-sixty-year-old "emotionally subnormal" men, Moore considers superheroes "abominations." He told blogger Pádraig Ó Méalóid their continuing dominance was "culturally catastrophic."

This from a self-professed anarchist who considers the shooting of government leaders a "lovely thought." Little wonder his first superhero was a revolutionary terrorist.

Moore and artist David Lloyd began *V for Vendetta* in 1981 for England's since-defunct *Warrior* magazine. I started reading it when the series moved to DC in 1988. I was twenty-two, Moore's age when he first conceived a story about "a freakish terrorist" who "waged war upon a Totalitarian State." But, he explains in the collection's introduction, it was Lloyd who transformed his freak into "a resurrected Guy Fawkes, complete with one of those paper mâché masks in a cape and conical hat."

Their plan was to create "something uniquely British," and, sure enough, the Fawkes reference meant absolutely nothing to this Pittsburgh-born college senior. When I'd read *The Handmaid's Tale* the year before, I thought Margaret Atwood was forecasting an original future: "they shot the president and machine-gunned the Congress.... The entire government, gone like that." But Fawkes beat her to the fuse by almost four centuries.

I didn't read up on the Gunpowder Plot until I was a student-teacher prepping *Macbeth* for a class of tenth graders. Shakespeare staged his tragedy of a regicidal antihero after Catholic terrorists tried to blow up King James during the 1605 opening of Parliament. They'd rented a storage space under the House of Lords and crammed in three-dozen barrels of gunpowder. Fawkes was arrested before he could detonate the plot, tortured into betraying his co-conspirators, tried, hanged, and his body displayed in pieces as a warning to sympathizers. He was still in prison when London lit bonfires in celebration of the king's survival, and Parliament later declared the anniversary an official holiday, complete with fireworks and newspaper-stuffed "guys" set ablaze.

Somewhere along the line the point of the celebrations got hazy. Guy Fawkes Night lost its official standing in the nineteenth century, around when penny dreadful writers were converting England's most abominable traitor into a romantic hero, a conspiracy Lloyd happily joined. "We shouldn't burn the chap every Nov. 5," he told his collaborator Moore, "but celebrate his attempt to blow up Parliament!"

I want to say the American equivalent would be championing John Wilkes Booth or Timothy McVeigh, but Fawkes's rehabilitation might be possible only because his assassinations failed. Benedict Arnold might be closer — except no one remembers what treason he was planning (and if even you do, surrendering West Point to the British doesn't have the same audacious charm).

So Lloyd wanted to "give Guy Fawkes the image he's deserved," but it's not clear Moore was committed to the plot. Although he told Margaret Killjoy he champions anarchy ("the only political standpoint that I could possibly adhere to would be an anarchist one") and longs for a society with "no leaders" (no archons), Moore doesn't "believe that a violent revolution is ever going to work." He doesn't hide his freakish terrorist's violence under POW! and BAM! bubbles either. It was Lloyd who banned the sound effects (along with thought balloons — probably the most important moment in Moore's development as a writer), but Moore's dialogue complicates the violence Lloyd renders otherwise bloodless:

> I've seen worse, Dominic, physically speaking. Like I say, it's the mental side that bothers me . . . his attitude to killing. Think about it. He killed them ruthlessly, efficiently, and with a minimum of fuss. Whatever their faults, those were two human beings . . . and he slaughtered them like cattle!

V the terrorist also enters quoting *Macbeth*, the usurper Shakespeare's audiences (including King James, for whom it was commissioned) would have linked to Fawkes. Moore's chapter one title, "The Villain," might be a subtle clue too.

V goes on to murder and maim his way through some thirty chapters, but the part that troubled me most at the time was the psychological torture he inflicts on his sidekick, Evey. Yes, he rescues the damsel from a back-alley rape in standard Batman fashion, but then he dupes her into believing she's been imprisoned by the fascist government, shaves her head, starves and waterboards her, all in the name of . . . what exactly?

By the end Evey is another good little Robin, taking on her mentor's mission, but there's more than a whiff of the Stockholm syndrome between the panels.

"The central question is," Moore says, "is this guy right? Or is he mad? I didn't want to tell people what to think, I just wanted to tell people to think and consider some of these admittedly extreme little elements." I'd call that a pretty good example of using a superhero to actively expand an audience's imagination. Moore's anarchy also overthrows the established order by unmasking the revolutionist at the explosive heart of superheroes.

Fawkes failed to free his fellow Catholics from the tyranny of their Protestant king, but that hasn't kept him from new adventures. The "hacktivist" network Anonymous adopted Lloyd's Fawkes mask for their 2008 Scientology protest, which they carried over to Occupy Wall Street and then a worldwide Million Mask March held on Guy Fawkes Day to protest government austerity programs. The group's anticorporate message, however, fades in the smoke haze once you know TimeWarner owns the copyright on the masks (via DC), which are manufactured in South American sweatshops and earn the company a killing on Amazon.

I don't know if that makes Anonymous a "champion of the oppressed," but I do know that Jerry Siegel didn't steal the Man of Steel's tagline from Guy Fawkes. He stole it from an entirely different revolutionist: silent film star, writer, and producer Douglas Fairbanks. *The Mark of Zorro* opens with Fairbanks's intertitle: "Oppression — by its very nature — creates the power that crushes it. A champion arises — a champion of the oppressed — whether it be a Cromwell or someone unrecorded, he will be there. He is born."

So oppression is radiation. It's the original cosmic gamma ray bomb of spider-bite mutation that births the superhero. I could quibble with the logic (is oppression always self-defeating?), but the word that made me pause (literally, I thumbed PAUSE on my remote) is "Cromwell." As in Oliver Cromwell, the man who chopped off King Charles's head in 1649 to become England's Lord Protector. Cromwell's kidneys betrayed him a decade later, and after the funeral, Charles's restored son dug up the usurper's body from Westminster Abbey for a belated beheading. Like Guy Fawkes's mutilated corpse, Cromwell's severed head toured England for years.

Johnston McCulley doesn't mention Cromwell in his original 1919 Zorro novel, *The Curse of Capistrano*, the *All-Story* pulp serial Fairbanks adapted the following year. Some American Fairbanks trace their name back to the Puritan Fayerbankes, proud followers of Cromwell since the 1630s, so maybe Douglas was carrying on family tradition. Except *The Mark of Zorro* isn't the first Cromwell shout-out in superhero prehistory. George Bernard Shaw lauds him in "The Revolutionist's Handbook," an appendix to *Man and Superman*. Shaw — via his alter ego, John Tanner, the handbook's fictional author — declares Cromwell "one of those chance attempts at the Superman which occur from time to time in spite of the interference of Man's blundering institutions." Shaw/Tanner is another disrespecting flouter of established authority. The devout eugenicist longed for a whole nation of Zorros, "an England in which every man is a Cromwell" (more on that in chapter five).

By the time Siegel was stealing Fairbanks's intertitles, "Cromwell" and "superman" were synonyms. Biographer John Buchan (better known for his Hitchcock-adapted *Thirty-Nine Steps*) called Cromwell "the one Superman in England who ruled and reigned without a crown." P. W. Wilson extended the comparison to modern times, ranking England's prime minister Stanley Baldwin "among the supermen," and likening his overseeing of Edward VIII's 1936 abdication to Cromwell's regicide.

Alan Moore traces his other superhero inspirations to seventeenth-century England too, when underground religious movements were espousing the heretical view that all men could be priests, "a nation of saints." Moore explained to Killjoy, "it was during the 17th century that, partly fueled by similar ideas, Oliver Cromwell rose up and commenced the British civil war, which eventually led to the beheading of Charles I."

Carlyle admits that Cromwell "seems an anarchist," but like "every Great Man," his "mission is Order," a restoration of divine will through a "true" king who — unlike the "ignoble, unvaliant, fatuous man" raised by a monarchy — "*has* a divine right." It's the ur-logic of Spider-Man's great power/great responsibility equation. Cromwell even answers a cry for help: "he comes out ... since no other is willing to come: in resistance to a public grievance." And though killing the king was an unfortunate solution, Carlyle says the guy was just being practical.

Fawkes would have gladly chopped off Charles's dad's head too, but Guy was no Oliver. He had the plot but not the superpower to execute it. Superheroes have to be executioners. Buchan celebrates Cromwell as "an iron man of action" with "no parallel in history." He ignored his own council of commanders during the civil war and, after making England a republic, ignored Parliament too. "It was too risky to trust the people," explains Buchan, "he must trust himself."

That's the übermensch Shaw and Emerson adore too. Not a champion of the oppressed, but a champion of the superself. It's a quality still central to superheroes, all those iron men of action who trust only themselves, ignoring and defying law enforcement to maintain their own Order. Zorro opposed the colonial regime of a corrupt California governor. Cromwell fought for religious freedom against a tyrant who persecuted anyone who did not conform to the Church of England. That's where superhero tales usually end. After crushing all that dastardly oppression, Fairbanks's movie Zorro retires into happy matrimony. McCulley kept his Zorro in more oppression-opposing adventures, ones inspired by Baroness Orczy's Scarlet Pimpernel, an iron man of action dedicated to rescuing noble necks from the kind of execution blade Cromwell wielded.

But once his authority was established, how could Cromwell continue to flout established authority? He had no choice but to convert to the villainous half of the superhuman spectrum — or, as Christopher Nolan's Batman sums it up: "You either die a hero or live long enough to see yourself become the villain." Like the regicidal tyrant Macbeth, the enthroned Lord Protector imposed his own, literally Puritanical order on England. He closed taverns, chopped down maypoles, outlawed makeup, fined profanity, and, as a real life Burgermeister Meisterburger, canceled Christmas. When Alan Brennert wrote his 1991 graphic novel, *Batman: Holy Terror*, he kept Cromwell on the throne an extra decade, creating an Elseworld in which the United States is an English commonwealth run by a tyrannical theocracy.

A superman in authority is never good for the common man. Superhero uniforms can be patriotic, but totalitarian blood runs under the superhero skin. Look at *The Boys* (2006), or *Kingdom Come* (1996), or *Squadron Supreme* (1986), or, best yet, Moore's *Marvelman* (aka *Miracleman*, but let's not go into that right now). I bought No. 16 from my college comic shop in 1989, a year after I graduated. It's the last issue before Neil Gaiman took over and I stopped reading the series. Gaiman is great, but the story was played out. Marvelman has rid the world of nuclear warheads, crime, global warming, money, childbirth pain, and, in some cases, death. He's not king of the world. He's its authoritarian God.

Marvel restarted the series in 2014, but my worship of Moore is over. I considered him the reigning writer of the multiverse, but his rule grew increasingly idiosyncratic and, less forgivably, dull. His last *Miracleman*, "Olympus," is a tour of the dystopic future. *From Hell* offers similar tours, literally horse-drawn, which, while aggressively nondramatic in structure, basically work. But my heart sank when the third volume of *The League of Extraordinary Gentleman* devolved into a balloon ride over yet more meticulously researched esotoria. Yes, the dreamlike Blazing World is ripe with 3-D nudity, but this is no way to conclude a revolutionary plot. When *Promethea*, my favorite of all Moore creations, plunged down the same rabbit hole, I stopped reading. Moore even established his own imprint, America's Best Comics, with no Parliament to ignore and no corrupt tyrant to oppose. His anarchic style had settled into its own oppressive order.

Of course readers rebelled.

⚡⚡⚡

So superheroes love oppression. It justifies their revolutionary instincts. Even Fairbanks's son, Douglas Jr., knew that. After his father's death, he wrote, produced, and starred in *The Exile*, a swashbuckler about Charles II, the son of the king Cromwell beheaded. The hero prince hides out on a Holland farm and falls in love with a flower monger while battling Cromwell's assassins before Parliament calls him home for his coronation. It's a happy ending made happier by the fact that Douglas Jr. didn't follow it with a sequel.

After the real Charles II started waging wars and suspending laws, Parliament regretted their invitation. But they didn't do anything about it till Charles's Catholic brother, James II, inherited the crown and Guy Fawkes's vision of a Catholic dynasty was slouching toward England. The Glorious Revolution of 1688 was at least bloodless. James fled to France, head attached, and William and his Dutch fleet docked permanently in London bay. Colonial America's archenemy George III took the throne a hundred years later because Parliament had outlawed Catholic heirs.

As far as tyrants go, George isn't much of a despot. I mean, sure, taxes suck, but the guy wasn't outlawing Santa Claus. Still, every mediocre Cromwell creates the mediocre Cromwell who crushes him, and so come 1773, a secret society of mildly oppressed middle-class colonists, aka the Sons of Liberty, were dumping tea crates into Boston harbor in defiance of Parliament's bailout of the British East India Company. The 2008 Tea Party reboot settled for Barack Obama for its inspirational tyranny, ready with their own Gunpowder tactics of debt defaults and government shutdowns. The new Tea Party follows the logic of the superhero formula too, championing personal definitions of America in defiance of the founding principles of compromise and majority rule. Like superheroes, they disrespect the established authority of elected government, flouting democracy in the paradoxical name of democracy.

I would never call them a Justice League, but I do feel affection for at least one member of their team. I recently reconnected with an old high school friend via (what else?) Facebook. Our cyber reunion wasn't entirely Friendly though. In the decades since we'd crammed Pre-Calc in his suburban basement, he converted to an aggressively libertarian brand of fundamentalist Christianity (or, as he terms it, simply "Christianity"). His profile picture is Obama photo-shopped as Stalin. I accused him of melodrama, but he remained literal in his belief that the Muslim president's reelection constituted a Socialist coup and collapse of the American experiment. Our email exchanges soon petered out. But I will honor him and his cohorts with a declaration:

The first American superhero was a Tea Party superhero.

"Oh! Lord of Hosts," cried a voice among the crowd, "provide a Champion for thy people!"

That's Nathaniel Hawthorne, 1835. Thy people are his pre-Revolutionary ancestors under the tyrannical yoke of King James and his New World minions, aka the governor of colonial Massachusetts and his nefarious Redcoat Guard.

> "There was once a time," declares Hawthorne, "when New-England groaned under the actual pressure of heavier wrongs, than those threatened ones which brought on the Revolution. James II, the bigoted successor of Charles the Voluptuous, had annulled the charters of all the colonies, and sent a harsh and unprincipled soldier to take away our liberties and endanger our religion."

Just to be clear, "Charles the Voluptuous" is Charles II, the guy Douglas Jr. played in *The Exile*. Hawthorne casts Charles's brother, James II, as America's first supervillain. Although the Revolution is a century away, Hawthorne is writing America's origin story, and that means retconning our first superhero. In answer to this cry of oppression comes the Gray Champion:

> Suddenly, there was seen the figure of an ancient man, who seemed to have emerged from among the people, and was walking by himself along the centre of the street, to confront the armed band. He wore the old Puritan dress, a dark cloak and a steeple-crowned hat, in the fashion of at least fifty years before, with a heavy sword upon his thigh, but a staff in his hand, to assist the tremulous gait of age.

A shaky old guy, not very superheroic sounding, I know, but hang on — he has superpowers: "while they marvelled at the venerable grandeur of his aspect, the old man had faded from their eyes, melting slowly into the hues of twilight, till, where he stood, there was an empty space." So, like Dumbledore, he can apparate. The wondering crowd whispers, "Whence did he come? What is his purpose? Who can this old man be?" Hawthorne is happy to answer:

> That stately form, combining the leader and the saint, so gray, so dimly seen, in such an ancient garb, could only belong to some old champion of the righteous cause, whom the oppressor's drum had summoned from his grave.

That's right; he's supernatural too. And while immortality is a nice trick, his real powers are rabble-rousing and monarch-busting: "his voice stirred their souls," and before "another sunset, the Governor, and all that rode so proudly with him, were prisoners, and long ere it was known that James had abdicated." The hero rises and another tyrant tumbles. The Gray Champion, the righteous spirit of democratic rebellion, is the ghost of Lord Protector Cromwell—or at least one of those Puritan Fayerbankes, proud followers of Cromwell since the 1630s.

I doubt my Tea Party friend read "The Gray Champion," though *The Scarlet Letter* was on our high school English syllabus. I won't declare Hester the first superheroine, but she's probably the first character in fiction to sport a letter on her chest, beating Shuster's Superman by nearly nine decades. The "A" starts as punishment, but Hester embroiders her own meaning into the symbol, and eventually the town rechristens her "Able" and "Angel" in appreciation of her selfless service.

The Gray Champ has her beat though. Midwife to the poor is noble and all, but even now he could rouse our whole land from its sluggish despondency. According to my Facebook Friend, the harsh and unprincipled administration of Obama lacks scarcely a single characteristic of tyranny, violating the rights of private citizens, taking away our liberties, and endangering our religion. These, as always, are evil times. Hawthorne agrees:

> "Satan will strike his master-stroke presently," cried some, bemoaning the deformity of any government that does not grow out of the nature of things and the character of the people. On one side the religious multitude, with their sad visages and dark attire, and on the other, the group of despotic rulers. Pray and expect patiently what the Lord will do in this matter!

A literal Godsend, the returning Gray Champion would forgo street protests and broadcast his message nationally these days. In fact, who needs the Gray Champion in the age of Facebook? My Friend shouts on his homepage: "Government of the people is GONE. People will only be ignored so long, then they will act. God help us all." That's why Hawthorne's tale ends as any comic book origin story should, with the promise of further adventures:

> Whenever the descendants of the Puritans are to show the spirit of their sires, the old man appears again. . . . His hour is one of darkness, and adversity, and peril. But should domestic tyranny oppress us, or the invader's step pollute our soil, still may the Gray Champion come.

Hawthorne even places the supernatural do-gooder at the Tea Party's namesake event, plus a couple of Revolutionary battle sites:

> When eighty years had passed, he walked once more in King-street. Five years later, in the twilight of an April morning, he stood on the green, beside the meeting-house, at Lexington, where now the obelisk of granite, with a slab of slate inlaid, commemorates the first fallen of the Revolution. And when our fathers were toiling at the breastwork on Bunker's Hill, all through that night, the old warrior walked his rounds.

The tyranny-fighting spirits of Guy Fawkes and Oliver Cromwell leaped the Atlantic in a single bound to animate America's first superhero. That's our nation's secret origin, written the year France's Alexis de Tocqueville first used the magic word "exceptional" to begin the transformation of a fledgling nation of Cromwells into a democratic superpower.

Hawthorne's Gray Champion is a two-dimensional adaptation of American history. It's how things would work in a black-and-white world sliced cleanly into righteous good and tyrannical evil. It's the simplified version you tell a six-year-old, the complex shadings flattened into superheroic poses. Our history and literature books are filled with such grayless Gray Champions.

Look at Paul Revere. That Son of Liberty died quietly at home in 1818 — before his resurrection four decades later gave him the strength of three men and the power of bilocation. He was both in the church tower swinging a lantern and on his horse across the river receiving the message. Fellow riders William Dawes and Samuel Prescott stumbled and vanished into the white space between the stanzas of Henry Wadsworth Longfellow's "Paul Revere's Ride," the poem that transformed the mild-mannered rebel into a larger-than-life American hero. When the actual human-sized Revere died, his obit didn't mention the not-yet-legendary midnight ride of 1775. With Dawes and Prescott out of the picture, he rose to ride beside his superheroic predecessors, Fawkes and Cromwell.

Paul Revere is one of several super-Americans Tarek Mehanna, a Pittsburgh-born pharmacist convicted of supporting Al-Qaeda in 2012, named as his role models. Batman was at the top of the list. "When I was six," Mehanna told his sentencing judge, "I began putting together a massive collection of comic books. Batman implanted a concept in my mind, introduced me to a paradigm as to how the world is set up: that there are oppressors, there are the oppressed, and there are those who step up to defend the oppressed."

After Batman, school field trips and high school history classes showed Mehanna "just how real that paradigm is in the world." He admired the oppression-fighting Paul Revere, Tom Paine, Harriet Tubman, Nat Turner, John Brown, Emma Goldman, Eugene Debs, Rosa Parks, Malcolm X, and Martin Luther King Jr. "Everything a man is exposed to in his environment becomes an ingredient that shapes his outlook," Mehanna explained. "So, in more ways than one, it's because of America that I am who I am."

"Are you a terrorist?" isn't on my superhero census bureau questionnaire, but Alan Moore might judge Mehanna "emotionally subnormal," and Judge O'Toole sentenced him to seventeen years. Glenn Greenwald calls that "one of the most egregious violations of the First Amendment's guarantee of free speech," one that history will condemn along with "the architects of the policies he felt compelled to battle." It could be a while before history makes its ruling, so meanwhile O'Toole's stands; a panel of judges rejected Mehanna's appeal.

Guy Fawkes's judges considered him a terrorist too. King George thought the same of Revere and his fellow Sons of Liberty, but Mehanna wasn't inspired by them. He was hero-worshipping Revere's comic book ghost. Like Henry Wadsworth Longfellow, Tarek Mehanna is a writer, supporting Al-Qaeda by pen not sword. Longfellow was the first American to translate Dante's *Divine Comedy* into English. Mehanna translated "39 Ways to Serve and Participate in Jihad" and posted it online from his bedroom in his parents' suburban Boston home. That's less poetic than a midnight gallop, but like his fictionalized hero, Mehanna is a messenger.

"I mentioned Paul Revere," he said,

> when he went on his midnight ride, it was for the purpose of warning the people that the British were marching to Lexington to arrest Sam Adams and John Hancock, then on to Concord to confiscate the weapons stored there by the Minutemen. By the time they got to Concord, they found the Minutemen waiting for them, weapons in hand. They fired at the British, fought them, and beat them. From that battle came the American Revolution. There's an Arabic word to describe what those Minutemen did that day. That word is: JIHAD, and this is what my trial was about.

That's not a definition most Americans want to hear, and only the most radical Muslims would conflate "jihad" with "terrorism," a term the FBI defines as "acts dangerous to human life that violate federal or state law" and that are intended to "intimidate or coerce a civilian population" and/or "influence the policy of a government by intimidation or coercion." There's a Spanish word to describe that too: ZORRO.

Johnston McCulley's grasp of colonial history is looser than Longfellow's, but he and Fairbanks knew what Americans loved. Their champion whips judges, disfigures soldiers, and kills at least one military officer in combat — all with the aim of coercing a tyrannous government into reversing its abusive policies. Batman cocreator Bill Finger was six when *The Mark of Zorro* stormed theaters. He included stills of the masked and swashbuckling Fairbanks in the scripts he handed Bob Kane. I don't know if Mehanna read *V for Vendetta*, but while he was collecting Batman comics in 1989, Michael Keaton was playing the caped crusader in theaters. Those three heroes share the same paradigm. They're all Gray Champions. "Muslims should defend their lands from foreign invaders — Soviets, Americans, or Martians," Mehanna told Judge O'Toole. "This is not terrorism, and it's not extremism. It's what the arrows on that seal above your head represent: defense of the homeland."

Whether you think Mehanna was unfairly convicted or not (my jury is still deliberating), he is a devout follower of Superheroism. He, like many of his fellow Americans, likes things simple. He sees the world through a six-year-old's eyes: the good guys and the bad guys whom the good guys battle, with all the poetically inconvenient nuances dropped into the stanza breaks and panel gutters. Longfellow sacrificed Dawes and Prescott to preserve the simplicity of his heroic vision. Madeline Albright, argues Mehanna, sacrificed "over half a million children" who died due to "American-led sanctions that prevented food, medicine, and medical equipment from entering Iraq." A 2012 Stanford Law School study estimates that drone attacks in Pakistan killed up to 881 civilians, including 176 children. Although the Department of Defense says such collateral damage differs from terrorism (because the deaths, while premeditated, are not the goal), I think Longfellow would leave the body count out of a poetic rendering of the War on Terror too.

We prefer our Sons of Liberty purified. Eugene Debs, another of Mehannna's role models, was six when "Paul Revere's Ride" was published in *Atlantic Monthly*. Debs grew up to be a champion of oppressed laborers and was sentenced to ten years in prison under the Espionage Act of 1917 because he spoke against U.S. involvement in the First World War. President Harding commuted the sentence after the war ended. Perhaps some future post–War on Terror president will do the same for Mehanna.

Meanwhile, Mehanna isn't the only patriotic terrorist to suffer from oppression-fighting Superheroism. Osama bin Laden's "Declaration of War against the Americans Occupying the Land of the Two Holy Places" bears a disturbing resemblance to "The Declaration of Independence." They both reflect the Batman paradigm. "The history of the present King of Great Britain," wrote Thomas Jefferson, "is a history of repeated injuries and usurpations, all having in direct object the establishment of an absolute Tyranny over these States." The list of oppressive offenses includes plundering, ravaging, and completing "the works of death, desolation and tyranny, already begun with circumstances of Cruelty & perfidy scarcely paralleled in the most barbarous ages, and totally unworthy the Head of a civilized nation."

Both of Bin Laden's pre-9/11 fatwas are the length of Jefferson's Declaration. He lists "crimes and sins committed by the Americans," calling them "facts that are known to everyone." Jefferson lets his "Facts be submitted to a candid world," detailing England's "abuses and usurpations" too. Like King George's "establishment of an absolute Tyranny over these States," America is "plundering its riches, dictating to its rulers, humiliating its people, terrorizing its neighbors." Both declare the "duty" and "honor" of the oppressed to fight for "justice," evoking Allah and "Nature's God" in support: "Our Lord, rescue us ... and raise for us from thee one who will help!"

Does that sound like a job for the Gray Champion? I hope America, like Cromwell, hasn't mutated into the tyrant that called itself into existence. I also understand why Longfellow rewrote history into the comforting beats of ballad stanzas.

⚡ ⚡ ⚡

George Washington could have been the first American übermensch. All he had to do was accept the call for his coronation after leading the colonies to victory. Instead, he declared, "I didn't fight George III to become George I," and settled for a two-term presidency.

If France hadn't backed the war, Queen Elizabeth II might still be our reigning constitutional monarch, as in Canada and New Zealand. Not that I'm accusing the God-appointed Louis XVI of egalitarian altruism. He sank over a billion livres into a rebel cause because those rebels were rebelling against his arch-nemesis, England. It seemed like a good idea at the time, though the financial crises that followed ended in the removal of Louis from his throne and Louis's head from his neck — to the retro-active cheers of Alan Moore.

"A common theory," writes Carlyle, is "that the French Revolution was a general act of insanity, a temporary conversion of France ... into a kind of Bedlam." *The Scarlet Pimpernel*'s author, Baroness Orczy, for example, calls the French Revolution a "surging, seething, murmuring crowd of beings that are human only in name, for to the eye and ear they seem naught but savage creatures, animated by vile passions and by the lust of vengeance and of hate." Carlyle disagrees. The hero-worshipper hails the Revolution "as shipwrecked mariners might the sternest rock," because it was prompted by "the one reason which could justify revolting": "You have put the too Unable Man at the head of affairs!"

I don't know if Victor Hugo would be on board with Carlyle's definition of hero-worship ("recognition that there does dwell in that presence of our brother something divine"), but the former monarchist fled France after Napoleon's nephew seized the throne. Hugo wrote some of his most influential work from exile, including political pamphlets, three books of poetry, and *Les Misérables*, the historical novel he "meant for everyone." Hugo described it to his Italian publisher as a superhero answering a cry for aid: "Wherever men go in ignorance or despair, wherever women sell themselves for bread, wherever children lack a book to learn from or a warm hearth, *Les Misérables* knocks at the door and says: 'open up, I am here for you.'"

I did not see *Les Mis*, either on stage or on screen, but my kids went with their Nana after my wife and I escaped for our own adventure: fancy dinner (turns out steak tartare is a raw hamburger), romantic movie (Jennifer Lawrence is a shape-shifting genius even when not playing a blue-skinned mutant), and historic B&B (former haunt of musical legend Oscar Hammerstein). We had a better time than the kids. My son was not wooed by Hugh "Wolverine" Jackman, and my daughter would not list on-set singing among his superpowers.

But the X-Men casting choice did spotlight some secrets in the musical's origin story. Both literary blogger Chrisbookarama and *Slate* culture editor David Haglund described Jean Valjean as a "superhero." They note his dual identity (alias "Monsieur Madeleine"), his superpowers (the strength of "four men"), and his arch-nemesis, Inspector Javert (inspired by real-life detective Eugène François Vidocq). Hugo also wrote one of the first superhero unmasking scenes:

"One morning M. Madeleine was passing through an unpaved alley" where an "old man named Father Fauchelevent had just fallen beneath his cart." A jack-screw would arrive in fifteen minutes, but "his ribs would be broken in five." Madeleine sees "there is still room enough under the cart to allow a man to crawl beneath it and raise it with his back," and he offers five, ten, then "twenty louis" to anyone willing to try. Javert, "staring fixedly at M. Madeleine," declares: "I have never known but one man capable of doing what you ask." Although Valjean is breaking the law by disguising his past as a convict, he "fell on his knees, and before the crowd had even had time to utter a cry, he was underneath the vehicle." Even the old man, "one of the few enemies" Valjean has made as Madeleine and then only from jealousy, is begging him to give up, when "Suddenly the enormous mass was seen to quiver, the cart rose slowly, the wheels half emerged from the ruts," and "Old Fauchelevent was saved."

"Just like a superhero," writes Haglund, "outed by the noble use of his super strength."

My daughter assured me the film framed it as a burst of Hulk-like adrenaline, but the Napoleon-loving Victor Hugo was going for much more. Although Valjean emerges in torn clothes and "dripping with perspiration," he "bore upon his countenance an indescribable expression of happy and celestial suffering" as the old man calls him "the good God."

It's the self-sacrificing yet self-ennobling choice superheroes make every day. This is another gospel in the New and Improved Testament we saw in chapter one. Even Jesus in Martin Scorsese's *Last Temptation of Christ* wants to hide in a mild-mannered lifestyle, before fully accepting the job of supersavior. Ditto for Tobey Maguire's Peter Parker, Michael Chiklis's Ben Grimm, and James McAvoy's pill-popping Professor X. A hundred years earlier, O. Henry's safe-popping Jimmy Valentine outs his Valjean past by saving a child from suffocating in the town bank vault. Philip Wylie's superhuman Hugo Danner longs for the quiet life too, but fate slams another would-be victim into another character-revealing bank vault.

And wouldn't you know, there's always a Javert standing right there trying to glimpse your secret self. Jimmy has detective Price on his trail (though in a typical O. Henry twist, he lets his Valjean go). That pesky tabloid reporter followed Bill Bixby for five seasons, always ready to snap a picture when Lou Ferrigno burst out during the emergency-of-the-week. Like *Les Mis* director Tom Hooper, the CBS team decided their

Incredible Hulk was just a burst of green adrenaline, the kind that allows Clark Kents to shoulder cars off endangered loved ones. That's the phenomenon Bixby's Banner is researching before his laboratory mishap, his atonement for failing to save his wife when fate dropped Fauchelevent's cart on her. Bruce Willis rescues his fiancée, Robin Wright, from their car wreck in *Unbreakable*, but then he fakes an injury and tries to live the quiet life of a Monsieur Madeline until Samuel L. Jackson's Elijah Price outs him too. It's hard for an Able Man to stay disguised when monarchy's broken oxcart keeps collapsing on the masses.

Nathaniel Hawthorne inserted his Gray Champion into the first American rebellion, and Victor Hugo retconned his superhuman Valjean into France's Napoleonic Wars. So what about political upheaval calls for retroactive superheroes?

The revolutions weren't just shifts in government. They shifted everyone's identity. It used to be we commoners had the aristocracy to look up to. Superhumaness was part of the king's holy job description, a fringe benefit of his larger-than-life nobility. According to Nietzsche scholar Walter Kaufman, the first superman was the tyrant Megapenthes from Lucian's second-century play *Voyage to the Lower World*. Not only was the ruler considered "handsomer than other men" and "a good eighteen inches taller," but he "seemed more than human," "neither more nor less than a God." Lucian's term is "hyperanthropos," and though Nietzsche read some Lucian, the übermensch has its own etymological origin story. But Kaufman is close. While he ruled, Megapenthes at least appeared superhuman. Unlike Paul Revere, who gained his superstature in the afterlife, Mega's obituary reduces him to a mere "monster" who had "established a lawless rule." His larger-than-life illusions vanish after Hermes drags him to the underworld where there are "Equal rights for all, and no man is better than his neighbor."

The thirteenth-century's Magna Carta was an early materialization, but the egalitarian spirit didn't fully escape Lucian's underworld until the American and French Revolutions summoned it Faust-like into the terrestrial realm. And once corporeal, the Gray Champion's ghost demanded a new species of ruler, one willing to seize rather than inherit Divine Rights. Fawkes haunted Cromwell, Cromwell possessed the Sons of Liberty, and their spirit overturned all of France until Napoleon Bonaparte, the nineteenth-century's first living superman, answered the call to action.

Napoleon crowns Carlyle's list of Great Men, one of those "natural luminary shining by the gift of Heaven." Emerson paints him in a superheroic glow too: "a man of stone and iron" with "the speed and spring of a tiger." "Men," says the American transcendentalist, "give way before such a man, as before natural events." That apparently explains how, unlike George Washington, the leader of France's revolutionary military seized control of his government and ruled his nation for a decade. The monarchy had to go, but the peasantry still needed a god to look up to. Emerson even has Napoleon fighting a "vampyre," the aristocrat class who "sucked [the land] of its nourishment." Napoleon used the less poetic phrase "hereditary asses," which may also explain why he is "the idol of common men," an "incarnate Democrat" whose grand talent and success enlist "an universal sympathy." By "transcending the ordinary limits of human ability," Napoleon "liberates us."

Shaw ranks Napoleon up there with Cromwell and Julius Caesar. Nietzsche's grandmother liked the guy too; she and little Friedrich lived near some historic battles sites in Saxony. Grown-up Nietzsche listed him among "the worthiest of individuals," "the more profound and comprehensive men" of the century. "I am apart from all the world," Bonaparte declared, "and accept conditions from nobody." When his wife accused him of adultery, he bellowed: "I have the right to answer all accusations against me with an eternal 'That's me!'"

Napoleon's adulterous penis has been apart from the rest of his body since his 1821 autopsy. Travel writer Tony Perrottet says it looks like "a little baby's finger." Nietzsche never discusses Napoleon's penis size, just his dickish will-to-power. He had the manly "instincts of a warrior," which Nietzsche credits "for the fact that in Europe the *man* has again become master over the businessman and the philistine." Nietzsche liked his supermanly ego too. After an early military victory in Italy, Napoleon "realized that I was a superior being and conceived the ambition of performing great things which hitherto had filled my thoughts only as a fantastic dream."

Supervillains often suffer from the same ambition. "I, Carl Kruger, will be dictator of the world!" bellows Bob Kane's Bonaparte knockoff in *Detective Comics* No. 33. As "Another Napoleon," Carl's fantastic dream involves a Dirigible of Doom. George Washington's was Democracy, and yet Nietzsche and Shaw saw Napoleon as an evolutionary step up from the villainy of the masses. Only a superheroic Napoleon could restore order to egalitarian anarchy.

The Scarlet Pimpernel answers the call too. Orczy opens her novel two years after the storming of the Bastille. Orczy's family lost its fortunes when Hungarian peasants stormed the family's estate, so the exiled baroness had a reason to invent an order-restoring hero. Jerry Siegel transformed the foppish half of Sir Percy into Clark Kent, but Superman stole from the Pimpernel too: "the man's muscles seemed made of steel, and his energy was almost supernatural."

Sir Percy isn't the only Napoleon-inspired superhero pulled into the gravity of postrevolutionary France. Alfred Burrage's rebooted *Spring-Heeled Jack Library* was published the same year, 1904, but is set as Napoleon claimed the throne, 1804. Accused of aiding France, a dashing but disinherited English lieutenant turns to a life of superheroic vengeance, complete with a proto-Batman alter ego, costume, secret sanctum, and a superpowered jumping range of thirty feet. Russell Thorndike sets *Dr. Syn: A Smuggler Tale of Romney Marsh* before the 1805 naval battle of Trafalgar, while "coast watchmen swept the broad bend of the Channel for the French men-o'-war." Syn is a mild-mannered vicar and ex-pirate who leads a semialtruistic smuggling gang and town protectors as the masked Scarecrow. The alias is designed to inspire fear in his foes:

> as the name of Napoleon was changed to Boney for the frightening of children by tyrannical nurses in England, so the title of the Scarecrow bore the like qualities on Romney Marsh, for it meant that the power of the smugglers was behind it, and would be used to force obedience to the Scarecrow's behests.

Isabel Allende can't resist the Napoleonic allure either. The majority of her *Zorro* prequel is set in Spain between 1810 and 1815, while the nation, fearing "Napoleon will convert Spain into a satellite of France," overthrows Napoleon's brother Joseph after Napoleon placed him on the Spanish throne. The young Zorro-to-be gains his superheroic education as the new democracy "approved a liberal constitution based on the principles of the French Revolution." Allende also liberally mixes her hero's blueblood, turning his "mestizo" stigma into the source of his powers. The novel is a sequence of romping adventures, each adding a new trait to the melting pot of his egalitarian character. A Gypsy sword, a pirate's attire, a Jewish fencing mentor, a cross-dressing Indian mother, they all coalesce in the swashbuckling amalgam of a democracy-championing superhero.

Allende understands those revolutionary principles from the vantage of the twenty-first century. But go back a hundred years and that bedrock of equality was still shifting under the weight of new Napoleons. The narrator of Owen Wister's *The Virginian* — riding across bookstore shelves as the Scarlet Pimpernel was strutting across the stage — explains:

> It was through the Declaration of Independence that we Americans acknowledged the *eternal inequality* of man. For by it we abolished a cut-and-dried aristocracy. We had seen little men artificially held up in high places, and great men artificially held down in low places, and our own justice-loving hearts abhorred this violence to human nature. Therefore, we decreed that every man should thenceforth have equal liberty to find his own level. By this very decree we acknowledged and gave freedom to true aristocracy, saying, "Let the best man win, whoever he is." Let the best man win! That is America's word. That is true democracy. And true democracy and true aristocracy are one and the same thing.

Carlyle makes the same democratically antidemocratic argument:

> Find in any country the Ablest Man that exists there; raise him to the supreme place, and loyally reverence him: you have a perfect government for that country; no ballot-box, parliamentary eloquence, voting, constitution-building, or other machinery whatsoever can improve it a whit. It is in the perfect state; an ideal country.

And the Best and Ablest Men, it turns out, are True Aristocrats like Bruce Wayne. Little men like Hitler-wannabe Carl Kruger end up in plane wreckage by the final panels. Carl, like Megapenthes and Louis XVI, is no super-man, and we need real supermen like Superman to guard us from them.

Then why is Napoleon, who was tall for his time, remembered as such a little man? Bob Kane draws his look-alike Carl in midget proportions. The impression was probably a result of his freakishly enormous body-guards. His tomb is freakishly large too and could fit a dozen emperors of any size. I dragged my family to see it during a vacation in Paris. Without him, I told them, *Action Comics* doesn't happen. Our guidebook said the tomb would be surrounded by a dozen "Amazon-like" figures celebrating his military victories, but they weren't Wonder Women. It's just a league of stony angels standing guard around the superman's larger-than-life remains.

As Allende's democratic Zorro trained in Spain, the most influential of the post-Napoleonic superheroes stood poised to seize the throne of the primordial genre.

Alexander Dumas's *The Count of Monte Cristo* opens in 1810, during Napoleon's decade-long reign. Dumas's father had been a friend and gen-eral to Napoleon since campaigning with him in Italy, where the future emperor suffered his superior-being epiphany. The two were so close that General Dumas was welcome in his emperor's boudoir while his emperor was naked in bed with Josephine. The friendship didn't last though. Du-mas's father later lingered unransomed as a prisoner-of-war, and so when a theater friend burst into the younger Dumas's boudoir with an idea for a play about Napoleon, Dumas refused: "The injuries Bonaparte had in-flicted on my family made me inclined to be unjust toward Napoleon."

But the theater friend (a proud Bonapartist) and the friend's lover (one of Napoleon's former mistresses and a star actress who enjoyed enter-taining guests topless) locked Dumas in her apartment until he com-pleted the twenty-four-scene *Napoleon*. The 1831 production flopped, so he expanded it into a book, published shortly after Nathaniel Haw-thorne's 1835 "Gray Champion." Both heroes embody their nations. At the hour of Napoleon's coronation, declares Dumas, "the Revolution had become a man," and when Napoleon relinquishes the throne a decade later, "the world seemed empty." Mary Shelley subtitled *Frankenstein* "The Modern Prometheus," the same subtitle Dumas choose for his exiled ex-emperor.

Edmond Dantès, Dumas's self-declared Count, owes his creation to Napoleon too — and not just because Dumas traveled around the Island of Monte Cristo with the emperor's nephew. The Count looks down at humanity, that "race of crocodiles," from Napoleon's superhuman height. According to Shaw, Napoleon regarded "mankind as a troublesome pack of hounds only worth keeping for the sport of hunting with them." A character also likens Monte Cristo to Byron's Manfred, a breed of hero who "by the force of their adventurous genius" is "above the laws of society" (more on Manfred in chapter three).

The recipe is elitist, but its ingredients are paradoxically egalitarian. The monte cristo, one of my favorite sandwiches, is named after Dumas's hero, but it does not appear in Dumas's *Great Dictionary of Cuisine*. Cookbooks, like early comics, delete most of the contributors from the credit box, but Dumas's cookbook may be the only one of his two or three hundred books he wrote himself. His most famous novels were collaborations. His hired assistants cooked up plots and pages for him to spice up and finalize to his own taste. Superman cocreator Joe Shuster employed a kitchen of artists to similar effect. Auguste Maquet, Dumas's most prominent sous-chef d'aventure, worked for him through the 1840s, co-authoring both *The Count of Monte Cristo* and *The Three Musketeers*. Bob Kane claimed similarly sole authorship of Batman, writing off writer Bill Finger with a paycheck. Maquet sued, but the French courts preferred Dumas's lone-wolf tale. Finger (a prolific plagiarist himself) stayed in the kitchen.

Neither Dumas nor Kane served up anything of much flavor without their collaborators, but *The Count of Monte Cristo* continues to be served across genres. If Maquet was the plotter, then he mixed convicted-of-a-crime-he-didn't-commit and revenge-is-best-served-cold recipes into a new stew. They're massive chapters in any contemporary *dictionnaire d'aventure*, spanning comics from *Batman* to *Oldboy* manga. Moore's V keeps a copy of Dumas on his bookshelf, and the film adaptation plays it on V's TV. The framed fugitive Edmond Dantès is also one of literature's earliest secret identity heroes and chameleon-like masters-of-disguise. Like "Alexander Dumas" on the cover, the Count is only the first ingredient in a tossed salad of Dantès's aliases, ranging from priest to bank clerk to Sinbad the Sailor. Also, like a comic book, the novel wasn't a novel — it was a serial, published in eighteen monthly installments beginning in 1844. It was already an international hit when the Count jumped the channel into English two years later.

Dumas was a mixed salad himself. His father the general was Haitian, a fact Alexander proudly championed. In the United States, even abolitionists had trouble believing a black man could produce Literature, thinking Frederick Douglass's editors must have ghosted his 1845 *Narrative of the Life*. President Polk had just won the 1844 election in part because of his promise to annex Texas as a slave state. France struggled over slavery too, abolishing it in 1794, reinstating it in 1802, and abolishing it again while *The Count of Monte Cristo* was sailing to American book stores where it would sell out despite its shady origins.

I'd like to think Dumas, not Maquet, decided the Count would marry Haydée, the Turkish princess he bought from a slave trader. Louis Hayward, star of *The Son of Monte Cristo*, doesn't look Turkish, and Douglas Fairbanks Jr., who was originally cast for the part, doesn't either. The Count, however, is taken for French, Arab, Roman, and Greek, and yet he claims no nation and no race. "I am," he declares, "a cosmopolite." His shape-shifting ability to "adopt all customs, speak all languages" is a product of his mixed nature, elevating him to the superhuman level of angels, those "invisible beings" whom God sometimes allows "to assume a material form." The only significant obstacle to his goals is his mortality:

> for all the rest I have reduced to mathematical terms. What men call the chances of fate — namely, ruin, change, circumstances — I have fully anticipated, and if any of these should overtake me, yet it will not overwhelm me. Unless I die, I shall always be what I am.

And what he is is a Napoleonic superhuman, a divinely self-made man embodying all democratic humanity — even while flouting all democratic principles.

The monte cristo, declares food critic Thadius Van Landingham, "is a jumble of contradictions," both sweet and savory, "a sandwich engulfed in controversy" and "clouded origins." It's a fitting tribute to the contradictory Mr. Dumas and the superheroic mix he brought to a boil. A dash of Guy Fawkes, a pinch of Cromwell, a teaspoon of Gray Champ, Valjean to taste, and as many twists of the Napoleonic pepper grinder as your supersenses can stand. Garnish with pimpernel, and skewer on a Spanish rapier. It's a revolutionary recipe, one still served in comic shops and movie theaters worldwide.

Such a steady diet of so-called Great Men is a paradox of democracy — the "one fixed point in modern revolutionary history," according to Emerson. His team of Representative Men includes Plato, Swedenborg, Montaigne, Shakespeare, Napoleon, and Goethe — which is much more difficult to pronounce than SHAZAM! (PSMSNG!). Carlyle's magic word is worse: OMDSLKJRBCN! They only agree on two of their superingredients (Napoleon and Shakespeare), but Marvel and DC fans have even fewer crossovers. The adoration is all the same.

A new government of representative greatness is assembling in chapter three, all monstrous ghosts of France's first supermanly emperor. Napoleon and his pop culture shadow opened the hellish door to the übermensch, and Faust flew through first, followed by a dark flock of Gothic Avengers.

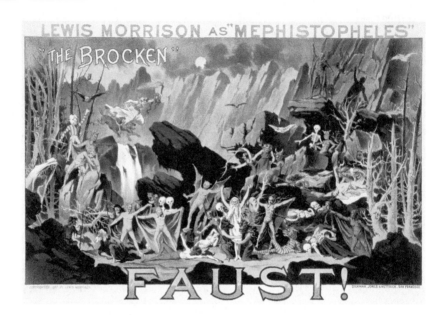

Dickman, Jones & Hettrich, "Faust!" c. 1887.

CHAPTER 3

A PARLIAMENT OF MONSTERS

All moveables of wonder, from all parts,
Are here . . . the man that swallows fire,
Giants, Ventriloquists, the Invisible Girl . . .
The Wax-work, Clock-work, all the marvellous craft
Of modern Merlins, Wild Beasts, Puppet-shows,
All out-o'-the-way, far-fetched, perverted things,
All freaks of nature, all Promethean thoughts
Of man, his dulness, madness, and their feats
All jumbled up together, to compose
A Parliament of Monsters.

That's my favorite bit of William Wordsworth's poetry, taken from *Preludes*, published from beyond the poet laureate's 1850 grave. It's a legion of superheroes, though a darkly disturbing one.

Most superheroes have a bit of the Dark Side in them. My students are startled by the devilishness of the original Superman ("a weird figure" who "leaps out into the night!") and the Shadow-inspired "Bat-Man" (another "weird figure of darkness"). To battle the darkness, they cross into it. It's a standard hero motif, one the historian Richard Slotkin sees in all frontiersmen:

Through this transgression of the borders, through combat with the dark elements on the other side, the heroes reveal the meaning of the frontier line (that is, the distinctions of value it symbolizes) even as they break it down. In the process they evoke the elements in themselves (or in their society) that correspond to the "dark"; and by destroying the dark elements and colonizing the border, they purge darkness from themselves and the world.

Judi Dench's M pleads a similar case for 007 in *Skyfall*:

I'm frightened because our enemies are no longer known to us. They do not exist on a map. They're not nations. They're individuals. Look around you. Who do you fear? Do you see a face, a uniform, a flag? No. Our world is not more transparent now. It's all opaque. It's in the shadows. That's where we must do battle.

So we elect heroes who best represent our fears. And no monstrous warrior can mirror more of our far-fetched madness than the marvelously freakish superhero. The Gothic 1800s are swarming with them. Their superpowered Parliament of post-Napoleonic demons includes a god of nightmares, a reanimated corpse, an aristocrat vampyre, an urban devil, ghost whisperers, occult detectives, and an ectoplasmic man who gives birth to the first living shadow. Like the godmen of chapter one, these supermen are supernatural, but instead of reaching toward heaven to assume divine powers, they split their humanity with hell.

Johann Georg Faust was the first. The sixteenth-century alchemist died in a laboratory explosion when, according to the German church, the Devil came to collect his soul. The two were business partners. An anonymous historian recorded their contract, complete with legalistic "whereas" and "whereof" jargon, in the first 1587 compilation of the legend. English playwright Christopher Marlowe introduced Faust to London audiences a decade later, but German poet Johann Wolfgang von Goethe's dramatic poem *Faust* is the most revered reboot. He published the first part in 1808, the year he met Napoleon, whom he considered "so brilliant" that "Mankind was certain to reach its goals under his direction." The dictator and the poet are the last two names on Emerson's roster of Representative Men.

Goethe praised the French Revolution as the beginning of a new era, but hated its violent price, democracy's deal with the Devil. When Mephistopheles offers to be Faust's "servant," the wizened scholar wisely asks, "how must I thy services repay?," demanding "the condition plainly be exprest!" In exchange for his soul ("under-signest merely with a drop of blood"), Faust wants superhuman knowledge. He exhausted all human study — philosophy, medicine, jurisprudence, theology — but was "no nearer to the infinite." Goethe introduces him brooding alone in his study, moments before conjuring his first spirit:

> Therefore myself to magic I give,
> In hope, through spirit-voice and might,
> Secrets now veiled to bring to light,
> ... That I the force may recognise
> That binds creation's inmost energies;
> Her vital powers, her embryo seeds survey,
> And fling the trade in empty words away.

Bruce Wayne was brooding alone in his study too when a bat answered his dark prayers.

That Faustian deal is still the vital power and inmost energy fueling superheroes.

The first time I lost a tooth, I ran to the top of our basement steps and yelled, "My tooth came out!" I couldn't see my mother in our laundry room, but she performed a reasonably convincing shout of excitement, ending with: "Looks like someone's getting a visit from the tooth fairy tonight!" My five-year-old body went rigid. Blood drained from my face. Tooth fairy? Who the hell was the tooth fairy? I must have a Gothic disposition because instead of picturing a friendly neighborhood do-gooder, I assumed the creature would be coming for the rest of my teeth.

One of Poe's narrators does that, plucks out all of his beloved's beautiful incisors and bicuspids with a pair of pliers. But Germany's E. T. A. Hoffman is the better source for malevolent fairies. A student in my senior English capstone course assigned the 1816 "Der Sandmann" to the class. Hoffman's Sandman doesn't bring sleep to dozy children. He's "a wicked man" who "throws handfuls of sand into their eyes, so that they jump out of their heads all bloody; and then he puts them into a bag and takes them to the half-moon as food for his little ones."

That's the guy Metallica is singing about. The Sandman is also my first Faustian candidate for the Parliament of Monstrous Superheroes. Hoffman's incarnation is a bit too malevolent, though the Hans Christian Andersen version isn't all good-night kisses either. Ole-Luk-Oie, the Dream-God, may be very "fond of children," but if you've been naughty, he holds a black umbrella over you all night so come morning you've dreamed nothing at all. His sibling is named Ole-Luk-Oie too, except

> he never visits anyone but once, and when he does come, he takes him away on his horse, and tells him stories as they ride along. He knows only two. One of these is so wonderfully beautiful, that no one in the world can imagine anything like it; but the other is just as ugly and frightful, so that it would be impossible to describe it.

The other Sandman isn't a Dream-God. He's Death.

I prefer Hoffman's eye-plucking fairy. He reveals "the path of the wonderful and adventurous" as the story's child-narrator tries to unmask him. This "terrible Sand-man" is a dual-identity supervillain. The kid recognizes his father's business partner, a satanic lawyer who practices alchemy by night. If the Faust allusions aren't clear enough, then note his "sepulchral voice" and the laboratory explosion that kills the hapless dad. Hoffman even quotes Goethe after strumming the Napoleon theme song: "Father treated him as if he were a being from a higher race." Hoffman actually says "*höheres Wesen*," superior Being. Like Lucian's "hyperanthropos," the übermensch is the idea forming at the edge of Europe's dreaming thoughts.

Enter Golden Age comic writer Gardner Fox. He must have spent a lot of time under Ole-Luk-Oie's other umbrella, the one with the pictures twirling on the inside. He dreamed up the Flash, Hawkman, Dr. Fate, and the Justice Society of America. Bill Finger usually gets credit as Batman's original writer, but Fox wrote six of the first eight episodes, each almost twice as long as Finger's introductory six-pagers. Instead of apprehending jewel thieves and serial killers, Fox's phantasmagoric Dark Knight faces down a werewolf-vampire and some guy who steals faces and puts them on talking flowers. The nineteenth-century Gothic lurks just under the skintight leotards of comic book superheroes.

When Finger returned Batman to the grit of Crime Alley, Gardner Fox dreamed up the Sandman, your standard fedora-wearing mystery man, except in a World War I gas mask. He stole his knockout pellets from Batman's utility belt (a Fox addition), though they'd already been field-tested by other heroes, including Johnston McCulley's Bat and WXYZ's Green Hornet (more on them in chapters four and six, respectively). When Jack Kirby and Joe Simon got tired of spinning Timely's umbrella of characters, they traded in the Sandman's business suit for a red and yellow costume and a sidekick named Sandy. They kept the color scheme when they revised him again in 1974, this time as the Sandman of Hans Christian Andersen lore, a protector of children's dreams. That's the dopey series Neil Gaiman reawakened in 1988. Gaiman confirmed to me (via the dream world of Twitter) that he read Andersen before starting.

Gaiman stripped off the leotard, but I still initially considered his white-skinned Morpheus just another superhero reboot, which I foolishly ignored. The *Sandman* series includes some of the most critically acclaimed, best-selling graphic novels of the 90s, branching beyond comics shops and into mainstream bookstores. When I attended a recent comics forum, it was the only work to receive its own three-scholar panel. Unfortunately, the forum was in Michigan after a bout of "snow thunder" had reduced the state to a lake of frozen slush, and none of the three panelists showed. Maybe the empty podium was their way of evoking a night spent under the Sandman's dreamlessly black umbrella.

Like Andersen, DC spun-off the Sandman's sibling Death, but when Gaiman killed *Sandman*, his contract stipulated that it would stay dead. Because, as Ole-Luk-Oie warns his listeners, "You may have too much of a good thing." I was paying enough attention to buy that seventy-fifth and final issue, a riff on Shakespeare's *Tempest*. It turns out the bard is a bit of a Faust himself. Carlyle's Great Man playwright signs a contract as the Sandman's front man, inundating the world with dream stuff for centuries to come. "There is nobody in the world," writes Hans, "who knows so many stories as Ole-Luk-Oie, or who can relate them so nicely."

I don't know whose "ugly and frightful" tale Ole-Luk-Oie's brother tells his damned listeners, but it should be Goethe's. Every Gothic parliamentarian knows the tale of the alchemist swapping eternal heaven for seven years of earthly omnipotence. He could have demanded invulnerability or superstrength, but his request sounds heroically noble to me:

> The scope of all my powers henceforth be this,
> To bare my breast to every pang, — to know
> In my heart's core all human weal and woe,
> To grasp in thought the lofty and the deep,
> Men's various fortunes on my breast to heap,
> And thus to theirs dilate my individual mind,
> And share at length with them the shipwreck of mankind.

Faust is also a superman. One of the spirits he conjures asks: "What vexes you, oh Übermensch!" Friedrich Nietzsche would adopt the term, but only after reading another Faustian dramatic poem, Byron's *Manfred*. The schoolboy Friedrich called Byron's knockoff "*übermenschlich*" (supermanlike), an "Übermenschen who controls spirits," and he felt "profoundly related to this work," preferring it over Goethe's.

I teach playwriting, so if either poet showed up in class, we'd have a discussion about the definition of "dramatic." Though equally difficult to stage, Manfred is Faust minus Mephistopheles, a subtraction that won over the impressionable Nietzsche. Byron substitutes in Arimanes, a Persian god of evil, but Manfred doesn't barter his soul to anyone but himself. Like Napoleon and the regicidal impulse that empowered him, the "Magian of great power, and fearful skill!" refuses to "Crouch!" before any monarch and instead employs his "superhuman art" to cast his own "tyrant-spell." Though Byron's Destinies echo *Macbeth*'s Weird Sisters, Manfred's powers were "purchased by no compact" but "by superior science," "strength of mind," and a whole lotta "daring." He accepts his approaching death, but still defies "The Power which summons me," refusing "to render up my soul to" the demonic spirit whom he orders "Back to thy hell! Thou hast no power upon me."

> Thou didst not tempt me, and thou couldst not tempt me;
> I have not been thy dupe, nor am thy prey —
> But was my own destroyer, and will be
> My own hereafter

The abbot at Manfred's side urges him to pray for salvation, but Manfred will have none of that either, content to "die as I have lived — alone." His soul takes its earthless flight, whither the abbot dreads to think. Hell presumably, which is where Marlowe sent his Faust in the last act of his tragedy. But the first part of Goethe's ends with the repentant Faust's arrival in heaven — another reason to prefer Byron's übermensch.

Byron first heard *Faust* the summer Percy Shelley and his mistress, Mary, visited him in 1816. As any self-respecting Goth can tell you, the teen-aged Miss Wollenstonecraft (she and the still unfortunately married Percy Shelley had been an item for a couple of years) spent the summer at Byron's Swiss lair. This was The Summer That Never Was, the summer England and New England weathered historic snow and an umbrella of sulfuric fog from Mount Tombora in Indonesia. It erupted the year before, during Napoleon's final Hundred Days that ended in his second exile. In Germany, Hoffman's Sandman was plucking eyeballs from children's heads. In Switzerland, they were breeding a new species of ghost stories for the inaugural session of the Parliament of Superheroic Monsters.

I don't know if Nietzsche read *Frankenstein*, but he should have, since Mary Shelley dreamed up a race of supermen before him. The man-made Creature would have lived with his bride in "the vast wilds of South America," but Dr. Frankenstein prevents their propagation. The name of Shelley's Faustian scientist usually conjures images a flat-headed Boris Karloff with those c. 1931 electric bolts bulging from his neck. Horror historians might tack on a corpse-sutured Christopher Lee or, more regrettably, Robert De Niro, but the original sports no stitches or jigsawed body parts. The guy is a god. Early stage productions draped him in Greek togas, his dark locks aswirl. Sure, his skin is transparent yellow and his face a fit of twitching muscles, but his "limbs were in proportion" (a big turn-on for early nineteenth-century readers), and the doctor "had selected his features as beautiful."

After returning to England, Percy's destitute wife found herself conveniently drowned in London's Hyde Park, allowing her adulterous husband to remarry and move to Bath. I taught a summer course there in 2015, not quite the centennial of *Frankenstein*'s publication, but close. She finished gestating the novel in 1817, while lodging near the Abbey, the one with the creepy angels crawling up and down its sides like a *Doctor Who* episode. Jane Austen's house is a few blocks north, but she moved out before the scandal-laden Shelleys moved in.

I lodged a few blocks south of the Abbey while teaching a creative writing course that followed Ms. Austen's and Ms. Shelley's literal and literary footsteps. The discordant pairing is especially fun, since the superhero is such a sutured corpse of a genre. We'll see in chapter six the hypochondriac Clark Kent that Austen was sketching while Mrs. Shelley was penning her monstrous superman. It would take later writers to weld the opposing impulses, love and horror, into a single cape-flapping creature, but Bath provided the embryonic fluid.

The semen and egg, however, met in Geneva. The four members of Byron's Gothic Parliament were nothing if not productive. Byron completed and published *Manfred* in 1817, a year before the anonymously published *Frankenstein* became an acclaimed hit — and not just because everyone thought Percy wrote it. Goethe was the godfather. Mary's mad scientist, like Byron's mad magician, inherited Faust's "ardent mind, / Which unrestrain'd still presses on for ever." All three o'erleaped the human sphere to know what "Doth for the Deity alone subsist!"

Percy might not have conceived much during that Summer That Wasn't, but his "Ozymandias" (yes, another Alan Moore allusion) appeared before *Frankenstein*, and he eventually upstages Byron's *Manfred* with his four-act poem *Prometheus Unbound*. John Polidori, Byron's much maligned traveling companion/physician, dreamed up a tale during the ghost gathering too. He gets credit for England's first supernatural dual-identity antihero, the Byron-inspired vampire, Lord Ruthven. A year after

Frankenstein's debut, *Vampyre: A Tale* was a hit in English bookstores too — and not just because everyone thought Byron wrote it. Polidori plucked the vampire from eastern European folklore and recast him as a seductive aristocrat feeding on high society. It sparked the first vampire craze (imagine Edward Cullen singing in two different but simultaneously produced operas) and the genre of the dashingly undead that's still haunting bookstores, TVs, and theaters.

I started reading *The Vampyre*'s spawn *Twilight* in an attempt to understand what was enthralling my then-tween daughter. I set her copy down just before the baseball scene. That was six years ago, but I recall how Ms. Meyer paints Lord Ruthven's descendant in superhero shades: Edward is a cursed but noble superhuman who uses his powers for good. It was, for example, very noble of him not to eat Bella when she smelled so delicious in science class. Some serious restraint for a soulless monster who lives to devour women.

That's the allure of the Gothic. Turn a monster against its nature and its struggle to do good is superheroic. When the monster is sexy, the formula is irresistible. The monstrous Lord Ruthven was no teetotaler when it came to blood, but he still spawned a colony of abstinent vampire hunks. The BBC's *Being Human* features three seasons of the AA-esque Mitchell struggling to stay on the non-blood-sucking wagon, followed by season four's equally valiant and tortured Hal. Before Joss Whedon turned his attention to men in unitards, the *Buffy the Vampire Slayer* creator sired not one but two vampires-with-a-soul, the angsty Angel and the bad boy Spike. Buffy owes both those lovers and most of her epithet to Marv Wolfman and Gene Colan, who introduced Blade the Vampire-Hunter to readers of Marvel's *Tomb of Dracula* in 1973. Warren Publishing's Vampirella arrived on Earth from her planet of blood-suckers in 1969, and soon she was battling Dracula's legion too. But the first vampire-trying-to-be-good award goes to Barnabas Collins of the Gothic soap opera *Dark Shadows*. Introduced as a subplot in 1967, the lovelorn Barnabas saved the show from cancellation and was soon taking a serum to restore his humanity (which Johnny Depp finished for him in 2012). Even James Malcolm Rymer and Thomas Preskett Prest's Varney the Vampire, a fiend for most of his 1845–47 penny-dreadful run, dies redeemed by the family he victimized: "what there is at all human in me, strange to say, all of you whom I sought to injure, have awakened."

Though there are enough of these soulfully soulless demons to constitute their own voting bloc, their vampire district remains one of hell's deepest testosterone pits. With a few very notable exceptions (Catherine Deneuve in *The Hunger*, the aforementioned Vampirella, Le Fanu's 1872 "Carmilla"), vampires are male. Octavia Butler's Shori from her novel *Fledgling* is the proverbial rule-proving exception. "Most vampires," Butler told the *Weekly Ansible*, "I have discovered are men for some reason. I guess it's because of Dracula; people are kind of feeding off that."

Feeding indeed. When I taught *Fledgling* in my contemporary fiction class, I asked my students to describe a typical vampire.

"A guy who hides in the shadows and jumps out and bites women."

And what would you have if you took out the fangs?

After a moment of awkward mumbling, an intrepid senior spelled it out: "A rapist."

The proto-vampire Byron did not have fangs. Just a penis. Which remains the not particularly veiled subtext of most vampire plots. Stoker's *Dracula* is about a foreigner buying the house next door and penetrating the neighborhood's fiancées. Lord Ruthven's bride is discovered dead on her wedding night, having "glutted the thirst of a VAMPYRE!" Frankenstein's monster commits a similar homicide. Victor finds his wife "lifeless and inanimate, thrown across the bed, her head hanging down, and her pale and distorted features half covered by her hair . . . her bloodless arms and relaxed form flung by the murderer on its bridal bier."

That sounds anything but heroic, and yet Marvel's *The Monster of Frankenstein* debuted in 1972, adapted by Gary Friedrich, the same writer who pulled the equally demonic Ghost Rider out of hell, and soon Shelley's no-longer-so-monstrous Monster was teaming up with Spider-Man and Iron Man. The human-vampire Blade teamed up with Spider-Man and Dr. Strange. All kinds of dark shadows swirl under a superhero cape, because that's what the genre feeds on: the heroically soulful suffering of an übermensch quelling his inner demons and redirecting his monstrous powers for good.

⚡ ⚡ ⚡

Shelly and Polidori invented two of our most enduring monsters, and comic books fitted them into spandex. It's an innocent-looking fabric, but when stretched too thin, it tears. The word "monster" comes from "*monstrum*," an omen, and "*monēre*," to warn. Monsters "demonstrate" our fears. A superhero protects us from those fears by holding them inside himself. But the darkness lurks just under the surface. Once bitten, England couldn't get enough of that demonic duality, electing more monster-fighting monsters to their nightmare Parliament.

I was recently quizzing a friend about living in Oxford as a kid. Ellen and her older brother attended Bishop Kirk Middle School, where she had Philip Pullman for a homeroom teacher. Pullman also gave her guitar lessons while not busy teaching English and Maths (the course is pleasantly plural in England). This was the late 70s, a couple of years after Marvel canceled *The Frankenstein Monster*, and a couple of decades before *His Dark Materials* made Pullman an internationally celebrated fantasy author. School plays were his main creative outlet. He wrote one a year and staged it in the lunchroom with a curtain draped in front of the food counter. Mrs. Dixon, the music teacher, composed the songs and thumped them out on the school piano.

Ellen remembers virtually nothing else about the 1978 *Spring-Heeled Jack*, just that her brother played a sea captain and got to kiss the prettiest girl in school (who became a supermodel and married Simon Le Bon of Duran Duran). Pullman later adapted the play into a children's book. It's part comic book too, which is appropriate, since Spring-Heeled Jack looks a lot like England's first superhero. "In Victorian times," writes Pullman, "before Superman and Batman had been heard of, there was another hero who used to go around rescuing people and catching criminals."

Pullman's illustrator, David Mostyn, draws Spring-Heeled in a cape and top hat — which is disappointing if you've seen the Victorian illustrations. I don't know how Pullman dressed his middle school actor ("the costuming was all very much pulled-together," says Ellen), but Alfred

Burrage's penny dreadful describes "the tight-fitting garb of the theatrical Mephistopheles," which "covered him from his neck to his feet" and "made him look like a huge bat, with a body of brilliant scarlet." This "most hideous and frightful appearance" also included a "black domino" mask, claws "of some metallic substance" (adamant?), a "small black cap" with a "bright crimson feather" (though he sometimes substituted a "large helmet" or "the head of an animal, constructed out of paper and paste"), a "high-heeled, pointed shoe" and "something like a cow's hoof, in imitation, no doubt, of the 'cloven hoof' of Satan" ("It was generally supposed that the 'springing' mechanism was contained in that hoof"), and a "capacious cloak," the flaps of which distended in flight "until they resembled a pair of wings."

Burrage wasn't the first author to dress up Jack. An anonymous serial sprung up in 1867, with a title lifted from John Thomas Haines's 1840 play, *Spring-Heel'd Jack, The Terror of London.* The title sounds as darkly fictional as "The Sandman" or *The Vampyre,* but the play was inspired by reports of a real-life assailant who terrorized the suburbs of London in 1838. According to the *Times,* a "young man in a large cloak" tore at one victim's "neck and arms with his claws" and "vomited forth a quantity of blue and white flames from his mouth." Police suspected a carpenter too drunk to recall anything of the night, but spreading rumors named the Devil and Henry de la Poer Beresford, the Marquis of Waterford, as Jack's alter ego. The mayor of London received an anonymous letter accusing an individual from "the higher ranks of life" of accepting a wager to garb himself "in three disguises—a ghost, a bear and a devil" and accost and so deprive "ladies of their senses."

True or not, the tally of senseless ladies climbed to thirty, with the *Morning Post* reporting "females" were "afraid to move a yard from their dwellings." The devilish Marquis was never arrested, but two of his imitators were. Spring-Heeled Jack, however, had already spun himself into Ole-Luk-Oie's umbrella of legends. The name—originally a reference to the culprit's elusiveness—reverse engineered itself the superpowered ability to leap over coaches and houses by supernatural and/or mechanical means. "Spring-Heeled Jack" also became a standard term for unsolved assaults and ghostly sightings, culminating with that 1888 Whitechappel serial killer "Jack the Ripper."

Spring-Heeled Jack traffics with the Faust legend too, but the Marquis's wager does the alchemist one better by becoming Mephistopheles himself. Burrage trades in the Marquis for a dashing young baronet, further ennobling the nobleman in the process. An aristocrat transforms himself into a man-bat to play "the part of the Good Samaritan," a Victorian Batman protecting distressed damsels from burglars, rapists, and swindling relatives cheating them of their inheritances.

Mephisto (the truncation he uses at Marvel) continues to terrorize the multiverse. He started tempting the Silver Surfer in 1968, before contracting the Ghost Rider, duping the Scarlet Witch and Vision out of parenthood, and, in a recently reviled retcon, swapping Spider-Man his aunt's life for his marriage. Mephisto also may or may not be responsible for the damnation-threatening hate mail Phillip Pullman received after his last dual-identity novel, *The Good Man Jesus and the Scoundrel Christ*. "The letter writers essentially say that I am a wicked man, who deserves to be punished in hell," Pullman told the *Sunday Times*. "Luckily it's not in their power to do anything like sending me there."

If Pullman did sell his soul for literary success, it was in the 80s when sales for his novels allowed him to quit his day job at Bishop Kirk Middle School. His *Spring-Heeled Jack* ends with a mad dash to a disembarking ship where the tale's middle school–aged children are reunited with their father, and then the "strange, devilish figure" vanishes without a parting word. "I wonder," says one of the kids, "what Spring-Heeled Jack will do tomorrow night?"

Jack began life as a real-world monster — at best a theatrical prankster, at worst a hysteria-spreading rapist — before warped into his opposite: a hero who rescues the victims his living incarnation attacked. The superhero genre loves that sort of metamorphosis, not just the transformation of the mild-mannered into the monstrously powerful, but that larger leap, the predator into the priestly protector.

But that's not quite true. The genre didn't transform Jack. That was Haines, Burrage, and Pullman. There's a tendency to talk about super-heroes as if they're Frankenstein creatures escaping the control of their creators. Writers wade through the same shadowy zeitgeist as their read-ers, so Spring-Heeled Jack and Batman and Edward Cullen seem to an-swer a democratic call to action when it's literary magicians animating our collective fears. After Byron, Polidori, and the Shelleys convened in Geneva, their Parliament sailed the Atlantic to call to order Edgar Allan Poe's Gothic imagination. I'll explain how Poe is a representative of dark superheroism, but first a quick detour.

Like Pullman, I taught English to teenagers. I didn't write any musi-cals about Mephistopheles-garbed adventurers, but I did have a Satanist in my class. Nice kid, polite, well-spoken, adept with a monochromatic wardrobe. I was a new hire in a Virginia high school, so as far as I knew the whole building was slithering with demon-worshipping students and staff, but this kid (I want to call him "Jack," but I've honestly forgotten his name) was the only one with *The Satanic Bible* on his desk. The even weirder thing was another kid (lost his name too) sitting two seats down. The Bible on that desk was the non-*Satanic* variety. Born Agains were as common as Confederate flags (a group met every morning by the fac-ulty parking lot to pray and smoke cigarettes), but this second, polite, well-spoken, fashion-neutral young man was joining the priesthood after graduation.

I figured God had been reading too many X-Men comics and wanted to see what a real-life Professor X vs. Magneto face-off looked like. He got His chance the morning of the first Poe assignment. I forget which title I'd typed on my English Honors syllabus, which body had been walled into which plot device, but discussion didn't get far. The Satanist raised his hand first:

"This story portrays a man working to fulfill his highest human potential."

The room was silent. The room was usually silent — it was first period — but normally all eyes didn't swerve to stare at our future priest so in-tensely. He blinked, not certain he'd heard correctly, his face probably a mirror of mine. His arch-nemesis was ready to elucidate his opinion, but then God chickened out, booming His voice over the P.A. speaker. Actually it was the secretary's voice, calling the Satanist down to the principal's office for reasons I never knew. I literally never saw him again.

The future priest went on to earn an A, and to write an end-of-year card thanking me, his agnostic teacher, for making room for Jesus Christ in the classroom. I don't think he believed me when I told him Poe was a Christian. I doubt the Satanist could have gotten his head around the yin and yang of that either. Poe, a founding father of both detective and science fiction, was a pro at combining opposing forces. Those same forces later recombine in the figure of the comic book superhero, making Poe a grandfather of the unborn genre.

He was a mostly monogamous author, so the bedchamber of both sci-fi and detectives is the Gothic. Those literary offspring, however, are promiscuous, and so the family tree gets knotty before it sprouts masks and capes. But Poe was writing about space travel a century before Superman rocketed away from Krypton, and there's a wonderfully obvious reason Batman premiered in *Detective Comics*. Poe is a superhero double origin point.

The term "detective fiction" was coined a few decades after Poe's death, "science fiction" almost a century later, but like any good retcon, the memory of their nonexistence has been erased from the multiverse. The two genres aren't patrolling polar ends of the literary axis, but their rosters, unlike the X-Men's and the Brotherhood of Evil Mutants', don't usually overlap. Detectives deal in crime, which means urban, which means right now. Expect grit in your blood puddles. That's why literature's first detective, C. Auguste Dupin, rarely leaves his Paris apartment, content to solve murders by combing clues from columns in the Parisian equivalents of the *Daily Planet*. Meanwhile, sci-fi is fantasy, is speculative, is otherworldly. The tech is early Victorian, so Poe needs a balloon to visit his city of telepaths on the moon, but it's still a bounding leap from the here and now.

In addition to ballooning and ratiocinating, Poe's superpowers include talking to mummies and hypnotizing corpses. Space tourism also spiked after he published his telescope hoax, and he even staffed his moon adventure with batmen ("Vespertilio-homo"). He loved masques, but his Gothic disposition required most of his guilt-hobbled monsters to apprehend themselves. Dupin's three cases are exceptions, including his debut in which the mother and daughter stuffed up a chimney in the Rue Morgue are victims of (SPOILER ALERT!) an escaped orangutan.

The revelation is as disappointing as it sounds, so you might want to skip ahead four-and-half decades to Arthur Conan Doyle's Dupin knock-off, Sherlock Holmes. Poe kept his detective from otherworldly adventures, but comic books pulled the two offspring together. Superheroes are fantastical detectives. They and their unearthly powers travel from far far away to fight crime in your urban backyard. Poe dug up the body parts, but it would take other mad scientists to assemble and animate them into a living character type.

Poe's 1844 short story "Mesmeric Revelation," published in New York while Spring-Heeled Jack was leaping off the London stage, provides a transcript of evidence for "the soul's immortality." Poe's patient, an invalid about to ride off with Ole-Luk-Oie's sibling, allows himself to be mesmerized (the term "hypnotism" had only been coined the year before) on his deathbed. "What we call 'death,'" he reports, "is but the painful metamorphosis." Upon reviving him, the patient's body turns suddenly cold and rigid. "Had the sleep-walker," the narrator wonders, "been addressing me from out the region of the shadows?"

My wife decided the question required further tests. She sent me to buy an Ouija board from the toy store in our local mall, and we set it up on our dining room table. She was teaching James Merrill's *The Changing Light at Sandover*, a postmodern epic composed from séance transcripts, and she wanted to give spirit communication a firsthand whirl. We rested our fingertips on the plastic planchette. Merrill and his lover used an upside-down teacup and barely had time to scribble each letter of dictation before it skidded to the next. Our planchette dribbled a few centimeters southwest. The yellow legal pad lay blank under my wife's uncapped pen. I could blame the board — a fault in the ectoplasmic wiring — but when she tried the experiment with her poetry students, a half-dozen ghosts elbowed onto their seminar table to chat. So I'm officially adding "talks to the dead" to my list of failed superpowers.

A real medium wouldn't touch a planchette anyway. Her hands would be tied behind her back as proof of her powers. And forget teacups. "A great physical medium," writes Sir Arthur Conan Doyle in *The History of Spiritualism*,

> can produce the Direct Voice apart from his own vocal organs, telekinesis, or movement of objects at a distance, raps, or percussions of ectoplasm, levitations, apports, or the bringing of objects from a distance, materializations, either of faces, limbs, or of complete figures, trance talkings and writings, writings within closed slates, and luminous phenomena, which take many forms.

It's a list worthy of Professor X, and Doyle witnessed them all. After creating the superrationalist Sherlock Holmes, Doyle converted to Spiritualism, a nineteenth-century pseudoreligion that transformed Gothic ghost tales into comforting parables of afterlife conversation. Like superhero comic books, Spiritualism soothed its fans' darkest fears.

Doyle's secondhand accounts are even more uncanny. Psychic researchers theorized that Eusapia Palladino grew a third "ectoplasmic limb" in the dark of her séance room. "Now, strange as it may appear," explains Doyle, "this is just the conclusion to which abundant evidence points." D. D. Home he dubs a "wonder-man," but Elizabeth Hope, aka "Madame d'Esperance," is my favorite of his superpsychics. Observers documented her powers of Partial Dematerialization, which may lack the BAMF! of Total Teleportation, but she could also materialize the spirit entities of an infant and a full-bodied "feminine form" named Y-Ay-Ali who held hands with séance participants: "I could have thought I held the hand of a permanent embodied lady, so perfectly natural, yet so exquisitely beautiful and pure." Y-Ay-Ali then "gradually dematerialized by melting away from the feet upwards, until the head only appeared above the floor, and then this grew less and less until a white spot only remained, which, continuing for a moment or two, disappeared."

Some cite eighteenth-century mystic vegetarian Emanuel Swedenborg as the father of Spiritualism (he trance-traveled to heaven and hell and to all of the planets of the solar system and several beyond), but Doyle looks a hundred years later. The year before Poe's 1849 death, twelve-year-old Kate Fox and fifteen-year-old Margaret Fox opened the door to the beyond in Hydesville, New York. They grew up in the western New York region that millennialists, Mormons, and sundry utopians "burned over" during the Second Great Awakening. The Fox sisters were latecomers to the antirationalist revival, equivalent of Silver or even Bronze Age superheroines, but they created their own genre as the first séance mediums when the Devil came knocking on their bedroom floor.

They later confessed "Mr. Splitfoot" was an apple tied to the end of a string, but by then they were both alcoholic celebrities in an international movement that had spawned as many imitators as *Action Comics*. Believers like Doyle claimed such confessions were forced and therefore false. Doyle also believed in fairies, famously falling for another pair of children's selfies posed with illustration cut-outs. The Partially Dematerializing Ms. Hope was exposed too — "literally," as debunker M. Lamar Keen puts it — when a séance sitter grabbed at some ectoplasm and instead caught the medium in "total dishabille." Except for the occasional TV psychic or afterlife memoirist, the flimsy world of Spiritualism has been stripped naked for decades. I doubt A. S. Byatt, for instance, is a convert, though her historical novella *The Conjugial Angel* pairs a warm-hearted fake with a dead-to-life spirit-seer. That's the faker/fakir dichotomy that's haunted the genre since its debut.

I used to teach Byatt in my first-year comp seminar I See Dead People, but my students prefer Henry James's *The Turn of the Screw*. James's father, Henry Sr., was a Swedenborgian theologian and James's brother William a psychic researcher. I've never tried to materialize the masculine form of Henry Jr. to ask what he did or did not believe, but his governess-narrator is my favorite study in Total Ambiguity. Is she a righteous medium battling demonic ghosts for the souls of her innocent wards? Or is she a victim of those not-so-innocents who, like fairy-fakers and foxy Foxes, are too damn good at playing grown-up? Or is the woman just batshit crazy? I wouldn't accuse her of possessing a Lord Ruthven–level of demonic duality, but the corpse of her ward does end the novel on the narrative equivalent of a bridal bier. Her imagination is also overcooked on fairy-tale romances and biblical struggles of good and evil — comic books basically — but however you diagnose her, the governess (James never unmasks her name) casts herself as a superheroine blessed/cursed with superpowers.

James Merrill never confessed the nature of his ghost chats either. Could teacup transcripts really produce a 560-page poem? Were he and his lover knowingly collaborating? Did the spirit of a first-century Jew named Ephraim really abandon their hand-drawn Ouija board to enter his lover's body for a séance threesome in bed? My wife's superpowers are sibling-based, because a bout of planchette-skidding in her sister's dining room ended in a telekinetically slammed door and a flock of cousins screaming upstairs. I was in the guest room reading, but, like Doyle, I believed every word.

I also believe superheroes are channeling those same spirits. It's their gloved fingertips on the Ouija board, animating our fears so they can absorb them again. Ole-Luk-Oie keeps spinning visions from The Summer That Never Was, but like Poe's nightmares, they keep assembling into new shapes. The Parliament of Monsters never sleeps.

I used to lie awake in bed as a kid imagining horrors perched beyond the threshold of my open door. My imagination was nonspecific, the reason the shadow frontier shifts so easily. It's not just devils and ghosts flitting beyond the door frame. Ole-Luk-Oie has bulbous-eyed aliens scribbled inside his umbrella now too.

Remember the *X-Files* episode when Scully is abducted? The scene was shot in Vancouver, but they pretended it was Afton, Virginia — which definitely does not have a funicular. I know because I drove over the Blue Ridge Mountains to the University of Virginia's Creative Writing Department three days a week, unaware that the university also housed a Division of Perceptual Studies (DoPS), the twenty-first-century equivalent of Doyle's and William James's Spiritualist department. DoPS founder Dr.

Ian P. Stevenson died a few months after I finished my MFA. Given his research area, I should place an asterisk next to "died," but his colleagues have yet to report evidence of his afterlife activities.

Dr. Stevenson became a full-time paranormal researcher when the inventor of the Xerox machine willed UVa's medical school a grant to open his own X-Files. The world's only university-based researcher of reincarnation was funded by photocopiers. If a medical school seems an odd place for a psychical investigator, know there's a venerable tradition of occult detectives with MDs. Stan Lee and Steve Ditko's world-renowned surgeon Dr. Strange abandoned his scalpels for astral projection two years after Lee and Jack Kirby's first attempt at a superhero, Dr. Droom, entered "that dark and mystical world which lies beyond the known and the unknown!"

That so-called dark and mystical world is actually Asia, but that's how Western writers transformed the Gothic into the superheroic: by scooping up a dark corner of the Sandman's dream world and transplanting it into the daylight of an earthly but still fantastically distant land. Like Dr. Droom, the real-world Dr. Stevenson visited India in 1961 to document the first of almost 3,000 cases of past-life experiences, more soothing adventures into the formerly Gothic afterlife. Stevenson was still finishing high school when Siegel and Shuster dreamed up comics' first occult physician, aptly named Dr. Occult. But Algernon Blackwood's 1908 Dr. Silence is probably the first general practitioner to accept the superhero job title "psychic doctor." Blackwood is best known for his ghost stories and other supernatural tales, but, like Doyle, he dreamed of real superpowers: "My fundamental interest, I suppose, is signs and proofs of other powers that lie hidden in us all; the extension, in other words, of human faculty."

If a medical degree doesn't sound sufficiently superheroic, then you should see the power-punching Hugh Jackman in *Van Helsing*. Joseph Sheridan LeFanu's Dr. Hesselius is another precursor, an occult Sherlock Holmes who administered to vampire victims and drinkers of hallucinatory green tea. All of these Hippocratic Oath–swearing health-care professionals reveal the superhero genre's most important if improbable Gothic-transforming superpower. Despite all those fist-thrown Ka-Pows!

and bone-bashing kicks, one of the boxes most often checked on the shadow-battling superhero checklist is altruism.

When told he won't be paid to treat the dying Lama, Dr. Droom answers: "I can't refuse to treat a sick man! If I must, I'll treat him for nothing!" And so he's rewarded because: "Only a charitable, self-sacrificing human would have done so!" Dr. Silence also takes "no fees, being at heart a genuine philanthropist." His wealthy friends are "puzzled" that he "should devote his time" not just to doctoring but "chiefly doctoring folk who could not pay." He possesses the "native nobility of a soul whose first desire was to help those who could not help themselves."

Hippocratic philanthropy extends to monsters too. Dr. Van Helsing can "pity" and "weep" for vampires during his "butchery" of their bodies, imagining Dracula's "joy" when "his better part may have spiritual immortality." When Dr. Silence faces an Egyptian fire spirit wrongly "torn from its ancient resting-place" and brought to England where it exacts revenge, he feels more for the mummy than its wealthy looters. He later worries about the well-being of a werewolf, a condition he terms an "infirmity," rare, but also "often very sad." He has no enemies, only patients. Though the ghost of a witch is beyond his help, he transmutes the "evil forces" she left behind "by raising them into higher channels." He doesn't destroy evil—he cures it.

Unlike the vampire-hunting Drs. Van Helsing and Hesselius, Silence has other superpowers, making him one of the first supermen to leap beyond the comparatively mundane realm of superhuman strength. He would be an ideal subject for Doyle's or Dr. Stevenson's studies in extrasensory perception. Not only does he possess the "power almost to see in the dark," "that special sensibility that is said to develop in the blind—the sense of obstacles," but "his psychic apparatus never failed in letting him know the proximity of an incarnate or discarnate being." His Watson-like narrator also wonders if he has "some secret telepathic method by which he knew my circumstances and gauged the degree of my need," a power that also "saw into the future."

These powers don't come from enchanted artifacts or mutating radiation. His magic isn't magic. It's an extension of his "humanity," his "spiritual sympathy." He can "absorb evil radiations into himself and change them magically into his own good purposes" because he's just an incredibly nice guy. He's not merely sensitive, he's "ultra-sensitive." "Thought-reading" just requires paying attention to and caring deeply about other people. Since "suffering always owns my sympathy," of course he's going to dedicate his life to helping others.

Dr. Stevenson's list of books he read numbered over 3,500. I'm sure it includes some of the same "Yoga books" Dr. Silence admires, the ones arguing "the necessity of man loving his neighbors as himself" because, says Silence, "men are doubtless not separate at all." Stevenson achieved that interconnected state of "perfect serenity" through the "mystical experience" of LSD. Whatever its source, he and Silence had the same goal, the same desire for "peace and quietness."

Usually that means putting the past and present back into balance. "Ancient pasts" and "ancient instincts" have a way of rising in Blackwood tales. Stevenson traveled the world to study the same phenomena, writing a 2,268-page monograph on past-life memories, including two hundred "in which highly unusual birthmarks or birth defects of the child corresponded with marks, usually fatal wounds, on the previous person."

Silence's filing cabinet is considerably smaller. He vanished in 1917, after Blackwood published his sixth and final case study. Given that *John Silence, Physician Extraordinary* was a breakout best seller that let the author quit his day job, it's weird the doctor never returned. The *X-Files* aliens returned Gillian Anderson after her maternity leave and Buddhist wedding. Blackwood was a student of Buddhism and believer in reincarnation, so his eventual reelection to the pop culture Parliament is probably inevitable. Either way, superheroes embody his altruistic ethic.

I don't have the selfless sympathy needed to transform the shadows of Gothic occultism into the comforting colors of comic book science. That kind of superhero sorcery requires a real magician. The nineteenth century's last Gothic experiment is Metamorphosis. I saw it on my sister's high school stage when I was fourteen. A magician is handcuffed, tied into a sack, and padlocked into a crate. An assistant stands on the crate, lifts a sheet above her head, and when she drops it on the count of three, the magician is standing in her place. When he unlocks the crate, there she is, handcuffed and sack-tied. Audiences tend to gasp.

When Harry Houdini performed the feat with his wife in Düsseldorf in 1900, a reporter explained the trick:

> In dematerialization, or the phenomenon of self-dissolving, the force of attraction and cohesion between molecules is overcome. As has been proven through innumerable examples, every body can in this way be brought in an aetheric condition and therefore, with the help of an astral stream, be transported from one place to another with incredible speed. In the same instant the power used for dematerialization is retrieved; the aetheric pressure again shows the molecules, which again take on their original local and former shape.

It could be a page torn right out a Dr. Silence tale.

Although he started his career as a medium, Houdini never claimed to have supernatural powers — except maybe "photographic eyes," but they only worked for memorizing locks. He did train himself to breathe so "quietly" he could last an hour and a half in a soldered coffin. His other learned skills involved inserting and removing objects from his throat and anus. His one real power, though, was the ability to withstand pain. Dislocated shoulders and handcuffs-gouged flesh meant nothing to him.

Germany called Houdini uncanny, a Napoleon, a limitations-defying Faust. Russians debated whether his powers were evil. Spiritualists in the United States and United Kingdom applauded his act, "one of nature's profoundest miracles," lamenting that audiences mistook it for just "a very clever trick." Drama queen Sarah Bernhardt asked him to grow back her severed leg. "She honestly thought I was superhuman," Houdini told reporters. He also told them "it is only right that what brain and gifts I have should benefit humanity in some other way than merely entertaining people." Jerry Siegel was only two years old at the time, but Clark Kent would similarly decide "he must turn his titanic strength into channels that would benefit mankind."

Houdini played a superhero of sorts in his 1919 silent film serial *The Master Mystery*. A mild-mannered lab tech is secretly Department of

Justice agent Quentin Locke. He battles Q the Automaton, a metal "Frankenstein" that "possesses a human brain which has been transplanted into it and made to guide it" as a "conscienceless inhuman superman." Houdini went on to battle a band of Bedouins serving a "hellish ghoul-spirit of the elder Nile sorcery"; H. P. Lovecraft ghostwrote the purportedly autobiographical sketch, but only after telling his *Weird Tales* editor that Houdini was a "bimbo" and a "boob." A friend of mine, poet-turned-horror-writer Scott Nicolay, mailed me a copy of "Imprisoned with the Pharaohs" padlocked in a tiny canvas bag that I still can't get open.

Houdini's other ghosts penned him into a detective thriller, *The Zanetti Mystery*, and contemporary author Daniel Stashower has been keeping that sleuthing spirit alive in a series of Houdini mystery novels, even pairing him with Sherlock Holmes in *The Adventure of the Ectoplasmic Man*. Sherlock does not believe Houdini can walk through brick walls "by reducing his entire body to ectoplasm . . . the stuff of spirit emanations," but Sherlock's creator did. "My dear chap," Doyle asked Houdini, "why go around the world seeking a demonstration of the occult when you are giving one all the time? My reason tells me that you have this wonderful power, for there is no alternative."

After his son's death and his wife's convenient discovery of medium skills, the evangelical Doyle toured the globe to lecture for his Spiritualist cause. Houdini toured too, debunking every medium he met as a fraud. The two were instant frenemies, each casting the other as his Moriarty. Like Professor X and Magneto, Doyle tried to persuade Houdini to use his powers for good: "Such a gift is not given to one in a hundred million, that he should amuse the multitude or amass a fortune."

Houdini listened. He dedicated his brain and gifts to fighting Doyle's ghoul-spirit religion. He amassed his own X-Files of criminal mediums and employed a band of undercover operatives, what he called his "own secret service department," to infiltrate Spiritualist congregations across the United States. He even turned himself into a real-life master-of-disguise, donning wigs and beards and plaster noses to sneak into séances and expose fakes swindling the bereaved. Like Batman, the memory of his dead mother drove him. If the dead could communicate from the shadows, surely she would have reached her doting son in at least one of his desperate attempts. Had her ghost succeeded to pierce the veil, Houdini's world would have transformed forever.

My sister was on stage during the Metamorphosis trick. She was one of those dancing distractions Houdini employed too. The cuffs were fake, the sack zippered at the bottom, and the crate lid pivoted on a hidden hinge, but it all looked real to me. The teen magician even invited an audience member on stage to inspect the phony equipment. Houdini gave a seventeen-year-old Walter Gibson that same privilege in 1915. Gibson would become one of Houdini's ghostwriters and succeeded him as president of the Society of American Magicians after Houdini's death in 1926. Gibson waited a respectful four years before publishing his illusion-stripping encyclopedia, *Houdini's Escapes and Magic*.

CBS's *Detective Story Hour* premiered in 1930 too. The radio show featured an omniscient narrator with a demonic laugh and knowledge of the hearts of men. The radio writers had invented "the Shadow" for convenience, so the publishers weren't ready when listeners looked for the character on newsstands. So they phoned Gibson and told him to rewrite some old tale featuring Nick Carter, the pre–Sherlock Holmes pulp detective they'd canceled over a decade earlier. Instead, Gibson invented a new character for *The Shadow Magazine*, in what would be the first of the 282 novellas he would pen for the pulp series. The Shadow turned into the biggest superhero of the Depression, an industry-transforming mystery man indistinguishable from the shadow world he polices.

He's a variation on Dr. Silence, but true to his Houdini mentor, Gibson kept his Shadow grounded as a down-to-earth master-of-disguise, even pitting him against a phony spiritualist in the novella *The Ghost Makers*. But when CBS hired Orson Welles to star in a 1937 radio reboot, they wanted mystical powers and so sent the Shadow on an Orientalist tour "to India, to Egypt, to China . . . to learn the old mysteries that modern science has not yet rediscovered, the natural magic." Dr. Silence and his fellow occult practitioners visited that half-real, half-mythic realm too. So did Spring-Heeled Jack, returning from India with his "magic boot," but he stole his costume from Mephistopheles, the shadow still haunting superheroes.

Faust's deal with the Devil lives on too. It's the curse contained in the blessing of superheroism, the human happiness you sacrifice to be humanity's savior. In *The Last Temptation of Christ*, Mephisto offered Jesus the chance to retire from his demigod mission and settle down with Mary Magdalene, but Jesus swapped his happy ending for superpowers. Faust wasn't planning on saving the world, but his descendants do regularly—even when it means damning themselves to live the lonely lives of monsters.

The Sandman's umbrella still shields us, spinning vampyres and reanimated corpses into a legion of good guys hell-bent on our protection. At least that's the illusion comic books help us believe. All superheroes are magicians, kindly metamorphosing our fears into bedtime stories, each a hero who, like Dr. Silence, can "absorb evil radiations into himself and change them magically into his own good purposes." Demigods descend from the heavens, pulling down a piece of that divine border with them. Hell is scarier, and so more powerful. Superheroes rise with the shadows of the infernal frontier inside them. They stand at the edge of consciousness, patrolling the darkness beneath.

Chapter four's heroes are dark frontiersmen too, though their border is slightly less mystical.

N. C. Wyeth, "The Battle at Glens Falls," *The Last of the Mohicans*, 1919.

INDIANS & COWBOYS

One of the economists in my book club has us reading Alex Mesoudi's *Cultural Evolution*. I'd voted for Colson Whitehead's zombie novel, *Zone One*, but the psychiatrist in our group vetoed it (great guy, but we couldn't even get him to finish *Maus*). I'm not complaining though, because a citation in Mesoudi sent me to my library to hunt down Peter Turchin's *Historical Dynamics*. Turchin is a historian and ecologist, which doesn't really explain all of those mathematical formulas and wave charts, but I think I pretty much follow the gist of his "Metaethnic Frontier Theory."

"Internally divisive issues," says Turchin, "will eventually destroy the asabiya [that's academic speak for 'collective action'] of the large group, unless it is 'disciplined' by an external threat."

My ridiculously simplistic translation: empires love frontiers. It's where group solidarity comes from. Why, as Turchin's charts show, do empires rise from frontier regions, and very rarely from nonfrontiers? Because Metropolis is a lazy den of in-fighting, a spreadsheet of special interests vying for attention. Border towns don't have that luxury. They've got all those swarthy aliens swarming outside their gates. And those fictionalized monsters give heroes an excuse to flex their steel.

Gunslinging cowboys like to hang out on America's mythical frontier, that quasi-historical territory writers reinvented as soon as historians decided the real thing had vanished, c. 1890. That frontier is the wellspring of American hero tales. Daniel Boone's fictionalized biographies turned the Revolutionary War vet into an international icon and inspiration for James Fenimore Cooper's Hawkeye in 1826. By the 1880s, the shrinking frontier had begun migrating east, giving detectives like Nick Carter a shadowy realm of city crime to patrol, right before science fiction writers catapulted the frontier into galaxies far far away. Super-heroes prefer the here and now of urban life, but they're frontiersmen too, importing their powers from the other side of the border.

The Shenandoah valley was more bus route than homeland in its pre-Virginian days, so my campus is only metaphorically built atop an Indian burial ground. And yet our student body chose "Lost Cities of Gold" for a fancy dress theme, interchanging Aztecs, Incas, and Mayans in publicity. Apparently they're all the same when you live in Metropolis. My colleague Deborah Miranda is an enrolled member of the Ohlone/Costanoan-Esselen Nation of California, former dominion of the Aztec Empire. Instead of Johnston McCulley's *Mark of Zorro*, you should read her *Bad Indians: A Tribal Memoir* for a tour of the colonial missions. That imperial tension is the radiation still transforming cowboys into superheroes.

This frontier tour kicks off in the thirteen original colonies, treks out to Kentucky, winds into Wyoming, veers back to the Virginian's Virginia, journeys into Jesse James's Missouri, meanders onto the Arizonian plains of Mars, corners a cattle-thief in the Oval Office, tails Tonto to Detroit, and finally splits paths with the cowboys who marshaled the superhero genre.

⚡ ⚡ ⚡

When a student asked world-renowned linguist and political commen-tator Noam Chomsky about the hordes of zombies swarming around our TV sets and theaters, Chomsky explained that in pop culture we're al-ways "about to face destruction from some terrible, awesome enemy, and at the last moment we're saved by a superhero." John Lawrence and Rob-ert Jewett call that the Myth of the American Superhero: "Spiderman and Superman contend against criminals and spies just as the Lone Ranger puts down threats by greedy frontier gangs. Thus paradise is depicted as repeatedly under siege, its citizens pressed down by alien forces too powerful for democratic institutions to quell." Therefore the superheroic cavalry is always riding to our rescue.

"So you go back to the early years," says Chomsky, "the terrible enemy was the Indians," those flesh-devouring zombies Thomas Jefferson called "the merciless Indian Savages." Jefferson blamed the supervillainous King George, who "excited domestic insurrections amongst us, and has endeavoured to bring on the inhabitants of our frontiers," "whose known rule of warfare, is an undistinguished destruction of all ages, sexes and conditions."

Those Indian Savages include the folks who mercilessly rescued the first boatload of Pilgrims from starvation. Also please ignore the fact that Jefferson's fellow founders signed a treaty with some of those said Savages that would have made the Delaware tribe the fourteenth state of the Union. Like the vast majority of U.S. treaties, things didn't work out as stated. "It turns out," continues Chomsky, "this enemy, this horrible enemy that's going to destroy us, is someone we're oppressing." He explains the reversal as "a recognition — at some level of the psyche — that if you've got your boot on somebody's neck, there's something wrong, and that the people you're oppressing may rise up and defend themselves, and then you're in trouble." Since its founding document, America has defined itself as a champion of the oppressed — even when it's been busy oppressing the oppressed.

Indians were our first metaethnic monster-victims. I grew up in Pittsburgh, home of the earliest recorded act of germ warfare in the Americas. When two Delaware chiefs visited Fort Pitt in 1763 to offer its besieged inhabitants safe retreat from Indian territory, the British commander declined but presented them with a gift of smallpox-infected blankets, hoping they would "have the desired effect." They did. Soon Rev. John "Fighting Parson" Elder was rousing hordes of merciless vigilantes to ride to the rescue and attack Indians living peacefully among settlers. "These poor defenseless creatures," wrote Ben Franklin, "were immediately fired upon, stabbed, and hatcheted to Death!" When the Pennsylvania governor posted rewards, no one turned in the murderers because, Rev. Elder explained, "the men in private life are virtuous and respectable; not cruel, but mild and merciful."

America still suffers from that same schizophrenia (or, as a psychology undergrad in my Superheroes course corrected me, dissociative identity

disorder). Our national psyche was founded on alter egos. Francis Parkman, while chronicling Pontiac's so-called Conspiracy in 1851, declared
the Indian to be full of "contradiction":

> A wild love of liberty, an utter intolerance of control, lie at the basis
> of his character, and fire his whole existence. Yet, in spite of this
> haughty independence, he is a devout hero-worshipper; and high
> achievement in war or policy touches a chord to which his nature
> never fails to respond. He looks up with admiring reverence to the
> sages and heroes of his tribe

That same liberty-loving hero-worship infuses the D.I.D. character of
comic book fans. Americans love identity-disguising alter egos because
they also mask ourselves.

Consider Doc Savage and the contorted narrative tricks his creator,
Lester Dent, plays. While sharing his name with those merciless Indians,
the superman is also a descendant of the real-life Colonel Richard Henry
Savage, whom Will Murray identifies as "a hero of the Spanish-American
War," in which the United States seized Puerto Rico, Guam, and the Phil-
ippines from Spain in 1898 — the same year the U.S. military fought its
last battle with a Native tribe. In his 1933 pulp debut, Doc Savage travels through Central America to find "the Valley of the Vanished" where
no "outside races have intermarried" with "the high class of Mayan" believed extinct since colonization. Though a Mayan princess, apparently
attracted by Savage's racially ambiguous bronze skin, would love to
intermarry, he returns to New York instead with a gift of gold from "the
treasure trove of ancient Maya" to finance his do-gooding missions. It's
a peculiarly American take on colonization, where the colonized are not
only willingly plundered but remain hidden in a static preserve unrelated
to any of those actual Indians openly impoverished within the borders
of the United States. John Carlos Rowe calls it our "contradictory self-
conceptions": "Americans' interpretations of themselves as people are
shaped by a powerful imperial desire and a profound anticolonial temper."

That duality might also account for America's "paranoid streak." "The
United States is an unusually frightened country," says Chomsky. "And
in such circumstances, people concoct either for escape or maybe out of

relief, fears that terrible things happen." Those fears unify the undisci-plined citizens of Metropolis, while entertaining them with the soothing fantasy of righteous heroes trampling the monster hordes.

The first merciless Indian Savages were a literary device by Thomas Jefferson to help justify the American Revolution. By the time that war ended in 1783, the United States had pushed its colonial frontier into Daniel Boone's Virginia territory, the future state of Kentucky.

That's also the setting of the first American superhero novel, Robert M. Bird's 1837 *Nick of the Woods*. Bird's Jibbenainosay is the premiere example of America's superheroic dissociative identity disorder when mythologizing our frontiers. According to Bird, the name means "Spirit-that-walks," and so he's "neither man nor beast, but a great ghost or devil that knife cannot harm nor bullet touch." Those who have glimpsed him describe "a great tall fellow, with horns and a hairy head like a buffa-lo-bull." Instead of patrolling the streets of Metropolis, he keeps the woods of Kentucky "under his friendly protection."

Despite the supernatural claims, Michael Lopez dubbed the Jibbe-nainosay "Batman in buckskins." The horns and hairy head are a cos-tume. The "wandering demon of the woods" is really mild-mannered Nathan Slaughter, "a poor Pennsylvany Quaker," the "only man in all Kentucky that *won't fight!*" It's an act of course — or split personality? Either way, Nathan looks like Clark Kent in buckskins. His eyes "beamed a good natured, humble, and perhaps submissive, simplicity of disposi-tion," and he stumbles "with a shuffling, awkward, hesitating step" like "a man who apprehended injury and insult, and who did not possess the spirit to resist them." His rifle and knife are "in a state of dilapidation," and even his horse seems "lame" and his dog a "coward."

Nathan has a Batman origin story. He is one of those "solitary men, bereaved fathers or orphaned sons, the sole survivors, sometimes, of ex-terminated households, who remained only to devote themselves to lives of vengeance," ranging "the woods, intent on private adventures, which they were careful to conceal from the public eye." At night Nathan leaves his real mark: "a good tomahawk dig right through the skull" and "a knife-cut . . . in the shape of a cross." That's his superhero emblem — only he puts it on the chests of his enemies instead of his own. Like the Punisher of the 70s or the 30s Spider, the Jibbenainosay is a killer.

Bird keeps Jefferson's merciless Indian Savages swarming, which is one of many reasons why I prefer my fictional Indians concocted by non-fictional ones. Deborah Miranda is one of a posse of Indian authors I admire. I've never met Sherman Alexie, but a half-dozen of his books roam shelves in my house: poetry in my wife's study, Young Adult in my daughter's room, more novels in the foyer. My wife and I share a contributors page with him in the superhero poetry anthology *Drawn to Marvel*, so I know he likes comics. He told the *New York Times* his favorite childhood hero was Daredevil, and since he grew up in a house "filled with cheap paperbacks," he's still drawn to "books that feature crime, criminals and justice." I've taught his novel *Flight*, a story about a body-swapping time-traveler, so he has no problem with flights of superpowered fancy. Bird didn't either; the novel he published the year before *Nick of the Woods* features a main character who, with a similar power of "metempsychosis," transfers his soul into other people's bodies. That's why I'd like Alexie to rewrite Bird's frontier superhero.

Alexie is also an expert on Indian killers. The phrase is ambiguous: a killer of Indians or an Indian who kills? Alexie's novel *Indian Killer* takes the second path, Bird's *Nick of the Woods* the first. Bird sets his killer loose on the "Injun" population surrounding a frontier fort, a decade before Kentucky reached statehood. Alexie's serial killer scalps white men in Seattle a century and a half later. Alexie and Bird have one opinion in common. They reject the romanticized image of the noble savage. Alexie told CBS News, "I just try to write about everyday Indians." The Indians Bird writes about aren't "wise" and "all about spirituality" either. They're "brutes," "evil creatures," and "the murderers of wives and children." Nathan is avenging his dead family. Alexie's killer isn't so different. He understands suffering. He leaves his mark at crime scenes too.

Scott Nicolay, editor-publisher of the now defunct lit mag *American Standard*, asked me to write a preface after he'd met Alexie at the Taos Poetry Circus and was featuring some of his love poetry. "In my copy of Alexie's *Indian Killer*," I wrote, "chapters start duplicating on page 329, just as Seattle is in a racial meltdown. Once again the Rush Limbaugh character imagines the Killer hunting him down a foggy alley. I spent several minutes bewildered by the post-modern gimmick, flipping pages — yes, it was word for word — till I realized my copy was defective."

History is a defective copy of itself too, trapped into repeating the same scenes. Comic books call that a reboot. I'd like a Jibbenainosay reboot from Alexie. His killer is already a version of Nathan Slaughter, a man so warped by hatred he transforms himself into a demon. *Indian Killer* was published in 1996, *Nick of the Woods* in 1837, just before John L. O'Sullivan coined the phrase "Manifest Destiny," the United States's justification for claiming (among other things) the Oregon Territory, which included the area around Puget Sound now called Seattle.

As a kid Alexie pretended Daredevil "was part Indian," the mixed fate suffered by so many Indian heroes, their dual identities as masked as the Lone Ranger. The little boy the Indian Killer kidnaps wears Daredevil pajamas. What origin story is he in? What blood quota drives a twenty-first-century Spirit-that-walks? Does he don the horned buffalo head by choice or compulsion? Is the secret avenger his Indian or his white half? Is there any difference?

"I am extremely conscious of my tribalism," Alexie told Bill Moyers. "I think a lot of people in this country, especially European Americans and those descended from Europeans, don't see themselves as tribal." Alexie was a "black and white thinker" too, "very us versus them," until 9/11, when he realized "the end game of tribalism is flying planes into building." Now he quotes F. Scott Fitzgerald instead: "The test of a first-rate intelligence is the ability to hold two opposing ideas in mind at the same time and still retain the ability to function."

When that Rush Limbaugh character thinks he's facing the killer in an alley, there's nobody there. It's his own ghost chasing him. I just pulled *Indian Killer* from my shelf and turned to page 329, startled to find no conservative radio commentator, no imagined stalker, no foggy alley at all. What happened to my defective copy? "The owner of my local bookstore," my preface reminds me, "exchanged it the next morning." I say,

"The pages of the book she handed me were yellowed along the edges from sunlight," and, a decade and a half later, they still they are. I wished I'd kept that first flawed copy, but I needed to know how it ended.

Nick of the Woods ends with Nathan displaying the scalp of his arch-enemy, Wenonga, the Injun who murdered his family, attached to his belt. Kentucky is safe, the frontier pushed beyond its colonial borders. "From that moment," concludes Bird, "the Jibbenainosay ceased to frequent his accustomed haunts in the forest; the phantom Nick of the Woods was never more beheld stalking through the gloom; nor was his fearful cross ever again seen traced on the breast of a slaughtered Indian." Instead the fearful emblems of superheroes appeared on their own breasts, as the Jibbenainosay's wooded paths gave way to metropolitan alleyways. Nick still stalks that gloom.

While Professor Miranda teaches Native American Lit, our colleague Professor Smout offers our English students a Cowboys & Indians course. I suggest journalist Emily Bazelon enroll next semester. Her 2013 *New York Times Magazine* article "The Online Avengers" shows how closely superheroes walk in frontiersmen's boot steps.

Bazelon chronicles the adventures of Anonymous hackers who use their powers to combat cyber-bullying. You may remember the Anons from chapter two, the ones in the Guy Fawkes masks from *V for Vendetta*. Bazelon says they tend to think in "polarized terms," viewing their cases as "parables with an innocent victim, evil perpetrators and ineffectual (or corrupt) law enforcement," all staples of superheroes. Bazelon enjoys some of those polarized terms too, describing how her aliased Avengers "team up" or "join forces" to expose "wrongdoers." In her defense, the rhetorical infection may originate with the tribe of Anons she interviews. "We wanted to strike fear into their hearts," declares a Batman wannabe. But it's Bazelon who draws him in comic book rhetoric: "He vowed that day he would do something about Rehtaeh Parsons's death."

In a comic book, an anonymous do-gooder would have swooped in and saved the fifteen-year-old Parsons before she was raped at a party. Though the teen boys documented their crime with cellphone pics they posted online, the police did nothing. Humiliated and shunned, Parsons changed high schools, but still suffering from depression a year and a half later, she committed suicide.

Bazelon spins that into a superhero's call to arms, but the metaphor's not quite right. These Anons aren't caped crusaders patrolling the mean streets of Gotham. Their streets are Facebook and Tumblr. Parsons and her rapists lived in Nova Scotia; her Avengers live in London and Scandinavia and never assemble except on Skype. Their superpowers are laptop-based. Many of the crimes they pursue — posting a video on YouTube or a message on Twitter — take place in the no-man's-land of the World Wide Web. The bad guys can live anywhere on the globe, but they elude justice by exploiting a virtual frontier.

What we have here is a Western.

The two genres are closely aligned. The first self-titled Avengers patrolled the frontier towns of colonial California in *The Mark of Zorro*. It's not entirely clear what Johnston McCulley thought his masked caballeros were avenging, but Zorro and his league of vigilantes impose order on their lawless if fictional land. Yes, California was once a Spanish colony, but McCulley's grasp of history ends there. Though superimposed on real space, the frontier of Westerns is always virtual. It spans the length of a Metropolis bookshelf. The first gunslingers and superheroes were both made of paper.

Professor Smout's syllabus includes McCarthy's *All the Pretty Horses* and Cooper's *The Last of the Mohicans*, but Bazelon should read Owen Wister's *The Virginian: A Horseman of the Plains* first. Published a year before *The Scarlet Pimpernel* and *Man and Superman* landed in London, the 1902 novel still shapes the Western and the superhero genre that grew from it. Instead of Indians, Wister's white-skinned bad guys disappear into the mountain sanctuaries of Wyoming:

> He that took another man's possessions, or he that took another man's life, could always run here if the law or popular justice were too hot at his heels. Steep ranges and forests walled him in from the world on all four sides, almost without a break; and every entrance lay through intricate solitudes.

Internet bad guys elude justice the same way. When journalist Amanda Hess dialed 911 after receiving death and rape threats via Twitter, the Palm Springs cop who arrived at her door dismissed them because the "guy could be sitting in a basement in Nebraska for all we know." The bad guy was safe in the intricate solitudes of his IP address.

Hess documents her experience, and dozens like it, in her *Pacific Standard* essay, "Why Women Aren't Welcome on the Internet." When Caroline Criado-Perez received similar threats after petitioning the British government to include women on its currency, she retweeted them until the international attention forced police to respond. They said it was Twitter's problem. Twitter said threatened users should contact local authorities. Wister's Wyoming faces the same failure of law enforcement, a failure that continues to justify superhero plots every month. Because "the law has been letting our cattle-thieves go," a former judge declares:

> We are in a very bad way, and we are trying to make that way a little better until civilization can reach us. At present we lie beyond its pale. The courts ... into whose hands we have put the law, are not dealing the law. They are withered hands, or rather they are imitation hands made for show, with no life in them, no grip. They cannot hold a cattle-thief.

Bazelon's Avengers are skilled at tracking cattle-thieves' user IDs through walled websites and forests of social media. When four teens in Texas tweeted gang rape threats at a twelve-year-old in New Zealand, the team of Anons unmasked their Twitter handles and forwarded evidence to the boys' high school administrators. The Virginian's punches are "sledge-hammer blows of justice." OpAntiBully forwards screenshots.

When Rehtaeh Parsons's mother received evidence of her daughter's rape, she turned it over to OpJustice4Rehtaeh, an Anonymous group she originally distrusted as masked vigilantes. But, she told Bazelon, "if pressure from this group is what it takes, let them do what they do." Wister's judge reasons similarly:

> And so when your ordinary citizen sees this, and sees that he has placed justice in a dead hand, he must take justice back into his

own hands where it was once at the beginning of all things. Call this primitive, if you will. But so far from being a *defiance* of the law, it is an *assertion* of it — the fundamental assertion of self-governing men, upon whom our whole social fabric is based.

Local authorities disagree. When badgered into reopening a rape case by OpMaryville and Justice4Daisy, the sheriff of Maryville, Missouri, complained: "They all need to get jobs and quit living with their parents." Parsons's alleged rapists — or at least the two who posted the YouTube video of the crime — now faced child pornography charges, though a police spokesman warned that OpJustice4Rehtaeh could come under investigation too. Technically, the Gotham police department is still investigating Batman, and J. Jonah Jameson has been editorializing against Spider-Man since his first issue: "We cannot allow that masked menace to take the law into his own hands!" He has "no business catching criminals by himself!"

Meanwhile, the Brotherhood of Mutant Cattle-Thieves has its advocates. The Electronic Frontier Foundation — a free speech and privacy rights group — lobbied against the Violence Against Women Act because of an amendment updating phone harassment to include email. When Hess received threats on her cellphone and police still refused to make a report, she took the law out of their withered hands. She tracked the guy's IP address, filed a civil protection order, hired a private investigator to serve court papers, and got a judge to approve a restraining order that included everything from Twitter to hot air balloon messaging.

Hess is no proponent of virtual justice leagues though. When the Virginian catches horse-thieves, he lynches them. That means Wister and his judge have to spend a lot of their frontier rhetoric differentiating this private but supposedly law-and-orderly form of capital punishment from the "semi-barbarous" lynching and burning of "Southern negroes in public." Apparently, the swift hanging of "our criminals" puts no "hideous disgrace upon the United States." The judge doesn't quibble over the definition of a "criminal" though, since the term denotes someone who has been tried and convicted, a luxury Wister's frontiersmen forgo.

By the end of Bazelon's article, her lead Avenger has lost his girlfriend of nine years — she complained he never turned off his laptop at night. Hess mentions her boyfriend but would rather write other articles about the "Frontier of Female Sexuality" and "the gun-toting, boob-grabbing douchebags who are subsidizing your online porn habit." She'd also like to see Internet harassment prosecuted as a civil rights issue, a wonderfully civilized aspiration far beyond the pale of the current U.S. legal system. Meanwhile, we're left with faceless superhero-wannabes trying to make our virtual frontier better until civilization reaches us.

Wister wraps up his ur-Western with an ultimatum ("I'll give you till sundown to get out of town"), a shoot-out, and then a honeymoon in the mountains that had secreted those cattle-thieves. But civilization isn't fully realized until the Virginian dons a suit special-ordered from the East and makes nice with his mother-in-law in New Hampshire. There's a couple of sentences about coming railroads and coal rights, but his adventures end after his once-skeptical love interest swallows his vigilantism. Superheroes would answer the same call-to-arms.

"What is become of the horseman?" asks Wister. "Well, he will be here among us always, invisible, waiting his chance to live and play as he would like."

⚡ ⚡ ⚡

The Internet is a Wild West, but the Kentucky frontier has changed a lot since Daniel Boone's and Nathan Slaughter's days. Since the District of Kentucky was still a part of Virginia in 1782, Wister's *Virginian* is a reboot of Bird's Virginians, those "colossal" frontiersmen who would "amaze the lesser mortals of the plains" as a "race of demigods." Now instead of hunting down merciless Indian Savages, Kentucky's leading demigods hunt down votes. The big game is the White House, but since the meta-ethnic frontier is closed, Metropolis is awash in internally divisive issues.

That's why Rand Paul fired his racist sidekick. In June 2013, the Kentucky senator accepted (by "mutual decision") the resignation of aide Jack Hunter, aka the Southern Avenger. Hunter's shoot-from-the-hip opinions on southern seccession, the Lincoln assassination, and whether "a non-white majority America would simply cease to be America" were a "distraction." Like Slaughter, Hunter had to stop wearing his Southern

Avenger mask, retiring the shock-jock alter ego he'd first adopted after a conversation with a bottle of Kentucky bourbon whiskey.

I teach at Washington and Lee University, in a smallville renowned as a War between the States tourist Mecca, so I'm familiar with all brands of Southern Avengers. Just as Kentucky began in Virginia, the mythic South is the secret origin point of the mythic West. Wister was a Virginian himself, descended from one of the South's largest slave-holding families, which included the senator who drafted the Constitution's fugitive slave clause. Southern Avengers are some of America's earliest superheroes, those rugged individuals too savage for life in Metropolis.

Thomas Jefferson and Francis Parkman projected that untamable energy onto their frontiers, and so their Indians' "wild love of liberty" and "utter intolerance of control" animates the frontiersman's character too, whether gunslinging or cape-flapping. Superman doesn't take orders from government officials. When Commissioner Gordon lights the Bat signal, he's begging for help, not dictating it. In Marvel's *Civil War*, even the flag-wearing Captain America rebels when the feds try to curtail his vigilante freedom. The Confederacy and the western frontier vanished into America's mythologized past, but Virginia rebels and Kentucky libertarians continue to champion the "Indian" spirit of "haughty independence" through their superhero descendants.

That spirit thrives in my Virginian town. The remains of not one but two Confederate generals rest within a half-mile stroll of my front door. Confederate flags are common too — though, unlike Mr. Hunter, most folks don't sport them on their faces. Even Captain Confederacy (a creation of sci-fi writer and former Minnesota gubernatorial candidate Will Shetterly) retired his mask when his series moved to Marvel's Epic. The comic was set in an alternate universe in which the Confederacy won the Civil War (apparently the same corner of the multiverse Newt Gingrich visited for his 2005 *Gettysburg* novel).

After Shetterly retired his first captain, a black woman took over the identity, draping Old Dixie across her breasts. If that sounds implausible, then you didn't attend my town's council meeting in which a regiment of Southern Avengers protested the banning of Confederate flags from city flagpoles. I can't criticize since I used to wear the same image across the back of concert T-shirts, believing it represented nothing more than a subgenre of rock. I was sixteen and still preferred Lynyrd Skynyrd's *Gimme Back My Bullets* over R.E.M.'s *Fables of the Reconstruction*.

Civil War reenactors, the most common brand of cosplayers in Lexington, Virginia, attended the council meeting too. My university borders the Virginia Military Institute, where I watched a legion of gray-clad and hoop-skirted extras cheer a regal Stonewall Jackson during the shooting of *Gods and Generals*. The chair of our theater department tells me they shot a scene in front of our colonnade too. While students are pulling down the American flag, you can see air conditioners in faculty office windows. For *Sommersby*, the film crew shoveled the historic downtown streets with dirt and angled the Exxon station out of frame. I'll watch Jodie Foster in anything, but I like *Sommersby* for its dual-identity plot (Richard Gere impersonates a Confederate vet who looks just like Richard Gere) and its time period. Reconstruction is way more interesting than the Civil War. It's also another superhero origin point.

Marvel movie guru Joss Whedon agrees. He started writing his pre-*Avengers* series *Firefly* after reading Michael Shaara's *The Killer Angels*. Whedon also took an undergraduate class from Richard Slotkin, author of *Gunfighter Nation*, my favorite study in American frontier mythology. Whedon sets his dystopic future six years after a civil war with a dispossessed Confederate-like soldier (Mal sings "We shall rise again" in the premiere) for a space captain. "Mal's politics," Whedon told interviewer Emily Nussbaum, "are very reactionary and 'Big government is bad' and 'Don't interfere with my life,'" tunes Senator Rand and his former sidekick sing too. But Whedon sees both sides:

> Sometimes he's wrong — because sometimes the Alliance is America, this beautiful shining light of democracy. But sometimes the Alliance is America in Vietnam: we have a lot of petty politics, we are way out of our league and we have no right to control these people. And yet! Sometimes the Alliance is America in Nazi Germany. And Mal can't see that, because he was a Vietnamese.

Actually, Mal is the thoroughly white-bread Nathan Fillion, but his second in command, like the second Captain Confederacy and at least one of the flag-wearing protesters at the Lexington council meeting, is an African American woman (though Latina.com identifies Gina Torres as Afro-Latina). Whedon's Confederacy never practiced slavery, which is why his take on the Reconstruction is both watchable and a complete cop-out. Whedon also avoids any metaethnic massacres by keeping his frontier unpopulated by aliens. It's just cowboys fleeing the stranglehold of the federal government. "Every story needs a monster," says Whedon. "In the stories of the old west it was the Apaches." His merciless Indian Savages are called Reavers, and though they'll rape you to death, eat your flesh, and sew your skin into their clothing (if you're "very, very lucky," quips Torres, "they'll do it in that order"), they were once fellow settlers driven into homicidal psychosis by secret, government experiments. No wonder libertarians hate Big Government!

As a Reconstruction-fueled space cowboy, Captain Reynolds is also a descendant of another rebellious libertarian hero, the ur-gunslinger and real-life southern avenger Jesse James. During the war, James fought as a Missouri bushwhacker against local Union militias. After Richmond fell and Lee surrendered, the pardoned general-in-chief served as president of my university. James kept fighting. He saw his campaign of train and bank robberies as resistance to Republican-led Reconstruction. Even before his 1882 death, journalists and dime novelists were converting him and his gang of "Gay Bandits" into gunslinging Robin Hoods. "In all the history of medieval knight-errantry and modern brigandage," the *Lexington Caucasian* reported in 1874, "there is nothing that equals the wild romance of the past few years' career of Arthur McCoy, Frank and Jesse James and the Younger boys. Their desperate deeds during the war were sufficient to have stocked a score of ordinary novels, with facts that outstrip the strung-out flights of fantasy."

Like the more recent Southern Avenger, James was also a political columnist. Jack Hunter wrote for the *Charleston City Paper*, where his articles remain online because his former editor refused to remove them. James wrote his diatribes for the *Kansas City Times*, where the owner was a fellow Civil War vet working to restore ousted secessionists to office. Missouri elected Democrat senator Francis Cockrell in 1875, who went on to serve five terms — evidence that the Radical Republicans (their term) had lost control of Reconstruction. The era formally ended in 1877 when President Hayes withdrew the last federal troops.

Their departure also marks the end of the South's most famous team of masked avengers, the Ku Klux Klan. They'd started as a social club of Confederate vets in Pulaski, Tennessee, but grew into paramilitary groups openly murdering opponents. The rebooted Klan of 1914 began their vigilante mission as The Knights of Mary Phagan (unfortunately echoed by the "white knight work" of Bazelons's Anonymous Avengers, OpJustice4Rehtaeh), avenging her death by kidnapping her murderer from a Georgia prison and lynching him. You can read more about the later KKK in chapter six, but the original team, like the original X-Men, wore identical costumes and were led by a man who called himself "Cyclops." They're all libertarian rebels exercising their rugged individualism outside federal law.

Superman battled the Klan on 1940s radio, and he's been followed by the Defenders, Black Panther, Batman, and both the Justice League and the Justice Society. Even the Southern Avenger fights racism now. In his *Politico* confession, Hunter blamed his old slurs on the mask: "Whenever I put on that wrestling mask, I took on a persona that was intentionally outrageous and provocative. I said many terrible things. I disavow them." The unmasked Hunter now criticizes fellow Republicans who dismiss "the idea that racism is actually a problem." Oscar Wilde might question the transformation ("Man is least himself when he talks in his own person. Give him a mask, and he will tell you the truth"), but a former high school friend of mine and former Ron Paul policy aide told me that "Jack is very committed to building a more inclusive, tolerant GOP."

I wouldn't call it a superheroic transformation, but the Southern Avenger Nathan Slaughter learned to live without his Jibbenainosay mask. Sherman Alexie, another former inhabitant of the "black and white world," tries "to live in the in between" now too. It's an alien terrain for all superheroic frontiersmen.

⚡ ⚡ ⚡

Joss Whedon's Captain Reynolds reveals another often forgotten fact about the superhero's frontier past: after migrating west, the South jumped to Outer Space. Edgar Rice Burroughs's dispossessed Confederate soldier, John Carter, heads to Arizona to dig gold but ends up on Mars, where he gains superpowers and champions a ruined race of aristocrats against four-armed apes and green-skinned heathens. How's that for metaethnic savages? *The Princess of Mars* gave me allegorical whiplash, but Burroughs's superhero politics aren't hard to decode. The South is dead, long live the South.

Since the Western's frontier was fictional anyway, Burroughs has no trouble relocating it to another planet, and the transformative leap mutates his frontiersman into a superman. In 1939, Jerry Siegel offered a "Scientific Explanation for Superman's Amazing Strength": "The smaller size of our planet, with its slighter gravity pull, assists Superman's tremendous muscles in the performance of miraculous feats of strength!" But Burroughs beat him by more than a quarter century. John Carter's powers are a product of "the lesser gravitation and lower air pressure on Mars." A "very earthly and at the same time superhuman leap" carries Carter "fully thirty feet into the air" and lands him "a hundred feet" away.

Disney released the novel's first film adaptation, *John Carter*, on the hundredth anniversary of its 1912 publication in *All-Story* magazine, back when it was titled *Under the Moons of Mars*. It also released a new edition of *A Princess of Mars*, with an intro by Junot Díaz, the second Pulitzer Prize–winning novelist attached to the project. "John Carter was also one of our first recognizable superhumans," writes Díaz, "and there is little doubt that his extraordinary physical feats inspired Superman's creators."

Michael Chabon (who has a thing for Martian sci-fi too) cowrote the screenplay, his first film credit since 2004's *Spider-Man 2*, once the high mark for Hollywood superhero excellence. Readers of *Thrilling Tales* (the retro-pulp issue of *McSweeney's* that Chabon guest-edited in 2003) know the first chapter of his sadly unfilmed screenplay "The Martian Agent: A Planetary Romance." Chabon told me he has no intention of completing the novelization, so his *John Carter* revisions are the closest we'll ever get.

Given that Burroughs's first Carter novel is one of the more entertainingly racist novels I've read, I trust Chabon had his delete key in full working order before opening director Andrew Stanton's script. The former

Confederate captain is a "southern gentleman of the highest type," whose "slaves fairly worshipped the ground he trod." Once he makes the magical leap to Mars (or "Barsoom," the quasi-Oriental name Burroughs gives his frontier), he wars with a race of green monsters, each a "huge and terrific incarnation of hate, of vengeance and of death." If the connection to the inhabitants of the United States' western plains is too subtle, then note that Captain Carter was battling a band of Apaches seconds before magically switching planets.

Burroughs further expands Jefferson's metaethnic tradition by giving his merciless Indian Savages four arms. Barsoom supports a species of four-armed gorillas too, funhouse reflections of those worshipping slaves freed after Captain Confederacy lost its War between the States. There's also a very human-looking race of a once great but now tragically fallen civilization. Burroughs doesn't describe any antebellum mansions in the ruins, but a 1912 reader would have recognized the vanquished South in Barsoom's rusty riverbeds.

Carter, yet another well-bred Virginian, arrives ready to rule. Those ferocious-looking Martians are "infinitely less agile and less powerful, in proportion to their weight, than an Earth man." Carter doubts "were one of them suddenly to be transported to Earth he could lift his own weight from the ground." Mars, with its impossibly arrested climate and cultures, is his to conquer. John Carter is the ultimate colonizer. Mars is literally made for him.

I was hoping Chabon would fix some of the colonial politics, but Disney's Martian women wear "flowing Middle Eastern garb," and their cities are modeled on the ancient ruins of Petra in modern Jordan. Chabon likens those four-armed Tharks to nineteenth-century "Afghani tribesmen," and Stanton gives them all the lean look of "desert-dwelling people," specifically "the Masai warriors" of Africa "and the Aborigines" of Australia. Plus, for musical icing, that's Led Zeppelin's "Kashmir" playing on the trailer. Lynn Collins, the once-titular princess, self-identifies as "Irish and Cherokee Indian." She also cried the first time she read the script, because she "felt its parallel to Earth was so poignant."

So what do North America, India, Afghanistan, Jordan, Kenya, and Australia have in common? They were all exotic territories of the British

Empire. Disney's Mars is the ultimate melting pot of non-Western "others." That's the sci-fi way of saying: "They all look the same to me."

Stanton and Chabon let their superman remain a Civil War vet, but the wars haunting their film are Iraq and Afghanistan. If Carter does not defeat his enemy on Mars, the enemy will attack Earth next. That's a one-sentence summary of President Bush's Middle East policy. The film portrays Carter as a reluctant warrior forced to finish a conflict he didn't start. Like Carter, a reluctant President Obama was dropped into the middle of a desert conflict with alien cultures he didn't understand.

Burroughs fans have a right to complain, but the allegorical update is oddly appropriate. Burroughs's novel was popular in part because it reflected U.S. foreign policy of 1912. England was done with imperialism, and America was its heir. Our internal frontier was closed, so we leaped to new borders. To expand our naval capabilities, we instigated the 1903 secession of Panama from Columbia and the construction of the Panama Canal. While Burroughs's Martian canals were premiering in *All-Story*, our canal was just two years from completion. America was the new superpower, and John Carter was our superpowered cowboy.

Carter isn't the only fictional frontiersman to enter the Oval Office. The *Village Voice* called George W. Bush a "fake cowboy," but when he moved from the Texas governor's office to the White House in 2000, he brought a bona fide cowboy painting. The 28 × 40 oil by Westerns illustrator W. H. D. Koerner had appeared on the back cover of his campaign biography, *A Charge to Keep*. The title is from a hymn, and a friend gave him the painting because it illustrated a 1918 short story of the same name. Bush thought the cowboy charging up a hill on horseback was a nineteenth-century Methodist evangelist spreading his faith across the West.

"He's a determined horseman," he told visitors, "a very difficult trail. And you know at least two people are following him, and maybe a thousand."

"Bush's personal identification with the painting," writes David Gergen, "reveals a good deal about his sense of himself . . . a brave, daring leader riding fearlessly into the unknown, striking out against unseen enemies, pulling his team behind him, seeking, in the words of Wesley's hymn, 'to do my Master's will.'" It's a plot common to Westerns and superheroes comics. It's also not true. Although the painting did appear beside Ben Ames Williams's "A Charge to Keep" in *Country Gentleman Magazine*, Koerner painted it in 1915 for the *Saturday Evening Post* to illustrate a story by William J. Neidig called "The Slipper Tongue." The horseman is not a galloping evangelist. He's a horse-thief fleeing a lynch mob. It could be a scene from *The Virginian*.

Whatever its title, the work has become the best known of Koerner's over eight hundred commissioned paintings and drawings. That includes "Hugo Hercules," the first comic strip superman, and further evidence of superheroes' cowboy origins.

Koerner immigrated from Germany at the age of three, and seventeen years later took a job as a staff artist for the *Chicago Tribune* earning $5 a day. His duties included producing a Sunday strip for the Comics Supplement. He came up with an urban cowboy with superstrength. If that's not enough to call him a superhero, Hugo calls himself "the boy wonder" while aiding a series of Chicago damsels-in-mild-distress. He has his own catchphrase too, "Just as easy," tossed off whenever he performs some superhuman feat, like ice skating with a boat on his shoulders or flinging a defensive line of football players across a goal post. Sometimes he adds, "I could do this forever," as if Koerner hasn't drawn him in a sufficiently effortless pose. Clark Kent wouldn't declare, "This is a job for . . . Superman!" for almost four decades, but Hugo knows when "It's up to me!"

Oval Office visitors commented how Koerner's Methodist horse-thief looked a bit like George W., but Hugo is the one with the cowboy hat — offset by a sports jacket, striped pants, and bowtie. The hat vacillated between white and black though, and Hugo vacillated too. Overall he was a force for good, but his altruism was random, and occasionally the good he did was correcting the harm he'd already done — like when he missed a football and accidentally punted a house across a field. But at least he lugged it back, right? And so what if he uses his strength to collect the bowling competition prize money after destroying a wall and a passing trolley? After catching a falling safe from crushing an old man as his daughter helplessly watched, he asks: "Am I glad I did it? Wid de doll's arms around me neck and de old gent coffing a three spot? Am I glad?"

Note that folksy way of talking. No wonder George W. liked Koerner. And if Hugo can be a bit destructive — did he really have to rip up a porch to carry it umbrella-like over a woman fretting about the rain? — he helps far more than he harms. Like when he catches that family jumping from a burning house, or when he carries a fire engine to another would-be disaster. He stops that runaway horse before it crashes its owner's carriage too, but more often he only saves damsels from inconvenience, halting trolleys and cable cars that refuse to stop, or lifting an elephant standing on a handkerchief. And how did the striking cabdrivers' union feel when he carried that woman on top of her pile of crates? Dragging a derailed train twenty miles is nice, but is lifting a young Romeo and his car to his Juliet's balcony for a parting kiss really the best use of one's superpowers?

As far as battling actual menaces, Hugo does wrestle a bear into submission — while dressed in Teddy Roosevelt buckskins. He was only saving himself though. Same with those three muggers who corner him at gunpoint. They look ready to abandon the criminal life after he lifts a cannon to their faces. Would their bullets have bounced off him? Could he have leaped tall buildings if they'd tried to escape? No idea. We'll never know how Hugo might have matured into the superhero genre. The strip ran from September 1902 to January 1903 when Koerner abandoned it for other work.

America wasn't quite ready for a comic strip superman. Wister's *The Virginian* roamed across national bookstores while Hugo stayed corralled in the Chicago funny pages. Soon Koerner was studying with illustrator Howard Pyle, creator of the 1883 classic *The Merry Adventures of Robin Hood* as well as varied adventures of Arthurian knights, noble pirates, and a modern Aladdin. It was a thorough education in superhero prehistory, but Koerner's interests turned west when the *Saturday Evening Post* commissioned his first frontier scenes. When he died at fifty-eight, the first supercowboy comic strip artist was one of the best known illustrators of the Old West. That was 1938, the year *Action Comics* No. 1 rode onto newsstands.

⚡ ⚡ ⚡

Superheroes still roam the frontiers, but not Jefferson's Indian Savages. They moved to Metropolis. While taking a break from grading Native American Lit essays, Professor Miranda Facebooked me a link to one of DC's newest characters, Equinox, a teen superheroine based on Cree activist Shannen Koostachin.

Equinox is a member of Jeff Lemire and Mike McKone's *Justice League United*. Like Marvel's *Alpha Flight*, the team is Canadian, so the character continues the U.S. publishing preference of placing Native America outside U.S. borders. But at least Equinox is from an actual tribe, her costume isn't red, her features aren't stoic, and she's not showing any thigh or cleavage. That helps offset the "her power stems from the Earth" cliché, and I like the idea of a character who has different abilities as the seasons change—never heard that one before.

DC has thrown unitards on Indians before (Black Condor in 2006, Dawnstar in 1977, Super-Chief in 1961), as has Marvel (Echo in 1999, Black Crow in 1984, Red Wolf in 1970). The appropriation fits the frontier logic of the superhero formula. Black Condor's superpower-bestowing Mayan spider goddess Tocotl? That's an all-American equivalent of a Tibetan guru handing out magic rings to Clark Kent tourists. Remember in chapter three when Richard Slotkin described frontiersmen merging with the shadowy border they police? That's why Nathan Slaughter chose an Indian name for his superhero identity. Frontiersmen are pioneers doused with Indian radiation.

The 1854 *Types of Mankind* tried to draw a line in the racial sand ("the white man seems fatal to the Red Indian, whose tribes fall away before the onward march of the frontier-man like snow in the spring"), but British explorer George Ruxton had already called those frontiersmen "White Indians," "a genus more approximating to the primitive savage than perhaps any other class of civilized man." Superheroes are those frontiersmen's mutant offspring, half-breeds who master their inner wilderness for the urban good of Metropolis. They absorb the thrill of the metaethnic border and fly it around our skyscrapers to entertain us.

That's why I prefer Wyatt Wingfoot. He doesn't have superpowers. No faux-Native pseudomythology hands him wings or a magic medicine bag. He doesn't commune with tree spirits either. His wardrobe is business suits and T-shirts, no cowboy boots, no buckskin jackets. He was born in *Fantastic Four* No. 50, cover-dated May 1966, on newsstands a month before my June-dated birth certificate. Wyatt's dad is "Big Will Wingfoot — the greatest Olympic decathlon star this country ever had!" Here on Earth-1218, that's James "Big Jim" Thorpe, Olympic gold medalist for the pentathlon and decathlon in 1912 — the same year John Carter premiered in *All-Story*. Stan Lee even lent Thorpe's name to the college coach trying to draft Wyatt: "I'm sorry! I'm not interested in athletics, Coach Thorpe!"

Wyatt is no superhero, but if you want a real-world equivalent to Bruce Wayne training "his body to physical perfection until he is able to perform amazing athletic feats," Jim Thorpe is your best bet. His Olympic records were still legendary when Finger penned that Batman origin, and in 1950 the Associated Press voted Thorpe the greatest athlete of the first half of the twentieth century. Thorpe was both a famous Indian and an Indian who was famous. Stan Lee romanticized him into Wyatt, but Wyatt is the first Indian in a superhero comic book to represent an individual instead of an ethnicity. He's the first Indian in Metropolis who didn't arrive via the Metaethnic Express.

Jack Kirby penciled Wyatt's premier, but I prefer Santa Fe painter Ben Wright's rendering of Thorpe. I picked *Jim Thorpe in His Carlisle Indian School Football Uniform* for the cover of my novel *School for Tricksters*. Wright's website says he "draws from Native American ceremony, symbolism, and tradition" and identifies himself as "part Cherokee," rarely promising signs, but I like the painting because the old-timey helmet sets the period, plus the slightly stylized Thorpe shades into the larger-than-life. The big "C" on his chest could be a superhero's. Carlisle Man! Thorpe is the original Indian superman, earning his fame as the Western genre was shading into the superheroic.

Biographer Kate Buford later told me Wright got it wrong. The cover of her *Native American Son: The Life and Sporting Legend of Jim Thorpe* features the original photo with an inside caption: "Jim Thorpe with the Canton Bulldogs, c. 1920, Canton, Ohio." So the "C" is for Canton, a team Thorpe played for after his career peaked. Ben painted over the facts—the way lesser-known inker Joe Sinnott thickened Kirby's lines for *Fantastic Four* No. 50.

That's how art works. It warps reality into a stylized version of itself. Superheroes are an extreme example and so useful for pointing out distortions. History books are a more subtle art form, but no more accurate. *School for Tricksters* is a historical novel, so I paint over a shelf of facts too. When my daughter's eleventh grade history teacher capped a Carlisle Indian School lesson with, "Oh, I'm sure those kids must have wanted to be there," my daughter grabbed a row of books from my office to write a rebuttal for her research paper.

I recommended *Chief Buffalo Child Long Lance: The Glorious Imposter.* I used to exchange emails with the author, Donald Smith, in Alberta. Thorpe is the Carlisle Indian School's most famed student, but I prefer the adventures of Chief Buffalo Child, aka Sylvester Long. He's the real Carlisle Man. He spent his superheroic life leaping racial skyscrapers while Metropolis applauded.

Race is the metaethnic fiction that has most thrilled and horrified America, and Sylvester Long wielded it like a superpower. Carlisle railroaded children from their western reservations to the middle of Pennsylvania to be transformed into working-class mainstream Americans. According to Long's autobiography, he was a full-blood Blackfoot born in a Great Plains teepee, and so an ideal student for the program. Except that his birth certificate says Winston-Salem, North Carolina, and both his parents were ex-slaves. Which still makes him the ideal Carlisle student, since Carlisle was all about painting over facts too. The real-life dual-identity Long graduated to Hollywood, where he performed a celluloid version of himself, until the movie exposure lead to his unmasking and suicide.

Sylvester, a mild-mannered library janitor and former Wild West circus performer, longed to be exceptional, a dangerously supeheroic dream for a mixed-blood Clark Kent in the Jim Crow South. But did he doodle over his real self, or did he become his disguise? That's a question to ask any superhero. When Dean Cain's Kent proposed to Teri Hatcher's Lane on the season two finale of *Lois & Clark: The New Adventures of Superman*, the network feared leaks and so shot three answers: "Yes," "No," and the one they aired, "Who's asking, Clark Kent . . . or Superman?" Smith documents at least a dozen Lois Lanes in Long's adventures, but no marriage proposals. His identity wasn't stable enough to settle down. That's the curse of all frontier-crisscrossing superheroes.

I ask my students Lois's question: what is the character's core identity? I see four options:

(A) the superhuman,
(B) the human,
(C) neither, or
(D) both.

For decades, Superman's answer was "A." Clark Kent is the pair of fake glasses he wears around humans. That officially flipped to "B" after John Byrne's 80s reboot. Clark lived a perfectly normal childhood until his superpowered puberty made him hide behind a cape and tights.

Sometimes students go with "C," arguing that both Clark and Superman are public faces worn by an inner Kal-El. It's a common idea outside of comics too, that we all have a secret private self who transforms according to social context: home, work, frat party. It fits the standard master-of-disguise trope too. Long could have wandered downtown any of his free Saturdays and leafed through a copy of *Nick Carter Detective Weekly* at a Carlisle newsstand in 1912. The master-of-disguise detective's banner illustration is a row of heads, "Nick Carter in Various Disguises," with the largest and literally central self in the middle (more on Nick in chapter eight).

"D" is the most daring choice. What if the center doesn't hold and we're all a series of shifting performances? Zorro admits as much when he unmasks himself as the languid Don Diego. The costume wasn't just a disguise; it made his whole body come alive — something Bruce Banner and the Hulk understand too. Are any of us the same person when we're angry? And is the goal to find a "golden mean" as Don Diego promises his fiancée? Like Teri Hatcher, Lolita is no polygamist. And yet who is the

Scarlet Pimpernel's wife married to? If Sir Percy is a foppish disguise, why does he keep laughing that inane laugh even after he unmasks?

All of that is too complicated an answer for early twentieth-century America. Heroes were starting to absorb the metaethnic radiation and paint stories layered with racial subtext, but readers still wanted to live in a black and white world. When his employers unmasked Sylvester, they only saw a dual-identity fake. He was a Negro disguised as an Indian infiltrating white America. Race was a row of tightly framed panels, no blood in the gutters.

Except then why did their private detective have to write over the facts, claiming he fingered rouge and hair-straightening gel from Long's corpse? Long was mixed race, more white than anything else, but that didn't suit American racial dichotomies. Long's alma mater had championed the dual-identity model too, doctoring "before" and "after" photos of graduating students. Sometimes you have to white-out a shirt collar to keep the world "savage"/"civilized."

Stan Lee invented the Keewazi Indian reservation for the Wingfoots and dropped Wyatt into the Human Torch's college dorm. Johnny looks up at his hulk of a roommate: "Say, whatever they feed you at home, I'd like it on my diet!" Wyatt is still wandering the borders of the Marvel multiverse. I think he's tangled with the Kree a few times too — an alien race Lee and Kirby created a year after Wyatt and who have only a phonetic resemblance to Equinox's tribe. Shannen Koostachin, Equinox's real-world alter ego, was fifteen when she died in 2010. Canada's House of Commons unanimously celebrated her superheroic achievements:

> In her short life, Shannen Koostachin became the voice of a forgotten generation of first nations children. Shannen had never seen a real school, but her fight for equal rights for children in Attawapiskat First Nation launched the largest youth-driven child rights movement in Canadian history, and that fight has gone all the way to the United Nations.

She made it all the way to *Justice League United* too.

⚡⚡⚡

The Canadian-U.S. border isn't exactly a Wild West frontier, but that new Justice League battles invading space aliens in its first issue. Metropolis is still swarming with metaethnic threats, and Equinox isn't the only Indian sidekick fighting them.

Undeterred by their colonialist sci-fi flop *John Carter*, Disney threw another $375 million over the frontier cliff in 2013. *The Lone Ranger and Tonto* earned back $260 million. I'll leave you to do the math, but if you're trying to calculate why Johnny Depp was wearing a dead bird on his head, look at painter Kirby Sattler's *I Am Crow*. The painting is to Tonto as Keith Richards is to Captain Jack Sparrow. It also has as much to do with Native America as the Rolling Stones have with the 1700s Caribbean.

According to Sattler's website, his "paintings are interpretations based upon the nomadic tribes of the 19th century American Plains." If you think that means the model for or at least the subject matter of *I Am Crow* is a Crow Indian, think again. "I," explains Sattler, "purposely do not denote a specific tribal affiliation to my paintings, allowing the personal sensibilities and knowledge of the viewer to create their own stories." Mr. Depp's personal sensibilities, for instance, told him the dead bird likes peanuts. Sattler's website also notes that he is of "non-native blood" and that he's neither a "historian" nor "ethnologist." And yet his "distinctive style of realism" avoids being "presumptuous" by giving his work "an authentic appearance" but "without the constraints of having to adhere to historical accuracy."

That makes Sattler a perfect source for Johnny Depp's equally nonaccuracy-adhering Indian fantasies. The actor said he may have a Cherokee or possibly Creek grandmother (how else to explain those cheek bones?) and told *Rolling Stone* that he hoped his portrayal of Tonto might "give some hope to kids on the reservations." He also had a Tonto-esque sidekick named "Nobody" in Jim Jarmusch's 1995 *Dead Man* (a film I really really tried to like), which apparently prompted Depp to direct himself in *The Brave* two years later. The film wasn't released in the United States, not even on video, so I'll have to trust the IMDb summary:

An unemployed alcoholic Native American Indian lives on a trailer park with his wife and two children. Convinced that he has nothing to offer this world, he agrees to be tortured to death by a gang of rednecks in return for $50,000.

If you replace "gang of rednecks" with "American pop culture," that's a decent allegory for Tonto.

Depp's performance was also based on Jay Silverheels, who played Tonto in the 50s TV series. He was born Harold Smith on a Canadian Mohawk reservation, but went with "Silverheels" when he moved to Hollywood. His performance in turn was based on John Todd, who voiced Tonto in the 30s radio show. Todd was seventy-seven and the last original cast member when the show went off the air in 1954. He was also Irish, but was happy enough to play dress-up for publicity shots. The network replaced him for public appearances, and briefly on air too, but, the story goes, the college-educated Native actor refused to read Tonto's ungrammatical lines, so Todd got the job back.

Tonto was originally Potawatomi, so he and his Michigan tribe (the program aired from Detroit) were a bit lost in the Southwest. Someone changed it to Apache, but Kee Mo Sah Bee, the summer camp the director enjoyed as a kid, is a better designation. Tonto means "stupid" or "silly" in Spanish, but that might be coincidence. The writers just needed someone for the Lone Ranger to talk to. The same creative team gave the Green Hornet a chauffeur for the same reason.

The Lone Ranger looks like someone grabbed a superhero, slapped a cowboy hat on his head, and dropped him in a Western, but the line of influence runs the other direction. *The Lone Ranger* premiered in 1933, five years before Superman landed in newsstands. It was a hit, so when the radio station demanded another show like it, they updated the formula. The 1936 Green Hornet is an urban Lone Ranger. His horse "Silver" morphed into the limo "Black Beauty." His Indian sidekick transformed into an Asian sidekick (Kato's shifting ethnic designations make as much sense as Tonto's). The Hornet's even a relative. His alter ego, Britt Reid, is the Lone Ranger's great nephew. Britt's father is the Ranger's nephew. John Todd voiced him too. The Shakespearean actor dropped Tonto's broken English to record the elderly Mr. Reid into the same microphone.

For twenty-first-century superheroes, the cowboy influence really is reversed. Seth Rogen's *Green Hornet* beat Armie Hammer's *Lone Ranger* to theaters by two years, both fueled by the killing Marvel and Warner Brothers were making on their assorted Avengers and Justice Leaguers. Even Kirby Sattler's interest in "the Indian" has more to do more with pop culture than "Indigenous Peoples of the Earth." The crow Johnny plopped on his head is, according to Sattler, a source of power:

> Any object — a stone, a plait of sweet grass, a part of an animal, the wing of a bird — could contain the essence of the metaphysical qualities identified to the objects and desired by the Native American. This acquisition of "Medicine," or spiritual power, . . . provided the conduit to the unseen forces of the universe which predominated their lives. . . . When combined with the proper ritual or prayer there would be a transference of identity. . . . More than just aesthetic adornment, it was an outward manifestation of their identity.

And that, Kirby, is what we folks of non-Native blood call a superhero: any object — a lantern, a ring, a bat, even an initial — contains the symbolic essence of the superpowers identified with the object and desired by the alter ego. Once acquired, unseen forces of the multiverse predominate the lives of the wearer. When combined with the proper ritual or prayer ("Shazam!"), there is a transference of identity ("Hulk smash!"). More than adornment, the superhero's costume is an outward manifestation of his identity. (I could quote some juicy bits from Michael Chabon's "Secret Skin: An Essay in Unitard Theory," but you get the point.)

I do give director Gore Verbinski credit for framing his reboot as a 1933 Wild West exhibit, a style of realism even less constrained than Sattler's. Tonto, "A Noble Savage in His Natural Habitat," is a magically talking mannequin. That almost but not quite makes up for the self-annihilating Comanche (Tonto's latest tribe) who aid Manifest Destiny by charging into the spray of Gatling guns (can you feel the hope surging through those reservation kids?).

Tonto's and the Lone Ranger's latest screen incarnations are probably no better and no worse than the black and white reruns I watched as a kid. I also attended "Indian Guides," where fathers and sons of my Pittsburgh suburb assembled plastic tomahawks and heard legends of

"Falling Rock," the mysterious brave whom yellow road signs still warned drivers to beware. So my "personal sensibilities and knowledge" of things Indian were right up there with Sattler's and Depp's. I'm just thankful it wasn't my dad in the headdress and war paint talking like Jay Silverheels at the front of the room.

Superheroes are similarly Silly Creatures best exhibited in a Habitat of Whimsy, so for the next reboot I hope Tonto is unmasked for what he's always been. A stupid white guy pretending to be an Indian.

There's one other frontier our country rests beside. American culture is an enormous sleeping brain, always on the threshold of waking. Movies, TV shows, comic books, those are the dreams and nightmares playing on its 24/7 screen. Like any sleeper, it wants to stay asleep. Which means inventing stories when noises from the periphery—slamming doors, gunfire, the Rape of Nanking—disturb it. When threatened, the great American unconscious tells itself tales of gun-toting cowboys and caped crusaders, maverick heroes who use their powers to protect their vulnerable nation.

The paths of the two linked breeds of very American heroes cross in and out of our country's anxieties. A year after the Lone Ranger started patrolling Detroit airwaves, a twenty-year-old in Cleveland dreamed up Superman. A fascist war loomed in Europe, and the fascist-fighting Man of Tomorrow was a bit of a fascist himself, discarding due process for a vigilante's dictatorial self-assurance. Hollywood responded with its own vigilante. The gunfighter, marooned in B movies during the Lone Ranger's Depression, leaped to feature films the year Germany invaded Poland. America snoozed more soundly to the sound of superheroes Ka-Powing Nazis across newsstands and the thunder of cavalry hooves riding to matinee rescues.

The mythic Old West is one of the superhero's spawning grounds, but his evolution doesn't end there. Before Superman's rocket can skid across the American plains, the superman has to battle evolution itself.

"The Irish Frankenstein," *Punch*, 20 May 1882.

CHAPTER 5

EVOLUTION

When I started researching superheroes, I assumed Nietzsche's declaration of God's death was the Big Bang event for the superman, and that Darwin was his John the Baptist crying out in the Galapagos wilderness. But Charles Darwin was only possible because God was already on his deathbed. Darwin didn't invent the Galapagos Islands, but he was the first Napoleon willing to see them for what they are: evidence of a world unanchored by Providence. The same revolutionary revelation sent Thomas Jefferson razoring up the gospels. Shelley, Polidori, and Byron descended into the same God-size void with their Faustian antiheroes.

It was scary times. Imagine a toddler waking to an empty house, Mom and Dad gone, not so much as a good-bye note on the fridge. No parents means no rules, no bedtime, no eternal timeouts, but all those orphans populating superhero tales are also embodiments of Victorian terror. We replaced the comfort of the Supernatural with the indifference of natural selection. Without God at the helm, humanity might founder in the shoals of devolution, be swamped by a flood of half-animal degenerates, its greatest aristocratic specimens drowned by their own parasitic degeneration.

The solution proved even worse. Seizing the helm meant breeding a new species of well-born demigods as indifferent to their creators as humanity had been to its own. The year Nietzsche discovered God's corpse, Darwin's cousin, social philosopher Sir Francis Galton, coined "eugenics," a pseudo-Greek term reverse-engineered from "well born." After studying the alumni lists of Cambridge, his and his cousin's alma mater, and documenting the apparent superiority of English families such as theirs, he decided he could evolve human thoroughbreds by selectively breeding top bloodlines. The United States imported the pseudoscience, distilled its own weed-killing variant of unfit breeding prevention techniques, and exported the killer mix to Germany where Europe's final Napoleon, Adolf Hitler, answered the call for the superman.

Superheroes answered that call too. They are Darwin's fossilized footprints.

⚡ ⚡ ⚡

Frankenstein's monster declares himself humanity's "arch-enemy" when his God-usurping creator refuses to make him a mate. The no-longer-mad doctor fears "a race of devils would be propagated upon the earth, who might make the very existence of the species of man a condition precarious and full of terror." Mary Shelley's Napoleonic imagination was fantasy in 1818, but Darwin made the terror real for Victorians. In his 1891 essay "Zoological Retrogression," H. G. Wells named humanity's predator the "Coming Beast," a "now humble creature" that "Nature is, in unsuspected obscurity, equipping . . . with wider possibilities of appetite, endurance, or destruction, to rise in the fullness of time and sweep *homo* away."

Superheroes were born to battle such Beasts. The Fantastic Four kept a subterranean world of monsters from rising up in their first issue. Atlanteans would have swept humanity away if the Human Torch hadn't doused Namor's Golden Age attacks. Blade is still staunching the destructive appetites of our vampire competitors. Every comic book portrays a survival of the fittest, ending with the superhero at the top of the food chain.

But Darwin had an arsenal of weapons to keep his readers on a perpetual cliffhanger. What if the Beasts don't attack but seduce? Robert Young observes in *Colonial Desire* how many nineteenth-century novels "are concerned with meeting and incorporating the culture of the other" and so "often fantasize crossing into it, though rarely so completely as when Dr Jekyll transforms himself into Mr Hyde." In comics, Jekyll/Hyde transformations are as common as cosmic rays and magic lightning bolts. "His costume marks him out as a proponent of change and exoticism," writes Richard Reynolds, but a superhero's split identity makes him "both the exotic and the agent of order which brings the exotic to book." Superheroes save the day not by destroying the racial threat, but by absorbing it. Like the "White Indians" of chapter four, they're Jekylls who master their superpowered Hydes to protect Metropolis from the fear of invading Hyde hordes.

Mutants and metahumans continue to threaten Homo sapiens. Magneto would sweep us all away and rule over Mutantkind. Mechanical übermensch are a problem too. One of my students argued how Skynet fits Nietzsche's model. The Avengers faced a similar foe in 1968 (and again on screen in 2015) when Ultron rebels against his superhero maker and plots the destruction of the human race. DC's Guardians of the Universe had similar trouble with their android police force. Cyborgs are worse, all those half-human Borg drones and Cybermen trying to assimilate us into their melting pot nightmare.

If these Darwinistic plotlines sound as quaintly absurd as Shelley's 1818 fantasy, you should stop by Darwin's alma mater. His ghost is still the thing-going-bump under the bed of the Centre for the Study of Existential Risk. The Cambridge superteam boasts Ph.D.s in philosophy, cosmology and astrophysics, and theoretical physics, and, oh yeah, one of them invented Skype. Yet they take robot supervillains seriously: "stop treating intelligent machines as the stuff of science fiction, and start thinking of them as a part of the reality that we or our descendants may actually confront."

By "Existential Risk" they don't mean soul-wrenching ennui. They mean human extinction. With the press drones are getting, those hovering Skynet bombers don't look so farfetched anymore. The Centre's website went online in 2013, and to aid the superheroic cause, I enlisted my book club to peruse the introductory links of articles and lectures on the Resources page. It's a reboot of a nineteenth-century sci-fi adventure novel.

Barring some steampunk time-travel plot, it's unlikely Darwin is going to invent the Matrix, but the Centre's A.I.-dominated future simmers with Victorian anxiety: "Would we be humans surviving (or not) in an environment in which superior machine intelligences had taken the reins?" As early as 2030, the Centre prophesies "life as we know it getting replaced by more advanced life" and asks whether we should view "the future beings as our descendants or our conquerors."

Either answer is a product of the same, oddly applied evolutionary paradigm that gave birth to superheroes too. Why talk about technology as a species? Darwin's ghost coauthors the Centre's analysis:

> we risk yielding control over the planet to intelligences that are simply indifferent to us ... just ask gorillas how it feels to compete for resources with the most intelligent species — the reason they are going extinct is not (on the whole) because humans are actively hostile towards them, but because we control the environment in ways that are detrimental to their continuing survival.

Natural selection is an allegory, but the Centre literalizes it by saying our "most powerful 21st-century technologies — robotics, genetic engineering, and nanotech — are threatening to make humans an endangered species."

To borrow a postcolonial term, the authors talk about A.I. as if it's a racial "other," the nonhuman flipside of an us-them dichotomy. We're supposed to worry "how we can best coexist with them," alarmed because there's "no reason to think that intelligent machines would share our values." The Centre describes technological enhancement as a slippery slope jeopardizing human purity because we are "going to become robots or fuse with robots." Our seemingly harmless smartphones lead to smart glasses and then brain implants, ending with humans "merging with super-intelligent computers." Moreover, "Even if we humans nominally merge with such machines, we might have no guarantees whatsoever about the ultimate outcome, making it feel less like a merger and more like a hostile corporate takeover." As a result, "our humanity may well be lost."

In other words, dirty mudblood cyborgs want to destroy our way of life. Once we allow machines to fornicate with our women, their half-breed offspring could become "in some sense entirely posthuman." Even if they think of themselves "as descendants of humans," these new robo-mongrels may not share our goals ("love, happiness") and may look down at us as indifferently as we regard "bugs on the windscreen." This is the fear that sold so many copies of Sax Rohmer's *Fu Manchu* novels from the teens through the 50s. The yellowly perilous supervillain's Hollywood incarnation commanded his swarthy minions to "kill the white men and take their women!" The Centre's future is swarming with Yellow Machines.

The term "posthuman" sounds futuristic, but it's another nineteenth-century throwback. Nietzsche's first translator went with "Beyond-man," but "posthuman" is an equally accurate rendering of "übermensch." When Vernor Vinge rewrote Wells to warn of "The Coming Technological Singularity" in 1993, he used Nietzsche too: "Within thirty years, we will have the technological means to create superhuman intelligence. Shortly after, the human era will be ended." When the Centre warns us not to fall victim to the "comforting" thought that these future species will be "just like us, but smarter," they're paraphrasing Shaw: "contemporary Man" will "make no objection to the production of a race of [Supermen], because he will imagine them, not as true Supermen, but as himself en-dowed with infinite brains." The superman will not share our human values: he "will snap his superfingers at all Man's present trumpery ideals of right, duty, honor, justice, religion, even decency, and accept moral obligations beyond present human endurance." Shaw, oddly, thought this was a good thing. He, like Wells, believed in scientific breeding, the brave new thing that, like the technologies the Centre envisions, promised to transform the human race into something superior. It didn't. But Nazi Germany gave it its best shot.

The Centre quotes the wrong line from Nietzsche ("The truth that sci-ence seeks can certainly be considered a dangerous substitute for God if it is likely to lead to our extinction"). I'd add *Also sprach Zarathustra* to the Resources page instead. Zarathustra advocates that most feared of futures, one in which "Man is something that is to be surpassed," and so we bring about our end by creating the race that replaces us. "What is the ape to man?" asks Zarathustra. "A laughing-stock, a thing of shame. And just the same shall man be to the Superman: a laughing-stock, a thing of shame."

Sounds like Existential Risk to me, one superheroes have been fighting for over a century. As far as the Centre's fears, the only humans who will be able to afford cybernetic upgrades are the ones who always capitalize on new technologies: the wealthy. Which means the Centre's future isn't a war between species — it's a class war, the one the Victorians were fighting. When racial others from the Empire's metaethnic frontiers migrate to Metropolis, they become the impoverished degenerates infesting Crime Alley. Superheroes have been battling them since the nineteenth century too.

$$\4\4\4$$

Evolution had more than one way to terrify Victorians. A Nietzschean Skynet can terminate the world population with the flip of a nuclear switch, but imagine that switch lurking inside every human skull.

When Congressman Daniel Sickles saw his wife's lover, the district attorney of Washington, D.C., standing outside their home waving a handkerchief to catch Mrs. Sickles's attention, the congressman grabbed three pistols, ran into the street, and murdered him. He'd only learned of the affair the night before, and the sight of the lawyer so enraged him, he acted "under the influence of a frenzy." That's what his lawyer told the jury before they acquitted him. It's the first successful use of a temporary insanity plea in U.S. courts. This is 1859, the year Darwin published *On the Origin of Species.*

James Holmes killed twelve people in a Colorado movie theater in 2012. He'd dyed his hair to imitate the Joker and opened fire thirty minutes into *The Dark Knight Rises.* His lawyers said he's crazy too. Four months earlier, Army Staff Sgt. Robert Bales shot sixteen people in their Panjwai homes. His attorney described him as "crazed" and "broken," and yet "his mental state [did] not rise to the level of a legal insanity defense." In exchange for a guilty plea, Bales received life without parole.

Dr. Jekyll couldn't re-create the monstrous serum that released his Mr. Hyde. The same is true of Sgt. Bales, but we know some of the ingredients:

contraband alcohol, snorted Valium, steroids, and the antimalarial drug mefloquine, which can induce side effects including hallucinations and psychotic behavior — that on top of PTSD and a traumatic brain injury from multiple deployments. Bales was also a loving husband and father of two. When asked by a judge why he massacred those Afghan families, he answered: "Sir, as far as why — I've asked that question a million times since then. There's not a good reason in this world for why I did the horrible things I did." He acknowledged that he "formed the intent" of killing each victim, but he didn't remember burning their bodies. When pressed, he said, "It's the only thing that makes sense, sir."

Sgt. Bales sounds like a confused observer of his own actions. Which he is. We all are. "Like a rider on the back of an elephant," argues psychologist Jonathan Haidt in *The Happiness Hypothesis*, "the conscious, reasoning part of the mind has only limited control of what the elephant does." Mostly we sit on top and watch what happens, recording the bumping and jostling of our emotions and actions. We're not steering the elephant. We just pretend we are. "Then, when faced with a social demand for a verbal justification," Haidt says, "one becomes a lawyer trying to build a case, rather than a judge searching for the truth."

"I thought I was doing the right thing," Bales said after his arrest. The elephant always does the right thing, and it's our job to prove it — to ourselves and everyone else. The counterevidence was too great for Bales's lawyer to challenge in court, but Haidt calls us all "intuitive lawyers" defending our elephant-size intuitions. I picture a blind lawyer, Daredevil's alter ego Matt Murdock, arguing why his vigilante-by-night job doesn't make his legal career complete hypocrisy. There are a range of available justifications (enforcement failure, police corruption, court incompetence), but none of them are the reason he runs around in a skintight unitard with little devil horns beating up bad guys. That's just something his elephant likes to do.

This sounds like a weirder form of dissociate identity disorder than most superheroes face, but two of Hollywood's biggest, Batman and Wolverine, encode the same human-animal duality. Comic books stock a zoo of animal-people, including, most obviously, Animal Man, and continuing down some of the alphabetized cages: Ant-Man, Badger, Beast, Black

Canary, Black Panther, Blue Beetle, Cat, Catman, Catwoman, Chameleon, Cheetah, Crow, Green Hornet, Hawkman, Hellcat, Lizard, Man-Bat, Man-Wolf, Nite Owl, Penguin, Rhino, Scorpion, Sabretooth, Toad, Tigra, Vulture, Wasp, and Yellowjacket.

Image Comics started publishing *Elephantman* in 2006, but the deformed and destitute Joseph Merrick became the first Elephant Man when he assumed the freak show moniker in 1884. Victorians ate him up. Even the Princess of Wales stopped by his bedside to ogle. Advertised as "Half-a-Man and Half-an-Elephant," Merrick believed his secret origin was the fairground elephant that frightened his pregnant mother. His doctor called him "the most disgusting" and "degraded or perverted version of a human being" he'd ever seen. Which explains ticket sales.

Victorians were busy being disgusted by all manner of animal men. H. G. Wells wouldn't get around to populating Doctor Moreau's island of half-men for another decade, but Robert Louis Stevenson began his vivisection of humanity's animal side with his 1882 play, *Deacon Brodie, or The Double Life.* Professor Brodie of my English department assures me she's only related to the real-life deacon by former marriage. Even so, you might not trust her with the keys to your house lest her inner elephant feels an atavistic urge to rampage. Deacon William Brodie was an upstanding member of his Edinburgh community until they hung him in 1788 for robbing by night the homes he woodworked by day. Stevenson expanded the two-faced deacon into *The Strange Case of Dr Jekyll and Mr Hyde.* The doctor is the ultimate elephant-straddling lawyer. Jekyll has no control over what his inner Hyde does. Drink, rob, rape, murder, he's a stampede of urges, and when he dies it is with a "dismal screech, as of mere animal terror."

Victorians were screeching too. Not just about Hyde, but about all such criminal degenerates hiding among their fellow Jekylls. Evolution, they believed, might be slipping backward into the animal mud that humans had once stood so divinely above. Weren't Joseph Merrick's elephantine deformities proof?

So who will save us from these animal men? Well, oddly enough, other animal men will. Superheroes aren't like the rest of us. Like a cyborg or a frontiersman, being "super" means you're only half-human to begin with.

Bruce Wayne would be another lazy socialite, but instead of abdicating control of his inner beast, he yokes it for his own moral mission. "Bat-Man" is comic books' first Jekyll-controlled Hyde.

Wolverine battles to keep his berserker frenzy under control too. It's a duality even the most evolved humans experience. Do you just make excuses for your elephant, or do you try to seize its reins? It's scary even admitting the elephant exists. We aren't so different from the Victorians. Instead of Darwin skinning our animal side, we have psychologists like Haidt poking their nonrationalist sticks through the bars of our cage. Who doesn't snarl when told their moral reasoning is an ad hoc rationalization for emotional reflexes? Who wants to work as hard as a self-caged superhero when it's so much easier watching from your animal's free-ranging back?

Perhaps James Holmes is a degraded version of a human being. Maybe Sgt. Bales doesn't deserve life, let alone parole in twenty years. They lost their inner battles against their berserker rage. They weren't human beings when they massacred those people. They need to be caged. I would like to believe that makes them unusual, that they're throwbacks from our animal past. I would like to think other human beings, if placed in Sgt. Bales's crucible of environment and chemical horror, would not commit the same atrocity. I want to believe I could never sit before a judge, with my lawyerly hands folded in front of me, and have to say:

"It's the only thing that makes sense, sir."

The Coming Beast, the inner beast, what more could Darwin throw at those poor Victorians? I'll tell you, but it first requires a side trip to Pittsburgh, c. 1975.

My sister and I spent every weekend at my mother's one-bedroom apartment, with afternoons at the zoo, swimming pool, or a matinee of that week's PG-rated flick, *Escape to Witch Mountain*, *Funny Lady*, *The Return of the Pink Panther*. Money — I realized later — was tight. My mother skipped lunches to balance the once-a-weekday dinner out with us. I don't know if her parents count as well-borns, but her father had been a well-paid corporate vice-president. After his early death, his trust-funded wife and daughters could still afford to live on their treed cul-de-sac in one of Pittsburgh's ritzier subdivisions. But that money was gone before my parents divorced. Instead of collecting alimony, my self-made mother started a research career as an entry-level lab tech feeding alcohol to rats, another of our Sunday adventures.

I've not seen *The Return of the Pink Panther* since, but the scenes are still vivid — that black-suited burglar creeping past museum security to pinch the precious diamond from its alarm-triggering pedestal. The Panther was the diamond, not the thief, which confused me. It should have been *The Return of the Phantom*. Though the Phantom didn't return either. That was his wife, Lady Claudine, in the black bodysuit, goading her husband, Sir Charles, out of his posh but boring retirement.

A life of luxury is a dangerous thing. Victorians feared it would destroy humanity, starting at the top of the ladder with the Aryan aristocracy. "The white races of Europe," warned E. Ray Lankester in his 1880 *Degeneration: A Chapter of Darwinism*, "are subject to the general laws of evolution, and are as likely to degenerate" and become "intellectual barnacles." Worse, any "set of conditions occurring to an animal which render its food and safety very easily attained seem to lead as a rule to Degeneration." Lancaster likens the process to how "an active healthy man sometimes degenerates when he becomes suddenly possessed of a fortune" or how "Rome degenerated when possessed of the riches of the ancient world." The problem is the "habit of parasitism" wealth produces: "Let the parasitic life once be secured, and away go legs, jaws, and eyes; the active highly-gifted crab, insect, or annelid may become a mere sac, absorbing nourishment and laying eggs."

Half of the rats we fed Sunday mornings were getting heavy doses of grain alcohol in their feeding tubes. They'd doze in the backs of their cages, lazily twitching with DTs. A philanthropic billionaire in Sir Arthur Conan Doyle's 1891 *The Doings of Raffles Haw* gets similar research results when he tries to save the world by sharing his fortune. An "ambitious, pushing, self-reliant" young artist, whose first words when you met him "were usually some reference to his plans, or the progress he was making in his latest picture," now "does nothing." By the final chapter, Raffles Haw recognizes the error of his ways, writing in his suicide note: "alas!

the only effect of my attempts has been to turn workers into idlers, contented men into greedy parasites, and, worst of all, true, pure women into deceivers and hypocrites."

So what is a well-meaning well-born to do? E. W. Hornung offered a very different strategy. He strips his cricket-playing protagonist of his riches, all that easily attained food and safety, and evolves him into a gentleman thief who has to risk imprisonment to maintain his lifestyle. "Why settle down to some humdrum uncongenial billet," asks A. J. Raffles, "when excitement, romance, danger and a decent living were all going begging together?" Sure, a life of burglary is immoral, but Darwin had already disposed of God, and Nietzsche said the superman would have to forge his own morality. Besides, wouldn't the aristocracy rather be robbed by a Keats-quoting "Amateur Cracksman" than a professional ruffian from the peasantry?

It's a pleasantly perverse solution, one Hornung crafted in defiance of his brother-in-law, Doyle. The author of Sherlock Holmes had yet to be knighted when Hornung published his first Raffles tale in 1898, but the gentleman thief turns Sir Arthur's knightly detective on his head. Hornung stole not only the name Raffles from Doyle's billionaire but a Watson too. After Raffles rescues another destitute socialite from suicide, the narrator sidekick rises to their new life: "The truth is that I was entering into our nefarious undertaking with an involuntary zeal of which I was myself quite unconscious at the time. The romance and the peril of the whole proceeding held me spellbound and entranced."

The Raffles mutation proved advantageous in the marketplace too, though usually with an added strain of Robin Hood do-goodery. Soon gentlemen thieves were relieving their boredom across magazine racks and bookshelves everywhere: R. Austin Freeman and John Jones Pitcairn's Romney Pringle (1902), O. Henry's Jimmy Valentine (1902), Arnold Bennett's Cecil Thorold (1904), Maurice Leblanc's Arsène Lupin (1905). Orczy's altruistic Scarlet Pimpernel steals fellow aristocrats instead of diamonds, but his League of sidekicks are just more thrill-seekers: "for this is the finest sport I have yet encountered. — Hair-breadth escapes, the devil's own risks! — Tally ho! — and away we go!"

Even the nefarious Raffles is a do-gooder in an evolutionary sense.

By helping himself he is helping humanity against aristocratic degeneration, and he gives birth to a whole breed of gentlemen-thief heroes. After the Pimpernel, other superhero aliases ascended the genre ladder: Louis Joseph Vance's Lone Wolf (1914), Frank L. Packard's Gray Seal (1914), Roderic Graeme's Blackshirt (1925), Leslie Charteris's Saint (1928). Masks had been seen before, but now signature emblems appeared too, from the Gray Seal's adhesive trademark found on the safes he cracks to the "P"-blazoned glove Lady Claudine left on that museum pedestal in the *Pink Panther*.

George E. Brenner preferred a literal calling card with his hero's catchphrase: "The Clock Struck." The 1937 Clock beat Superman to comic books by a year, but it took Bob Kane and Bill Finger to raise a parasitic well-born into full superhero status. The "young socialite" Bruce Wayne signs his notes with a bat stamp, while affecting Lankester's habit of parasitism: "Well, Commissioner, anything happening these days?" When Gordon invites him to a crime scene, Bruce yawns: "Oh well, nothing else to do, might as well." That's from Batman's first 1939 page. The avenge-the-dead-parents motive was an afterthought spliced in months later. The original Bruce was just bored. Beating up degenerates keeps him from degenerating into one.

Doyle's Raffles faces the same problem. As a billionaire, "perhaps the only one in the world," he feels a great responsibility: "I have not been singled out to wield this immense power simply in order that I might lead a happy life." That was 1891. The world population of altruistic billionaires has risen since. Bill Gates is worth about $78 billion, and, like Raffles Haw, he wants to give it away. "My full-time work will be the foundation for the rest of my life," he said after retiring from corporate life in 2014. If that doesn't keep him happy, Lady Melinda will have to slip into that Phantom outfit, a variation on the female thief played by Grace Cunard in the 1914 *My Lady Raffles*.

My mother was no bored burglar. She had the ambition, push, and self-reliance to evolve her rat-feeding job into a Ph.D. in epidemiology, but when she lost her multimillion-dollar research grant, her life devolved into Alzheimer's. I helped move her to an assisted living facility, where her food and safety needs are easily attained. She used to talk about the progress she was making on her latest art project, but she hasn't touched her pens and drawing pad for months now. She says she's gotten quite good at bingo though, a game of chance not unlike a raffle or the stock market. Her retirement portfolio is making a killing. I drive over every month for lunch and dinner out, plus shopping errands. I can't remember the last time we saw a movie together, but I might suggest a matinee next time. Everyone needs an afternoon adventure to stave off boredom.

Gregor Mendel, assuming he entered his abbey a virgin and kept his vows, died a virgin. And yet the nineteenth-century monk is best known for his adventures in reproduction. He's the guy who gave us dominant and recessive traits. His "Experiments on Plant Hybridization" sprouted six years after *On the Origin of Species* and then quietly withered — before British physician Archibald Garrod dug it up in 1901 and transplanted it into English to take root in the early eugenics movement.

England and the United States were rich soil for the superman. The American Breeder's Association blossomed in 1903, followed by Sir Francis Galton's School of Eugenics in London and the Carnegie Institute–funded Station for Experimental Evolution and the Eugenics Record Office in Long Island. Shaw, an enthusiastic Galton lecture attendee, published *Man and Superman* the same year, applauding the engineered "changes from the crab apple to the pippin" and demanding the same process be applied to human reproduction. It was time to "weed out the human race."

Orczy's Sir Percy Blakeney, a foppish hothouse flower, answered Shaw's call to arms when he strutted across Nottingham's Theatre Royal in 1903. Although he was a "descendant of a long line of English gentlemen" of near-royal standing and wealth, Percy's mother was a "hopelessly insane" and "hopelessly incurable" "imbecile," and so her son a "hopelessly stupid" "nonentity" with no "spiritual attainments" and "the air of a lazy, bored aristocrat indifferent to matters of honor and justice." Shaw, through his eugenics-advocating John Tanner, declares such members of the Idle Rich useless parasites, literal degenerates prophesized by Lankester two decades earlier. And yet Orczy transforms Sir Percy into a superman.

"If two plants which differ constantly in one or several characters be crossed," explains Mendel, "each pair of differentiating characters... unite in the hybrid to form a new character." "Thus," reasons Shaw's eugenicist, "the son of a robust, cheerful, eupeptic British country squire, with the tastes and ranges of his class, and of a clever, imaginative, intellectual, highly civilized Jewess, might be very superior to both his parents."

Orczy selects the same characteristics. Percy is robust ("Tall, above average, even for an Englishmen, broad-shouldered and massively built") and cheerful (with a "perpetual inane laugh" and "good-humoured" air), while his "plebeian" wife, Marguerite, is "the cleverest woman in Europe." Marrying them produces a figurative offshoot, the Scarlet Pimpernel, "the best and bravest man in all the world" and yet also a "humble English wayside flower."

Since "those characters which are transmitted entire... are termed the *dominant*, and those which become latent in the process *recessive*" because they "disappear in the hybrids," the new and improved Percy absorbs his wife's *dominant* cleverness, imagination, and intellect, while breeding out his own *recessive* "foppish manners." But Mendel's "hybrids, as a rule, are not exactly intermediate between the parental species." They are a new and superior breed. So what happens when you mix a hothouse flower with a hardy weed? As the Scarlet Pimpernel, Percy has "superhuman cunning" and "almost superhuman strength of will," and, you'll recall from chapter two, his "muscles seemed made of steel, and his energy was almost supernatural." Eugenics prophesied that the superman would sprout after generations of selective breeding, but Orczy produces him in the turn of a page.

And she doesn't stop with Sir Percy. She transforms a "Secret Orchard" of Shaw's "good-looking, well-born and well-bred Englishmen." Tanner calls his Idle Rich Class useless, and so the Pimpernel gives them a purpose: "The idle, rich man wanted some aim in life — he and the few young bucks he enrolled." Sure, a member of the League says they're just in it for the thrill, but Marguerite knows better. They're in it for "the sheer love of the fellow-men."

It would take another quarter century for eugenics to wither. Come 1928, Waldemare Kaempffert would be planting very different seeds, warning his *New York Times* readers that selective breeding "would establish an artificial aristocracy, which, like all aristocracies, would seek to perpetuate itself," and therefore "specimens of humanity that fail to meet the aristocratic standards" would "become 'weeds.'" Which was exactly what Shaw and Orczy had in mind. Her novelization of *The Scarlet Pimpernel* leaped to bookstores in 1905, the same year *Man and Superman* premiered in London's Royal Court Theatre.

Superman was blooming.

My father's parents never learned much English. Their newspaper included only one comic strip, *Tarzan*, translated into Slovak. Mutineers didn't maroon them on the jungle shores of rural Pennsylvania, but like Tarzan's parents, they settled on a strange continent an ocean from their homeland. Tarzan swung into newspaper comic strips on January 7, 1929, the same day as Buck Rogers, and so yet another Big Bang moment in superhero history. The strip expanded to a full Sunday page in 1931, the year my father was born. Jerry Siegel parodied it in his school newspaper with "Goober the Mighty," the oldest and least promising of Superman's siblings, but also proof of the eugenics' leap into pop culture.

My grandparents were still new to the United States when *All-Story* serialized Edgar Rice Burroughs's novel *Tarzan of the Apes* in 1912. It was an instant, imitation-spawning hit. Charles Stilson's 1915 *Polaris of the Snows* swapped Africa and apes for Antarctica and polar bears, but it's the same formula (there are no polar bears in Antarctica and no "anthropoid apes" anywhere). Stilson wrote two more Polaris novels (and his own ending to *Tarzan of the Apes* since Burroughs's marriage-plot cliff-hanger annoyed him so much), but as the King of the Jungle expanded his reign to stage, film, and radio, imitators stopped disguising their loin-clothed knockoffs: Bomba the Jungle Boy (1926), Morgo the Mighty (1930), Jan of the Jungle (1931), Bantan (1936), Ka-Zar (1936), Ki-Gor (1939).

Tarzan was a knockoff too. He's a lost-worlder, the genre H. Rider Haggard explored in 1885 with *King Solomon's Mines* and into which Doc Savage and Superman boldly followed. Burroughs also swapped out Rudyard Kipling's India and wolves, but his jungle isn't that different from Mowgli's. W. H. Hudson preferred Venezuela for his 1904 jungle girl Rima in *Green Mansions*. DC adopted Rima in 1975, after the soft-core jungles were well endowed with leopard-draped females. Eisner and Iger's Sheena, Queen of the Jungle, beat Superman to comic books by a year, with dozens swinging behind her. Stan Lee offered Lorna the Jungle Queen in the 50s and Shanna the She-Devil in the 70s. Shanna later married Ka-Zar, Marvel publisher Martin Goodman's first pulp jungle man. Ka-Zar re-premiered in *Marvel Comics* No. 1 beside Namor and the Human Torch, before Stan Lee transplanted him to Polaris's Antarctic lost world, swapping out ancient Romans for ancient dinosaurs.

But Tarzan remained Lord of the knockoff jungle. My father and his childhood friends debated who would win in a fight: Tarzan or Buck? Tarzan or the Phantom? Tarzan or Batman? If you don't think a loin cloth counts as a superhero costume, remember the ape-man is also secretly the English aristocrat Lord Greystoke. If that's not enough of an alter ego, read chapter twenty-seven, "The Height of Civilization," in which the former savage transforms into "Monsieur Tarzan," a French-speaking socialite who on a gentleman's wager can strip off his tux, wander naked into the wild, and return two pages later with a lion across his shoulders.

Burroughs terms him a "superman," proof that eugenics was widening its cultural domain. Corn flakes tycoon John Kellogg founded the Race Betterment Foundation in 1906, and Indiana, with a boost from future president Woodrow Wilson, passed the nation's first sterilization law a year later. In 1911, the American Breeder's Association added immigration restrictions, segregation, and anti-interracial marriage laws to their fight against unfit breeding, while the First International Eugenics Congress met at the University of London the following year to discuss the same agenda.

Burroughs did not attend, but he was a fan. Biographer John Taliaferro describes him as "obsessed with his own genealogy" and "extremely proud of his nearly pure Anglo-Saxon lineage," believing in the "extermination of all 'moral imbeciles' and their relatives." The October 1912 issue of *All-Story* hit stands a few weeks after the Eugenics Congress convened. I doubt Winston Churchill ever touched an American pulp, but he and his fellow attendees shared Burroughs's delusions about genetics. I always show chapter twenty, "Heredity," to my class. Despite being reared by apes, young Lord Greystoke knows how to bow in a courtly manner, "the hall-mark of his aristocratic birth, the natural outcropping of many generations of fine breeding, an hereditary instinct of graciousness which a lifetime of uncouth and savage training and environment could not eradicate."

DNA wouldn't be discovered for a couple more decades, so eugenicists thought they could weed out everything from crime to promiscuity by stopping unfit parents from giving birth to unfit babies. One of those babies was my father. His parents hailed from the degenerate regions of the Austrian-Hungarian Empire and were among what anti-immigration advocate Francis Walker called "beaten men from beaten races; representing the worst failures in the struggle for existence," men with "none of the inherited instincts and tendencies which made it comparatively easy to deal with the immigration of the olden time." That's why Congress capped the 1924 quota for eastern Europeans at 2 percent of their 1890 U.S. population. My grandparents had already weaseled in.

Adolf Hitler had been a private in the Austrian-Hungarian army at the same time and in the same city as my grandfather, but rather than accept a second conscription, Stefan Gavaler bounded over the Tatra Mountains to land in Carrolltown, Pennsylvania. He died in the kind of mining accident Superman tries to prevent in *Action Comics* No. 3 ("Months ago, we know mine is unsafe — but when we tell boss's foremen they say, 'No like job, Stanislaw? Quit!'"). One of Stefan's sons went on to marry the daughter of a corporate vice-president of good German stock and produce exactly the sort of Aryan-diluting mongrel Burroughs feared: me.

Tarzan, however, marries well. Even if you accept Phillip Jose Farmer's "biography," *Tarzan Alive*, in which the adolescent man-ape accepts the open sexual norms of his adopted tribe, the adult Greystoke changes his degenerate ways. After learning he's not a half-ape but an undissipated carrier of high English blood, he foregoes both his kingdoms to pursue the eugenically fit daughter of an American professor to the woods of Wisconsin. It takes a second book for Jane to marry him, and a third to produce a son. Burroughs wrote a sequel almost every year until 1939, the year Germany invaded Poland. Tarzan (the name means "white skin" in anthropoid ape language) could wrestle a gorilla into submission, but Hitler proved too much for him. He only published one more Tarzan novel before his death in 1950.

A Nazi puppet government ran the Slovak half of Czechoslovakia during the German occupation, but Tarzan wouldn't make it there till Disney's invasion. I recently found a Slovak-dubbed version of the *Tarzan* soundtrack song "Son of Man" on YouTube. I can't understand a word of it, but I think my grandparents would be pleased it exists.

Burroughs, like many people in the United States, would annul his love for eugenics. His 1938 serialized novel *Carson of Venus* lampoons the Nazis ("Zanis" on Venus), and his Earthman hero laments: "There is nothing more annoying than to commit an egregious error of judgment and have no one but yourself upon whom to blame it."

But the 1910s was still a booming decade for fans of Tarzan and his new race of supermen. As a historical researcher, my first mistake is thinking the past is the present, only in funny clothes. But immerse yourself in the period (I recommend the *New York Times* online database) and you realize you're looking at a planet more alien than Krypton. That's why I give my students a crash course in eugenics, a term, for those who've heard of it, they associate with Germany, not homegrown America.

They also think mutant supermen only exist in comic books. The biological term "mutant" was coined in 1901, but it's so ubiquitous now it includes Lady Gaga and the human-motorbike cyborg on the cover of *Born This Way*. Stan Lee first imported the concept, a staple of post-Hiroshima sci-fi, to the world of comics, and it's since become such a Marvel term, I'm hesitant to use it outside their multiverse. I remember the narrative nausea my adolescent self felt when ex-Marvel writer-editor Marv Wolfman buckled under the popularity of *X-Men* and shoehorned DC's first mutant into *Teen Titans*. It didn't help that the character was a joke, a mute mutant (is that a pun?). I had to Google his name (Jericho) and his powers (mind control?), but remembered his dorky blonde curls too well (I sported similar ones in the 80s).

Lee's first use of the term wasn't impressive either. After two years of cranking out his Silver Age pantheon (Fantastic Four, Hulk, Spider-Man, Thor, Iron Man, Dr. Strange), he hit his limit for origin stories. So the X-Men, "The Strangest Super-heroes of All!," were all Born That Way. Professor Xavier professed in their first issue: "You, Miss Grey, like the other four students at this most exclusive school, are a MUTANT! You possess an EXTRA power ... one which ordinary humans do NOT! That is why I call my students ... X-MEN, for EX-tra power!"

The first "extra-man" was born a half-century earlier. *Alias "The Night Wind"* crawled out of the primordial pulp goo of *Cavalier* magazine in 1913, six months after *Tarzan of the Apes* set the new standard for super-human adventuring. Like Superman, Bing Harvard, aka the Night Wind, has no problem tying "bow-knots in crowbars." Instead of crash-landing from Krypton to be reared by midwestern farmers, or shipwrecked from aristocratic England to be reared by anthropoid apes, Bing is a foundling reared by a New York banker. He also possesses "a wonderful, God-given strength," which is his "birthright," what "his unknown father and mother had bestowed upon him as an inheritance."

Peter Coogan terms him an "anomaly." That's a pretty good synonym for "mutant," but the superhero scholar is talking genre tropes, few of which the character fits. The first time I showed my class an excerpt, someone said it read like a supervillain origin story. Hard-working orphan framed for embezzlement turns his powers against the powers that be. It's true, Bing snaps the wrists of any cop who tries to arrest him, but after he clears his name (with the help of an aristocratic lady cop who later marries him), he settles happily into law-abiding domesticity. The truly anomalous gene in the series is the never-solved mystery introduced in its opening chapters: Who are Bing's parents?

Jericho, it turns out, is the son of the supervillain Deathstroke, his powers the product of the biological experimentation inflicted on his father. All Marvel mutants can be traced back to Celestial tampering in the gene pool millions of years ago. But Bing? Frederick Van Rensselaer Dey (writing as his alter ego Varick Vanardy) didn't care. Dey had cranked out Nick Carter dime novels for decades, but the Night Wind dies after only three sequels. The fact is frustrating, but even if I could sit down with Frederick over coffee in Dr. Doom's time machine, I'm not sure I would steer him differently.

Bing's real superheroism is only visible when you step out of the time machine and wander the 1910s. Where did the idea of killing the genetically unfit come from? Not Auschwitz. American eugenicists recommended installing a gas chamber in every town in America to "euthanize" the locally unfit. This was two years before the Night Wind started snapping police wrists. Those sterilization programs became state laws while Dey was writing. Everyone knew the human race would devolve if Aryan supremacy wasn't maintained. That was common sense. If your parents weren't Anglo-Saxon, if you weren't from good, reliable Protestant stock, you were in trouble. Your parentage defined you. The cop who frames Bing says it:

> Who are you, anyhow, I'd like to know? It ain't nothin' out uh the way that you should be a thief. I guess you inherited it all right. It's more'n likely that his dad is doin' time right now, in one uh the prisons, an' his mother, too, maybe. It's the way uh that sort. He don't know who his antecedents was.

Who was Bing? Who were his parents? Dey doesn't care. His hero was just born that way. And Dey blesses him for it. He declares Bing's powers "God-given." They're not the result of scientific breeding. He's an accident, a genetic anomaly. He's homo superior. Not the well-born superman eugenicists were obsessed with, but an up-from-the-muck mutant, defying the prejudices America was inhaling. Dey was singing "Born This Way" a hundred years before Lady Gaga.

I don't know which social house Darwin and Sir Francis belonged to at Cambridge, but I can guess. "I always knew Salazar Slytherin was a twisted old loony," says Ron Weasley, "but I never knew he started all this pure-blood stuff. I wouldn't be in his house if you paid me."

And yet the House of Slytherin has no shortage of new applicants. It's a Who's Who of Recent Movie Supervillains, including Magneto, Sebastian Shaw, the Lizard, Aldrich Killian, and the Red Skull. Oh, and Lord Whatshisface minus Ralph Fiennes's nose. Also, if you don't mind a little song and dance with your supervillainy, Broadway's Green Goblin. But Stanton Parish, of the short-lived Syfy series *Alphas*, has the best advertising slogan of the batch: "Better people, Better world."

The semi-immortal Parish had been honing his PR skills since the Civil War, so he may have cribbed the phrase from Kentucky eugenicists in the 1930s: "Fewer Babies, Better Babies." That was when contraception was about preventing more unfit. Or as Margaret Sanger phrased it on a 1921 cover of *Birth Control Review*: "To create a race of thoroughbreds." The American branch of Slytherin House, the Eugenics Society of the United States, was sponsoring national "Fitter Family" contests then too, with winning families receiving medals inscribed with the slogan: "Yea, I have a goodly heritage." The pamphlet writers over at the Carnegie Institute Department of Genetics were lesser word wizards, but no less dedicated: "Eugenics Seeks to Improve the Natural, Physical, Mental, and Temperamental Qualities of the Human Family."

Other eugenics admen focused on the flipside: "Some people are born to be a burden on the rest." Ads for *The Black Stork*, a 1917 documentary about a pediatrician who allowed unfit babies to die, cut to the chase: "Kill Defectives, Save the Nation." The Night Wind, probably the one and only anti-eugenic superhero, stopped adventuring in 1919, the year the highly eugenic Zorro was born. Zorro and Tarzan and the Scarlet Pimpernel and rest of their League of Well-Borns expanded into the 20s and 30s, until the Nazis mortally wounded eugenics as a mass culture movement. All that "pure-blood stuff" would be forever associated with the über-Aryan Adolf Hitler and the war Hollywood is still fighting.

Lord Voldemort is the tip of the white-hooded iceberg. Contemporary culture is still full of Salazar's supremacist heirs. In 1999, just months before the Y2K virus was poised to wipe out human civilization, Hugo Weaving's Agent Smith explained to *The Matrix* fans: "As soon as we started thinking for you, it really became our civilization. Which is of course what this is all about. Evolution. . . . The future is our world." Ian

McKellen's Magneto complained that "nature is too slow," in the 2000 *X-Men*. Michael Fassbender's Magneto was still complaining in the 2011 *X-Men: First Class*, but under the tutelage of Kevin Bacon: "We are the future of the human race. You and me, son. This world could be ours." A month later, Hugo Weaving's Red Skull was giving Captain America the same lesson: "You pretend to be a simple soldier, but in reality you are just afraid to admit that we have left humanity behind. Unlike you, I embrace it proudly. You could have the power of the gods!"

Iron Man 3 joined the inductee list with supergenius Aldrich Killian turning himself and his minions into the "new iteration of human evolution." *Harry Potter* alum Rhys Ifans, aka Dr. Curt Connors, aka the Lizard, wanted to "enhance humanity on an evolutionary scale" and "create a world without weakness." "This is no longer about curing ills," he assured Peter Parker in *The Amazing Spider-Man*. "This is about finding perfection." Unfortunately, "Human beings are weak, pathetic, feeble-minded creatures. Why be human at all when we can be so much more? Faster, stronger, smarter!"

Dane DeHaan played Green Goblin in the sequel, but only after declaring himself an "apex predator" in *Chronicle*. Robert Cuccioli's Green Goblin was singing the same song nightly, plus weekend matinees. According to Bono's lyrics, "The crossroads of the world just need a little tweak from a freak." He studies "enhanced genetics" and "super-human kinetics" to create "new men," a "new species." The military only wants a "new breed of Marines," but the Goblin's "designer genes" lead him into a much bolder "do it yourself world" in which human beings are the new "masters of creation," claiming "powers once reserved for the ancient gods."

On BBC America's *Orphan Black*, Dr. Aldous Leekie is cloning the future into existence through "Neolution: The New Science of Self-Directed Evolution," the refrain the Second International Eugenics Congress sang in 1921: "Eugenics is the self-direction of human evolution." They're all singing harmony to the House of Slytherin theme song:

> *For each of the four founders had*
> *A house in which they might*

Take only those they wanted, so,
For instance, Slytherin
Took only pure-blood wizards
Of great cunning just like him.
Said Slytherin, "We'll teach just those
Whose ancestry's purest."

Maybe Rowling just borrowed eugenics for a set of boilerplate bad guys, same as all those other screen and TV writers. There's no twisted old loony bigger than Adolf. But then why did it take till 2013 for my state to introduce the Justice for Victims of Sterilization Act? Virginia was once the cutting edge of eugenics. The future chancellor of Germany admired our 1924 Racial Integrity Act while dictating *Mein Kampf* in his prison cell. He used its DNA for the Nazi's own Law for the Prevention of Hereditary Diseased Offspring.

Hitler removed himself from the gene pool in 1945, but Virginia eugenicists kept sterilizing the so-called unfit until 1979. Governor Warner apologized over a decade ago, but only now is the legislature even considering paying for its Death Eater history. The bill would compensate each victim $50,000, for an estimated grand total of $76 million. If that sounds like a lot, imagine living your muggle life under the reign of Voldemort. Yes, Virginia, there are supervillains, and they didn't come from comic books.

I was sitting in a Thai restaurant with my recently Alzheimer's-diagnosed mother when my son texted me:

"In dungeons and dragons I created hawk-eye, Hulk and Thor."

It was even bigger news than his downloading superhero mods into Minecraft, because it required his own creative mixing. His über-Aryan is a human paladin with a demigod destiny and an epic-tier artifact hammer. For the Hulk, you start with a human warden and multiclass him to get a monk's unarmed strike while wearing bloodweave armor. Mix enchanted arrows and a throwing shield with bow-mastery and brawler talent, and both Hawkeye and Captain America are set to go. I think he chiseled Iron Man from living metal, though apparently warforging with a high charisma score works too.

It's the best thing about superhero teams, how cyborgs and mutants and magicians can combine forces, all their discordant realities merged in the melting pot of action-packed fantasy. Tolkien would take it farther with *Lord of the Rings*, but his first team of adventurers mixed dwarves with a hobbit and a human wizard. It was 1937. *The Hobbit* made a case for racial diversity in a time of Aryan purity.

Hitler had barred Jews from the German Olympic team the summer before. The "part-Jewish" fencer Helene Mayer was Berlin's token exception, and she medaled, along with nine other Jewish athletes from other nations. The biggest winner was African American Jesse Owens with four golds, including a relay record set with his white teammates. Hitler left the stadium rather than shake a non-Aryan hand. In Berlin, Owens stayed in a whites-only hotel, but back home, he had to use a freight elevator to attend his own banquet. FDR, afraid of losing the southern vote, snubbed him.

Hitler wanted to cleanse Europe of ethnic diversity, believing it would return the splendor of ancient Greece and Rome. But go farther back, and evolutionary geneticist Mark Thomas calls ancient Europe a "*Lord of the Rings*–type world," with multiple human races coexisting for dozens of millennia. In addition to Early Modern Humans (including the hominid formerly known as Cro-Magnon), you have your standard Neanderthals, plus their recently discovered neighbors, the Denisovans. Instead of segregating themselves on separate continents, the three hung out together in Spanish and Siberian caves. "It is possible," writes Carl Zimmer for the *New York Times*, "that there are many extinct human populations that scientists have yet to discover."

Old school theories don't like the idea of Homo sapiens coming in flirting range of lesser breeds, but analysis of a Neanderthal toe bone proves ancient races didn't keep to their prudish selves. If you have type 2 diabetes, you probably have a branch of Neanderthal relatives on your 50,000-year-old family tree. The gene is biggest in the Americas, so the colonists of Virginia were way too late when they passed my hemisphere's first antimiscegenation law in 1691. Since early humans didn't discover

Neanderthal love until after they'd exited Africa, Virginia's slave population was the genetically purest on the continent. Even Englishman Ozzy
Osbourne flunked the one-drop rule. The heavy-metal Neanderthal descendant had his DNA sequenced in hopes of finding a "plausible medical
reason why I should still be alive" given "the swimming pool of booze"
and drugs he'd guzzled. The answer wasn't racial segregation.

Denisovans are crashing family reunions now too. Europeans carry
some Denisovan blood, but the biggest pockets are in Australia and New
Guinea, with Brazil and China claiming some of the best Neanderthal-
Denisovan mixes. Denisovans also share about 8 percent of their genome
with some million-year-old species, so that's more bad news for Houses
of Slytherin worldwide. We are all, says computational biologist Rasmus
Nielsen, "connected to other species."

Conan the Barbarian creator Robert E. Howard agrees. The father of
sword and sorcery renamed ancient Eurasia "Hyboria" and populated it
with a mixed-race of arctic warriors descended from the lost continent of
Thuria. The survivors of Atlantis devolved into ape-men, and the former
Lemurians came westward, "overthrowing the pre-humans of the south."
This is about 20,000 years ago, after Neanderthals and Denisovans had
given way to Homo sapiens. Howard published his first Conan story
in 1932. Conan's people, the Atlantean-descended Cimmerians, would
evolve into Celts by 9,500 B.C., and Conan into Marvel Comics in 1970.
"The origins of the other races of the modern world," Howard writes,
"may be similarly traced. In almost every case, older far than they realize,
their history stretches back into the mists of the forgotten Hyborian Age."

Howard committed suicide in June 1936, three weeks before Jesse
Owens took his first Olympic gold. That left the *Weird Tales* realm of
sword and sorcery undefended when Tolkien invaded the following year.
Like any conqueror, he renamed everything, so Hyboria became Middle-
earth. Both ages took place in Earth's lost history, though Tolkien admits
"it would be difficult to fit the lands and events (or 'cultures') into such
evidence as we possess, archaeological or geological, concerning the
nearer or remoter part of what is now called Europe."

My wife and son and I watched all three *Hobbit* installments, but
skipped the *Conan the Barbarian* reboot, as did most of the world's

Cimmerian-descended population. Rumor has it Arnold Schwarzenegger will be returning to Hyboria soon. His last superteam included Grace Jones and Wilt Chamberlain, but I'm hoping Hollywood assembles an even more discordant cast. That's what superteams are about.

⚡ ⚡ ⚡

Racial purity was always a fiction—whether traveling to the ancient past or the distant future. As you know, I like Dr. Doom's time machine, but Superman is a kind of time machine too. In *Superman: The Movie*, Christopher Reeve appears to spin the earth backward on its axis to save Margot Kidder from having died in an earthquake, which gets stupider the longer you think about it. Marlon Brando's God-sized head appears in the clouds to boom a command at his disobedient son: "You must not alter the course of human history!"

Or something like that. It doesn't matter. Superman does what he wants and nothing bad comes of it. But it was his dad who spun him backward in the first place:

> In his laboratory, the last man on Earth worked furiously. He had only a few moments left. Giant cataclysms were shaking the dying planet, destroying mankind. It was in its last days, dying. . . . The last man placed his infant babe within a small time-machine he had completed, launching it as the laboratory walls caved-in upon him. The time-vehicle flashed back thru the centuries, alighting in the primitive year, 1935 A.D.

That's the script Siegel mailed Buck Rogers artist Russell Keaton in the summer of 1934. Siegel later swapped the time-vehicle for "a hastily devised space-ship" and Earth for a "distant planet destroyed by old age." Leap forward a year to *Superman* No. 1, and "Superman comes to Earth from the planet Krypton whose inhabitants had evolved, after billions of years, to physical perfection!" In Superman's newspaper comic strip premiere, Krypton is "a distant planet so far advanced in evolution that it bears a civilization of supermen—beings which represent the human race at its ultimate peak of perfect development!"

But how exactly can aliens "represent" the human race? After the German invasion of France, William Marston wrote that Siegel "believed that the real superman of the future would be someone with vast power who would use his invincible strength to right human wrongs." That phrase, "the real superman of the future," is literal. Siegel's Superman was the superman foretold by eugenics.

When Zack Snyder rebooted Krypton in his 2013 *Man of Steel*, he transformed it from a chunk of ice to a pinnacle of selective breeding, a planet whose inhabitants had taken the reins of evolution and engineered themselves into a race of violently amoral übermensch. They reproduce scientifically, culling only the best from their gene pool Registry. One of General Zod's sidekicks quips: "Evolution always wins."

That's not a galaxy far far away. That's us. The Registry, the Codex of the genetically fit that General Zod wants so desperately, that's not a sci-fi fantasy. That's Long Island. The Eugenics Record Office amassed records of the fit until closing three months after Germany invaded Poland. A review panel from its founding funder, the Carnegie Institute, had declared its work without scientific merit in 1935, the year South Carolina became the thirty-first and last state to pass a sterilization law. Germany had already adopted the American model and was slouching its way toward Auschwitz.

Abandoning selective breeding didn't mean Americans were done with the superman. They just changed tactics. Rather than "pick out a few superior children and make supermen of them alone," explained Rockefeller Institute researcher Dr. Alexis Carrel, "we would improve all of mankind." Newly egalitarian but increasingly bizarre means for superhuman transformation included hormones (1929), glandular stimulation (1931), chemistry (1934), vaccines (1934), nutrition (1935), diet (1936), and, my favorite, the transplantation of ape glands into children (1936) — that last researcher was confused why no parents were supplying nine-year-olds for his study. In contrast to "the Hitler program of race purification," Carrel wondered if mixed breeding might be the new ideal: "It may be that crossing civilizations as we do in America produces the best minds."

Siegel published his first take on superman in *Science Fiction: The*

Advance Guard of Future Civilization No. 3. "Publishing" in this case means hand-cranking pages of his fanzine on his school's mimeograph machine. Shuster illustrated. In "The Reign of the Superman," a homeless man given the powers of telepathy and mind control by a mad scientist plots world domination — until God answers a newspaper reporter's prayers and the meteorite-extracted serum wears off. This was January 1933, the month Adolf Hitler was appointed chancellor after performing well in presidential elections. *Times* correspondent Norman Ebbutt warned that Germany, despite Hitler professing "a peaceful foreign policy," intended "to recover all it has lost and has little hope of doing so by peaceful means." Like Hitler, Siegel's superman plots war. "The Superman" disrupts the "International Conciliatory Council," "the greatest Peace Conference of all time," by mentally "broadcasting thoughts of hate" that would "send the armies of the world to total annihilation."

Siegel didn't make the leap in a single bound. The word "superman" already suggested German aggression. A 1935 *Time* article, reporting the League of Nation's response to Germany's violation of the Treaty of Versailles, was simply titled "THE LEAGUE: Superman!" The one-word exclamation encapsulated international protest against Germany's rearmament. It was an old story. The 1916 *New York Times* editorial "Two Years of the Superman" had declared that, although the first year of the Great War ended with "Superman everywhere in ascent," "the common men" were now "coming towards their own," proving that Germany's "arrogance, egotism, cruelty and tyranny cannot conquer the world."

So when Siegel rebooted the übermensch into a superhero, he was spinning the swastika backward on its Axis. Superman was the end of the superman. The first comic book superhero is the eugenic superman plucked from the future and redirected to fight the Nazi superpower that would create him. In comic books, evolution lost. Humanity did not devolve into mental barnacles. Degenerates did not topple Metropolis. Mongrels did not trample the delicate flower of Aryan supremacy and plunge the human race into animal anarchy. Darwin and Nietzsche peeled God's cold, dead hands from evolution's helm, but the rudderless universe did not capsize.

But those decades of evolutionary terror did leave a permanent mark on pop culture. The history books my children read in their public schoolrooms have erased the horror of American eugenics, but the lowly comic book preserves the secret history of the superman. Those well-born, dual-identity, superpowered do-gooders are all Darwin's ghosts.

Fantômas, 1911.

CHAPTER 6

THOU SHALT NOT KILL

Does your emblem hide the heart of a serial killer? Are you the KKK but in a cooler costume? Are you really just a supervillain in disguise? These aren't questions you expect on a superhero census questionnaire, because the short answer is always an emphatic "No!" Superheroes are fundamentally good — even while fighting the bad. The Lone Ranger's creators Fran Striker and George W. Trendle laid down the law for their radio writers: "When he has to use guns, The Lone Ranger never shoots to kill, but rather only to disarm his opponent as painlessly as possible."

Striker and Trendle didn't explain their masked man's motives though. Why not shoot the bad guys? Martin Parker's 1656 "Robbin Hood" didn't kill; he merrily separated clergymen from their money and their testicles:

> No monkes nor fryers he would let goe,
> Without paying their fees;
> If they thought much to be usd so,
> Their stones he made them leese.

Does that castrating vigilantism still infuse superheroes?

Part of the confusion is the term "vigilante." Some see a toggle switch: either you're a lawful hero or you're a lawless vigilante. I see a spectrum. The 70s Avengers became a department of the U.S. government, each employee earning a tax-financed salary of $1,000 a day. The 70s Punisher, however, constituted his own legal system, marshal-judge-executioner. Spider-Man, like most superheroes, swings somewhere in-between, chasing crooks while cops chase him. But whether the hero kills, castrates, or leaves criminals tied to lampposts outside police stations, my question is the same: Why?

Before Mark Waid took the job of rewriting Superman's motivations for the twenty-first century, he'd always thought of the first comic book superhero as simply "the epitome of unselfishness," a guy who "invariably puts the needs of others first." When his DC editor asked why, Waid didn't have an answer: "Because . . . because doing the right thing is . . . is . . . is the right thing to do."

It's not a question you're supposed to ask. According to the Napoleon-loving Nietzsche and Shaw, it's not even true. Supermen aren't good. They're outlaws, self-fulfilling villains who act pro-socially only if it happens to suit them. "We are bold robbers," the real-life outlaw Jesse James told the *Kansas City Times* in 1872, "and I am proud of the name, for Alexander the Great was a bold robber, and Julius Caesar, and Napoleon Bonaparte." James also felt that any man "enough fool to refuse to open a safe or a vault when he is covered with a pistol ought to die"—though he did apologize for accidentally shooting a little girl and offered to pay her doctor's bill.

Comic book supermen fly above the law too, including the Sixth Commandment. My students are startled by the death count in *Action Comics*. A gang of "would-be murderers" watch their bullets ricochet off Superman: "Good Heavens! He won't die!" "Glad I can't say the same about you," he answers. "A moment later a dozen bodies fly headlong out the window into the night, the machine-guns wrapped firmly about their necks!" Shuster doesn't draw any corpses, but just how high is that window? And what are we to think happens a few pages later when he tells a "torturing devil" he's going to "Give you the fate you deserve" and then "tosses him away as tho he were a javelin" and "the torturer vanishes from view behind a grove of distant trees with a pitiful wail"?

Detective Comics is worse. In his six-page debut, "Bat-Man" punches a killer into an "acid tank" and declares it "A fitting end for his kind." A thug or two vanish off rooftops too, but Kane is more direct than Shuster. He drew his own "SNAP!" when illustrating Finger's caption: "There is a sickening snap as the Cossack's neck breaks under the mighty pressure of Batman's foot." By *Batman* No. 1, he's machine-gunning bad guys from the batplane: "Much as I hate to take human life, I'm afraid this time it's necessary."

Siegel's and Finger's lawyers could shrug those deaths off as collateral damage, but Spider-Man cocreator Steve Ditko considers superheroes "moral avengers" who kill criminals in order to champion "a clear understanding of right and wrong," even if that means violating the "pervading legal moral" code. DC censors' code put a halt to heroic homicides in 1940, but there were no philosophers on their editorial advisory board to address the underlying dilemma: Do any human laws apply to supermen? Napoleon didn't think so. "They charge me," he said, "with the commission of great crimes: men of my stamp do not commit crimes." Since superheroes have no peers, their crimes go untried — which is okay because they're helping humanity, right? And yet superheroes are guided by the same self-determined morality as any supervillain. The two are members of the same above-the-law species.

Self-serving killers or homicidal saviors? This chapter traces the coin edge dividing those two faces of the übermensch. We'll begin the philosophical tour in ancient Greece, follow the murderous implications to nineteenth-century Russia, stop in Washington State to weigh some contemporary vigilantism, and then settle into early twentieth-century cinema to weigh superheroic villainy against villainous superheroism.

Assuming superheroes are good, is that goodness a product of their superness? Does great power, as Stan Lee argues, really come with great responsibility? Or, if power corrupts, do superpowers supercorrupt?

When Plato asked those questions in 380 B.C.E., his older brother Glaucon answered with a supervillain origin story:

> Gyges was a shepherd in the service of the king of Lydia; there was a great storm, and an earthquake made an opening in the earth at the place where he was feeding his flock. Amazed at the sight, he descended into the opening, where, among other marvels, he beheld a hollow brazen horse, having doors, at which he stooping and

looking in saw a dead body of stature, as appeared to him, more than human, and having nothing on but a gold ring; this he took from the finger of the dead and reascended. Now the shepherds met together, according to custom, that they might send their monthly report about the flocks to the king; into their assembly he came having the ring on his finger, and as he was sitting among them he chanced to turn the collet of the ring inside his hand, when instantly he became invisible to the rest of the company and they began to speak of him as if he were no longer present. He was astonished at this, and again touching the ring he turned the collet outwards and reappeared; he made several trials of the ring, and always with the same result — when he turned the collet inwards he became invisible, when outwards he reappeared. Whereupon he contrived to be chosen one of the messengers who were sent to the court; where as soon as he arrived he seduced the queen, and with her help conspired against the king and slew him, and took the kingdom.

Moral of the story? Give a mild-mannered shepherd superpowers, he turns into a homicidal tyrant.

Glaucon has a disturbing number of latter-day Gyges to support his argument. Tolkien devolved his hobbity little Sméagol into a murderous Gollum with a similar ring of superimmorality. Invisibility did the same number on H. G. Wells; in *The Invisible Man*, a perfectly law-abiding medical student morphs into a psychopath who wants to "terrify and dominate." Nicholas Baker conducted a similar experiment while writing *The Fermata*, a novel about a man who can freeze time; when imagining what they would do with that superpower, everyone Baker interviewed "divided pretty evenly between something sexual and stealing money." Before Steve Ditko worked up the character, Jack Kirby's first-draft of Spider-Man would have gained his arachnid powers from a ring, not radiation, but either way, those godlike abilities are corrupting; Peter Parker learns the hard way, too busy cashing in on TV appearances to apprehend his uncle's future murderer. Even Bruce Banner and Ben Grimm in Lee's original treatment turned into conquest-minded monsters after their first doses of greed rays.

So with great power comes great shitheadedness. "No man," Glaucon concludes, "would keep his hands off what was not his own when he could safely take what he liked out of the market, or go into houses and lie with any one at his pleasure, or kill or release from prison whom he would, and in all respects be like a God among men."

So in a Glaucon comic book, everybody with a superpower is a super-villain. Plato, however, disagrees. So do the PR departments for every masked hero. They fight the good fight despite their anonymity — the invisible superpower Glaucon thinks fuels everyone's inner supervillain. Superheroes don't kill kings and seduce queens. They also don't offer any philosophical explanations to Mark Waid's editor. Why be good? They have no idea. Fortunately, a friend of mine wrote the book on the subject. Duncan Richter's *Why Be Good?* interviews the superheroes of philosophy, Plato to Wittgenstein, quizzing each with that most fundamental of ethical quandaries: Isn't Plato's big brother a total douchebag?

For most superpowered philosopher-kings, the answer is a cosmically dull and wholly unexamined sense of civic duty. "We have more power than any humans have ever possessed!" declares Mr. Fantastic, before the Thing cuts him off, "You don't have to make a speech, big shot! We've gotta use that power to help mankind, right?" Clark Kent was the first to leap to that cosmic conclusion, deciding he "must turn his gigantic strength into channels that would benefit mankind."

But why?

To answer, Duncan chopped the multiverse in half for me. On one side stand the Utilitarians, the Ends-Justify-the-Means League, those caped thinkers who calculate morality according to results. Opposite them, Emmanuel Kant and his philosophically impractical sidekicks don't care about consequences. You do good because good is good even if doing good could end up doing bad, which it won't. It's the principle that matters. That's the idealistic motto of the traditional superhero. Be good for goodness sake. Any parent could tell you that. When Siegel and Shuster expanded Superman's origin story for *Superman* No. 1, they inserted a retroactive panel in which the Kantian Kents give a prepubescently round-faced Clark a talking to about the proper use of superpowers, a lesson he enacts after Shuster sketches in the Kents' superego tombstones.

Nietzsche would be appalled to find his übermensch associated with such a cowardly allegiance to dead gods. Nietzsche is disgusted by Jesus because Jesus is a superman who submits to the will of his Father and accepts self-sacrifice to aid second-rate humanity. Right or wrong, a true superman imposes his own selfish order. The result might be tyranny, but Duncan says Thomas Hobbes can live with that too. In fact, a gloved fist of authoritarianism is exactly what the planet needs. Doesn't matter much if it's Superman or Lex Luthor on the throne. If he keeps the blood-thirsty masses secure and docile, then more superpower to him. And that means none of those masked, chaos-loving vigilantes challenging government authority.

John Locke, on the other gloved hand, would never sign the Superhero Registration Act. He's the first to whip on a mask and shine the Bat Signal against oppression. Not that Locke or any other philosopher is going to endorse Bruce's vengeance-motivated war on crime. Alan Moore, however, one-ups the Dark Knight's punishing Old Testament idealism with an even darker plunge into night. Like Hobbes and Glaucon, the *Watchmen*'s nihilistic Rorschach thinks humans are amoral shits, but he responds like a nitpickingly principled Kant who refuses to lie even when lying will save the world. Because when the masses find out the giant squid that attacked New York wasn't really from another dimension, there goes Ozymandias's new world order. Ozy is the pharaoh of the Utilitarians. John Stuart Mill would look at his bizarre (a giant squid, really?) but ends-justifying scheme to stop nuclear Armageddon and say, "Job well done!" Because it worked (sort of). The scam unites the United States and the U.S.S.R. against a common squid enemy. The mob-fearing Hobbes would applaud too. Authority is authority is authority. Even Plato trusts the watchmen to watch themselves. A well-born class of über-rulers — what could possibly go wrong?

But what does Socrates think? Depends who you think Socrates is. The hemlock-guzzling father of philosophy may just be Plato's mask — like the could-be Robin assuming Batman's identity in *Batman Beyond*. But Socrates would make a great alter ego for any superhero. An adolescent Clark Kent is reading *The Republic* when he allows that gang of bullies to taunt him in *Man of Steel*. I even know what page he was on:

"Is it, then, the role of a just man to harm anyone?"

Glaucon says Peter Parker behaved in his rational if small-minded self-interest when his blood first ran with radioactive greed: "From now I just look out for number one — that means — ME!" But Plato's wholesome veins run with the blood of a twelve-year-old comic book reader. It takes him most of the book to Socratically clobber philosophy's first supervillain, but by the end, Plato saves humanity by ripping out its amoral heart and making visible the do-gooding rationality inside us all. He gives every person the superpower of reason and so makes everyone heroic.

That sounds nice, but Plato may be dodging the bullet fired at Superman's chest. If it's rational to be good, then villains are irrational, and so supervillains are superirrational. And if superheroes are superrational, does superrationality work the same way as rationality? Might superrationality look immoral to those of us who are merely rational? Shaw did warn in the last chapter that the superman will ignore all our "ideals of right, duty, honor, justice, religion, even decency." He would call superheroes "sham Supermen," those "Heroes" readers love because we think they're us only "endowed with infinite brains, infinite courage, and infinite money." But a true superman's "moral obligations" go "beyond present human endurance."

So maybe no human philosophy applies to superhumans. What does Gyges care about principles or utilitarianism? His Napoleonic crimes go unpunished, and his kingly reign uninterrupted because with Great Power comes only Greatness. The laws of morality and rationality don't govern true supermen.

So does that mean Superman is *not* a superman? Are superheroes good because they're everyguys but with supermuscles? To answer that, I need to add two more philosophers to the superhero philosophical advisory board: Russian novelist Fyodor Dostoyevsky and American screenwriter Blake Snyder.

I started reading *Crime and Punishment* in A. P. English as a high school senior (I finished it too, a dubious honor my adolescent self did not award *Moby Dick*). No caped men flap through Saint Petersburg, but the novel says a lot about superhero morality. Rodion Raskolnikov, Dostoyevsky's pawnbroker–murdering philosophy student, chops the world in half:

> Men are in general divided by a law of nature into two categories, inferior (ordinary), that is, so to say, material that serves only to reproduce its kind, and men who have the gift or the talent to utter a new word. . . . The first category, generally speaking, are men conservative in temperament and law-abiding; they live under control and love to be controlled. To my thinking it is their duty to be controlled, because that's their vocation, and there is nothing humiliating in it for them.

So that's us, the grass-grazing denizens of Gotham and Metropolis, no surprise there. But the second category, "extraordinary" men, is key to understanding the difference between superheroes and supervillains because, according to Raskolnikov, there is no difference.

Extraordinary men "all transgress the law." By "making a new law, they transgressed the ancient one handed down from their ancestors and held sacred by the people." So

> all great men or even men a little out of the common, that is to say capable of giving some new word, must from their very nature be criminals — more or less, of course. Otherwise it's hard for them to get out of the common rut; and to remain in the common rut is what they can't submit to, from their very nature again, and to my mind they ought not, indeed, to submit to it.

When the Flash breaks the sound barrier, he's defying more than just a law of nature. All supermen are supervillains because their superness is their crime. The superpowered are an inevitable offense to the ordinary, and so those law-abiding masses will try to "punish them or hang them (more or less), and in doing so fulfill quite justly their conservative vocation."

At least that's how things look in nineteenth-century Russia. Dostoyevsky published *Crime and Punishment* in 1866, but how would he fare in twenty-first-century Hollywood? When a friend of mine — a former script reader for a California production company — wanted to collaborate on

THOU SHALT NOT KILL

a screenplay, he handed me Blake Snyder's *Save the Cat!* The how-to screenwriting guide explains why the Sandra Bullock vehicle *Miss Congeniality* is a better movie than *Memento*. It comes down to formula: *Miss Congeniality* hits all fifteen beats on The Blake Snyder Beat Sheet, while Christopher Nolan's directorial debut "is just a gimmick that cannot be applied to any other movie." If Snyder were a poetry professor, he would lecture on the superiority of sonnets to free verse, while defining the greatest works of literature by the uniformity of their iambic beats.

Raskolnikov would classify Snyder as "ordinary." Hollywood spec writers play by the rules. But in Snyder's defense, he understands those rules exceptionally well. He chops the multiverse into ten idiosyncratic genres. His "Dude with a Problem," for example, includes *Die Hard* and *Schindler's List*, while "Superhero" goes beyond *Batman Begins* to claim *Gladiator* and *A Beautiful Mind*—and probably anything else staring Russell Crowe. Snyder's ur-Superhero is "Gulliver tied to the beach by the Lilliputians." For Snyder, capes and crime-fighting aren't the heart of a superhero movie; it's the focus on "a super being" and "what it must be like to have to deal with the likes of us little people." So Batman, Frankenstein, and Dracula are all superheroes "challenged by the mediocre world around them," because it's really "the tiny minds that surround the hero that are the real problem."

Raskolnikov would agree. Dracula and Batman are both superhuman and so above the morality of the ordinary. Raskolnikov's extraordinary men and Snyder's superheroes belong in the same law-transgressing category. Though I'm not sure Snyder's mind is beautiful enough to recognize the connection. He fulfills his Lilliputian vocation for Christopher Nolan when he shouts "screw *Memento!*" and dismisses all the "hullabaloo" because of its low box office revenue. That was in 2005, the year *Batman Begins* premiered, and three years before Heath Ledger won the Oscar for Best Supporting Actor for *The Dark Knight*. Raskolnikov warns that "the same masses set these criminals on a pedestal in the next generation and worship them," and sure enough, Snyder later lauds Nolan's caped crusader for following "the beats down to the minute."

Or does that mean Nolan is a superhero who overcame his Gulliverness by conforming to the Lilliputian Beat Sheet? Either way, the director, like his Bruce Wayne, "is admirable because he eschews his personal comfort in the effort to give back to the community." That, says Snyder, solves the problem of "how to have sympathy for the likes of millionaire Bruce Wayne or genius Russell Crowe." They save the cat.

And Raskolnikov agrees again. His "extraordinary man" has "an inner right to decide in his own conscience to overstep" if overstepping "is essential for the practical fulfillment of his idea," an idea that might be "of benefit to the whole of humanity." That's how he rationalizes killing and robbing that nasty old pawnbroker to a cop. He argues (faux hypothetically): "Kill her, take her money and with the help of it devote oneself to the service of humanity and the good of all. What do you think, would not one tiny crime be wiped out by thousands of good deeds?"

It doesn't matter how the cop answers, because a real Gulliver wouldn't have asked a Lilliputian for his opinion. That's Raskolnikov's downfall. He's reading from the wrong page in *Save the Cat!* He wants to be a superhero ("An extraordinary person finds himself in an ordinary world"), but he's really just a Dude with a Problem ("An ordinary guy finds himself in extraordinary circumstances"). Worse, his circumstances are self-inflicted. He fell for Snyder's superhero formula because it "gives flight to our greatest fantasies about our potential."

Raskolnikov fails to be "a man of the future," but Nietzsche (who ranked reading Dostoyevsky "among the most beautiful strokes of fortune in my life") took his wanna-be Napoleon and renamed him the übermensch. After Siegel and Shuster adopted the character type, DC completed the circle by calling Superman "The Man of Tomorrow." But Dostoyevsky was no law-breaking innovator either; Carlyle and Emerson had been fawning over Great Men for decades. After explaining his theories, even Raskolnikov admits: "there is nothing particularly new in all that. The same thing has been printed and read a thousand times before." Or as one of Snyder's studio execs told him: "Give me the same thing... only different!"

That's Raskolnikov: a repentant Gyges punished by his own platonic rationality. Even if Raskolnikov had worn a magic ring while committing his murders, he wouldn't have escaped his own Lilliputianism. Napoleon should have suffered from his crimes too, but instead of invisibility he wielded the superpower of moral indifference.

Philosophically, superheroes fall into the same two categories: Raskolnikovs and Gygeses. The first are Dudes with Superpowers who fight for Lilliputian justice because in their hearts they're Lilliputians too. The second are actual supermen who get around their Gulliver woes by conforming to the Lilliputian Beat Sheet. Or mostly conforming. Fighting for law and order doesn't mean a superman has to obey every rule. As long as you stay on this side of homicidal Napoleons like Moore's Rorschach and Ditko's Mr. A, the Lilliputian justice system won't punish your Gulliver vigilantism.

Gyges's magic ring is irrelevant. Supermorality and superimmorality are internal powers, ones indistinguishable to mere mortals. So to continue to pursue the philosophical quandary of superhero goodness, we need to look beyond superpowers and focus on the physically human. Strip away flight and X-ray vision, and what's left? More important, how do those superheroic remains differ from supervillainy? To answer, we need to remove the superhero formula from its comic book and Hollywood context and judge real-world remakes of *Crime and Punishment*. That means removing ourselves temporarily from the historical tour and focusing on the here and now.

The first case study is set in Washington State, and on its surface, it doesn't look much like a superhero tale. Like Raskolnikov, serial-killer Patrick Drum doesn't pull on spandex when exercising his superhuman rights. When police arrested him in 2012, he was wearing a white tank top and khakis. However, like the Punisher or Dexter or the 1930s Spider, Drum is dedicated to killing bad guys. Oliver Queen on season one of *Arrow* crossed off names from a checklist of targets he murdered. Drum only x-ed out the first two on his list of sixty registered sex offenders before the Lilliputian authorities ended his adventuring.

Drum lived about eighty miles outside the patrols of a team of spandex-wearers, Seattle's "real life superheroes" Buster Doe, No Name, and Phoenix Jones. RealLifeSuperheroes.com (RLSH) insists its members "are not 'kooks in costumes,' as they may seem at first glance." According to RLHS.com, these folks "seek to inform, and, most importantly, inspire" through "charity work and civic activities." Since these organizations, like noncostumed neighborhood watches, work within the law, they usually do no harm, and their "safety patrols" might even deter a crime or two. But they're not superheroes. They can't fill enough boxes on even my checklist. They're self-designed cosplayers staging theatrics on city streets.

RLSH members "believe in due process" and "are certainly not vigilantes," but Drum told a courtroom, "This country was founded on vigilantism." He makes a disturbingly accurate point about U.S. history. Flip back to chapter two. What's the Revolutionary War but an enormous act of vigilantism against King George? Lexi Pandell details Drum's adventures in the *Atlantic*, but doesn't connect the benday dots. Though Patrick Drum can't fly or turn invisible, he is a modern superhero.

Bruce Wayne needed a defining emblem before starting his war on criminals. A bat didn't fly through Drum's window, so he looked to his childhood. In the note he left beside his victims' corpses, he explained how he'd once watched scorpions in a pet shop aquarium circling "in full battle ready posture" to protect a pregnant female. "This spirit always impressed me." He left his emblem, a scorpion encased in a lollipop, with his signed notes. After his second murder, Drum planned to go off the grid and "live in the wild," the site of his origin story. When he was ten, a stranger got him drunk and lured him into the woods for oral sex. Bruce's childhood ended in Crime Alley, a wild zone he never emotionally escaped either. Like Batman, Drum is about pro-social vengeance.

"My actions were not about me," he explained in superheroic grandeur. "They were about my community. I suffered many failures and my overall view of things was one of hopelessness. I took that hopelessness and in turn threw myself away to a purpose. I gave myself to something bigger than myself." And, as in so many superhero sagas, the community championed him. The county prosecutor abandoned the death penalty because she doubted she could convince a jury to execute. Drum has too many fans, including the National Rifle Association (NRA). "The only thing that stops a bad guy with a gun," says NRA vice president Wayne LaPierre, "is a good guy with a gun."

That's the logic that armed the Golden Age of superheroes. Not just the good vs. evil mentality, but the gun part too. In the 30s and 40s, holsters were as common to superhero costumes as masks and capes. The Shadow, the Phantom, Captain America, even Batman gunned down his share of bad guys. LaPierre would reholster them all. The pair of police officers patrolling Columbine weren't enough to prevent that travesty, so the NRA's National Model School Shield Program (no relation to Nick Fury's S.H.I.E.L.D.) calls for "armed volunteers." Good guys motivated by selfless altruism to protect their communities.

In comic books, you call them superheroes. In real life, they're the morally ambiguous George Zimmerman. Insurance underwriter by day, by night Zimmerman was a self-proclaimed neighborhood watchman, the definition of the Spanish word "vigilante." He was an armed volunteer patrolling the mean streets of his gated community when he shot Trayvon Martin in 2012. The judge called him "mild," a "run of the mill" Clark Kent kind of guy, an upstanding student earning a degree in criminal justice with dreams of becoming a judge himself. Prosecutors called him a "wannabe cop." Because his second-degree murder charge required evidence of a "depraved mind," one "brimming with ill will, hatred, spite or evil intent," his jury called him innocent.

What would Plato call him? Rational? Irrational? What about Drum? His Lilliputian judge sentenced him to life without parole, but an imprisoned Gulliver is still a Gulliver. Does Drum's ability to carry out murders without suffering Raskolnikov's guilt prove he's a superman — or is he just a soulless serial killer? Philosophically, is there a difference? "The actions of the just," says Glaucon, "would be as the actions of the unjust; they would both come at last to the same point."

Perhaps the problem is individualism gone too far. Steve Ditko's superheroes are homicidal because they enact the anticollectivist philosophy of Ayn Rand. "What are your masses but millions of dull, shriveled, stagnant souls that have no thoughts of their own," she wrote the year

Action Comics debuted. Like her hero-worshipping predecessors Carlyle, Emerson, and Wister, Rand believed "men are not equal in ability and one can't treat them as if they were." Drum and Zimmerman agree. They acted alone and so relied on no one else's moral judgments. But Zorro and the Scarlet Pimpernel recruited teams of like-minded vigilantes to adventure with them. Even Batman had Robin and Alfred to pull him back from Nietzsche's abyss. Maybe morality is in the numbers.

So what would a team of Zimmermen and Lollipop Scorpions look like? Would it be a Justice League or a Brotherhood of Evil Mutants? RLSH cosplay team Michigan Protectors currently patrols Detroit, but in the 1930s the city was under the protection of the Black Legion, a splinter group from the Ohio KKK. The Protectors' Adam Besso, aka Bee Sting, retired from superheroing in 2012 after pleading guilty to attempted assault with a weapon (his "stinger" was a shotgun). But that's nothing to the 1936 conviction of nine Black Legion members for the kidnapping and murder of alleged wife-beater Charles Poole.

According to the historian Peter H. Amann, Black Legion founder William Shepard supplied his superhero team with secret rites and costumes: "You have to have mystery in a fraternal thing to keep it up," he said; "the folks eat it up." His Legionnaires sported black hoods, pirate hats, and robes with cross-and-bones on the chest — the same emblem *Exciting Comics'* superhero Black Terror would use in the 40s. Despite the Black Legion's self-proclaimed passion for "crime fighting," in "real life," Amann concludes, their actions "were neither glamorous nor likely to reduce crime." The *Detroit News* thought so too: "Hooey may look like romance and adventure in the moonlight, but it always looks like hooey when you bring it out in the daylight."

The number of annual lynchings dropped to single digits for the first time the year of the Black Legion trial. They'd dropped from triple digits in 1902, the year Thomas F. Dixon Jr. published his first best seller, *The Leopard's Spots*. Dixon's state of North Carolina only amassed a fifth of Georgia's and Mississippi's lynching totals, but Dixon made up the difference fictionally with his second novel, *The Clansman: An Historical Romance of the Ku Klux Klan*, in which a knightly team of Night Hawks hunt down and kill a Negro officer responsible for the deaths of two white women who virtuously threw themselves from a cliff rather than be raped.

I was maybe ten when someone threw a burning cross in a front yard down the street from my house. I didn't know the family who lived there, just the fact they were black. My dad doubted it was the Klan, just some local Neanderthals. Maybe the same ones who egged our house and wrote "Niger Lovers" on our garage when my parents were suing the township to integrate the local police. Presumably real Klan members would have spelled the slur correctly. I was too busy reading Marvel Comics to think much more about it, but I mention the event as an apology for one of the most unpleasant discoveries I made while tracking superheroes back to their origins. KKK hooey runs deep in the genre.

When hunting for superhero ground zero, many scholars point to Orczy's Scarlet Pimpernel mostly because of McCulley's Zorro imitation, which in turn influenced Finger's Batman. But the Scarlet Pimpernel lacks one of the superhero's most defining characteristics. He has no costume, no repeating physical representation. He's just a name and a series of ordinary disguises. He's also extraordinarily nonviolent, preferring to deter an enemy with a snuff box of pepper than a blow to the jaw.

Dixon's 1905 historical novel, published the same year as Orczy's, is a more convincing predecessor. His homicidal Klansmen are the first twentieth-century dual-identity costumed heroes in American lit. Like other superheroes, they keep their alter egos a secret and carry their costumes with them ("easily folded within a blanket and kept under the saddle in a crowd without discovery"). They change "in the woods," the nineteenth-century equivalent of Clark Kent's phone booth ("It required less than two minutes to remove the saddles, place the disguises, and remount"). Their powers, while a product of their numbers and organization, border on the supernatural (their "ghostlike shadowy columns" rode "through the ten townships of the country and successfully disarmed every negro before day without the loss of a life").

Gus, the would-be rapist and the team's inaugural target, wasn't so lucky. Dixon does not depict the execution of the "vicious scoundrel," but his corpse is left "lying in his full uniform in Lynch's yard" and across the breast "was pinned a scrap of paper on which was written in red ink the letters K. K. K." The Jibbenainosay left his signature mark on his victims' corpses too, as would Zorro and the Spider. The Klan also nailed a notice to the courthouse:

> The Negro Militia now organized in this State threatens the extinction of civilization. They have avowed their purpose to make war upon and exterminate the Ku Klux Klan, an organization which is now the sole guardian of Society. All negroes are hereby given forty-eight hours from the publication of this notice in their respective counties to surrender their arms at the courthouse door. Those who refuse must take the consequences.

If the scoundrels refuse to heel, the order of southern supermen will deliver more of their homicidal justice.

Though history has tossed the Klan into LaPierre's bad guys bin, Dixon sees them as patriots overthrowing the tyranny of Negro Rule and rising like Napoleons to the dictates of their evolutionary supremacy. He even gives them the first superhero mission statement: "To protect the weak, the innocent, and the defenceless from the indignities, wrongs, and outrages of the lawless, the violent, and the brutal; to relieve the injured and the oppressed."

Compare that to Superman deciding to become a "champion of the oppressed" and "to devote his existence to those in need!" Or the Phantom's vow "to devote my life to the destruction of piracy, greed, cruelty, and injustice, in all their forms!" Or Doc Savage's oath: "Let me think of the right and lend all my assistance to those who need it, with no regard for anything but justice." Green Lantern even makes it rhyme:

> In brightest day, in blackest night,
> No evil shall escape my sight.
> Let those who worship evil's might,
> Beware my power, Green Lantern's light!

Green Lantern belongs to a corps of identically costumed vow-takers dedicated to fighting for their version of truth and justice. The supervillain Sinestro started his own corps too, and their oath is almost the same:

In blackest day, in brightest night,
Beware your fears made into light
Let those who try to stop what's right,
Burn like his power, Sinestro's might!

Patrick Drum pledged himself to doing "what's right" too. So did Detroit's Black Legion and every other incarnation of the KKK—which means they're not just a team of Gyges. Perhaps their intent to do good supports Plato's belief that wrong-doers are simply mistaken, that if their faulty reasoning could be corrected, then even the worst villains would abandon their villainy.

But would supervillains?

Dixon's superheroes use a warped definition of "oppressed," but that's what Shaw and Nietzsche demand of a superman. Accept no judgments but your own. That's a disturbing philosophy since supervillains live by it too. The Klan's noose is the tightrope supermen walk before tipping into heroism or villainy. Either way, we ordinary dudes can't understand the logic of their extraordinary minds. If they seem moral, we happily applaud them. If they seem immoral, well, we applaud them even more.

"Both the Joker and Hannibal Lecter were much more fascinating than the good guys," says Talking Heads singer David Byrne. "Everybody sort of roots for the bad guys in movies." Byrne was explaining why he wrote "Psycho Killer," the opening song from the Heads' concert movie, *Stop Making Sense.* Jonathan Demme also directed Anthony Hopkins as Hannibal in *The Silence of the Lambs*, but that was almost two decades after Byrne wrote about his psycho killer, so Hannibal couldn't have influenced the song. Maybe Byrne's explanation doesn't make sense because Byrne is also a fan of Dadaism. He adapted a Hugo Ball poem for the song "I Zimbra." Its string of nonsense syllables reflects Ball's Dada Manifesto: "to dispense with conventional language" and "get rid of everything that smacks of journalism, worms, everything nice and right, blinkered, moralistic, europeanised, enervated."

That sounds more like a supervillain mission statement, but to understand superheroes we need to understand their superhuman brethren too. The original Lex Luthor types are easy: inflated Gyges trying to rule a worldwide kingdom. But an agent of chaos like the Joker, that's harder to get your philosophical head around. Immoral? Irrational? Do the terms apply to the dark side of the übermensch? My D&D-playing son might label him "chaotic-evil," as opposed to Lex's "lawful-evil," but the terms are just another roll of the descriptive die. Maybe the bigger question is:

Why be evil?

The surreal answer may be found in Paris of the early 1910s, where Hugo Ball's avant-garde cousins were rooting for France's first pulp-fiction psycho killer, Fantômas. I'm no expert in French surrealism, but I've stood mesmerized in front of more than one Magritte painting. He, like Jean Cocteau and Guillaume Apollinaire and André Breton, was mesmerized by the figure of a "masked man in impeccable evening clothes, dagger in hand, looming over Paris like a somber Gulliver." That's John Ashbery's description of the iconic cover art for Pierre Souvestre and Marcel Allain's 1911 *Fantômas*, the first in a series of thirty-eight novels featuring the seemingly psychotic *empereur du crime*.

A side mystery is how a Pulitzer Prize–winning poet came to write the introduction to the reissued translation. Maybe it's because Ashbery is, according to Ashbery, "sometimes considered a harebrained, homegrown surrealist whose poetry defies even the rules and logic of surrealism," a description that also suits Souvestre (a failed aristocrat-lawyer turned automotive journalist) and Allain (Souvestre's secretary, ghostwriter, and later husband to Souvestre's flu-widowed wife). Ashbery calls them both "hacks," their prose "hackneyed," and their narratives "crude." Yet Ashbery's harebrained forefather, Guillaume Apollinaire, declared *Fantômas* "extraordinary," its lyricism "magnificent," and the serial a "modern *Aeneid*."

Apollinaire's review also included "lamely written," so the surrealists' praise isn't entirely surreal, but it doesn't explain the supervillain's Napoleonic impact on pop culture. One clue may be that modest domino mask the villain wears on his debut cover. "Masks are a way of leaving the self, breaking connections imposed by morals, intelligence and customs," writes yet another French surrealist, Michel Leiris. "They are a way of conjuring evil forces and defying God."

The gentleman serial killer may have stolen his mask and top hat from A. J. Raffles, but there's no hint of Robin Hood in him. Ashbery mentions other influences (*Manfred*, *Les Misérables*) and the popularity of Nick Carter in France at the time, but he misses how much Souvestre and Allain pilfered from that American pulp. The authors allude to "Cartouche and Vidocq and Rocambole," but their psycho killer's most immediate predecessor is Nick Carter's arch-nemesis, Dr. Quartz.

Carter's "hack," Frederic Van Rensselaer Dey, introduced that psychopathic genius in 1891. Quartz "wished to defy the police; to defy mankind, because he believed himself to be so much smarter than all other men combined." He is Raskolnikov's extraordinary man, indifferent to "rightdoing and wrongdoing, as we define the two terms" and to "anything human, animal, moral, legal, save only his own inclination." If you like the scene in *Silence of the Lambs* where Dr. Lecter displays his gutted guard like an art installation, you'll just love "Dr. Quartz II, at Bay" when the doctor embalms a whole railroad car of victims and arranges them like waxworks playing a game of cards. Or if you like Alan Moore's *Killing Joke* when the Joker rigs a funhouse ride to project photos of Commissioner Gordon's raped and crippled daughter, wait till you see Fantômas tie a corpse inside a clock bell so blood rains down with the clanging of the hour.

It would be easy to call them all "evil." It's the term we like to use for supervillains Adolf Hitler and Osama bin Laden. But the word doesn't make sense. It pretends to define what it merely describes. The real horror, the thing that should keep you awake at night, is the absence of evil in the motives of those who commit it. Adolf and Osama were trying to make the world a better place. They thought they were the good guys. David Byrne finds the Joker and Hannibal Lecter fascinating because they don't make sense. There's no understandable cause to their überdepravity. There's no mystery to be solved, just endless installments brimming with ill will, hatred, spite, and evil intent.

Fantômas is the messiah of circular evil, the Antichrist of hierarchal order. He overturns all meaning. Though they exist solely in "conventional language," Souvestre's and Allain's novels still answer Bell's mission to "get rid of all the filth that clings to this accursed language . . . your stuffiness, this laughable impotence, your stupendous smugness, outside all the parrotry of your self-evident limitedness." Replace "Dada" with "Superman" and Bell's Manifesto reads:

> How does one achieve eternal bliss? By saying Superman. How does one become famous? By saying Superman. With a noble gesture and delicate propriety. Till one goes crazy. Till one loses consciousness. How can one get rid of everything that smacks of journalism, worms, everything nice and right, blinkered, moralistic, europeanised, enervated? By saying Superman. Superman is the world soul, Superman is the pawnshop. Superman is the world's best lily-milk soap. Superman Johann Fuchsgang Goethe. Superman Stendhal. Superman Dalai Lama, Buddha, Bible, and Nietzsche. Superman m'Superman.

Ultimately Ashbery declares Fantômas a Cubist charade (Picasso and Gris were fans too), and yet one whose "popularity cut across social and cultural strata." Like a dagger's blade, he might have said. The best monsters are never slain, never contained, are forever plotting new and paradoxically comforting horrors between episodes.

A story's meaning only emerges when it's over, and so Fantômas was meaningless to the generation who embraced him, and his supervillain successors remain incomprehensible to us. They make everything stop making sense. Ball calls for new words, for an invented language of nonsense, which is what I hear when David Byrne sings his chorus: "kiss kiss say." I don't understand French (*"qu'est-ce que c'est"*), but nobody, not even France, understands a superman like Fantômas.

The superheroes of Blake Snyder's definition are amoral. Batman, Dracula, Frankenstein, the good, the bad, the ugly, they're all superbeings stuck with the likes of us. Batman and Superman cope by riding to our rescue. Dracula and Fantômas share a strategy too: they kill us. Dracula needs the nourishment, and Fantômas, like the Scarlet Pimpernel, is in it for thrills ("the devil's own risks!").

But some superhumans swing both ways, saving/feeding according to whim. Catwoman's moral compass is in a constant spin. Like Two-Face, she seems guided by chance, which may be further proof of her superhumanness: "morality" isn't on her vocab list. I missed Halle Berry's 2004 *Catwoman*, so I'll look at cinemas' first catwoman. Not Michelle Pfeiffer — not even Lee Meriwether from the 1966 *Batman* spoof. The original catsuited superwoman padded across screens a century ago.

Nick Carter, le roi des détectives arrived in Paris cinemas in 1908 to rain down multiple sequels and knockoffs, including Louis Feuillade's 1913 *Fantômas* serial and his acclaimed follow-ups, with scripts improvised with the same actors, costumes, plots, and character types. Actress Musidora next played the antiheroine Irma Vep in the 1915 *Les Vampires*. Fantômas had traded in his domino mask and top hat to become "The Man in Black" during his second serial installment, and Musidora stripped the outfit off him and tightened the seams before slinking into it herself. Though brutally deadly, the anagramic Irma Vep is not a vampire of Dracula's blood-sucking variety but the leading member of a crime syndicate terrorizing Paris. They were inspired by an actual crime syndicate, a gang of automobile-driving anarchists whose murder spree paralyzed the city in 1911, the year *Fantômas* appeared.

By monarchial standards, France had been in anarchy since the Revolution, but by the early twentieth century, some superanarchists also embraced "Illegalism," committing crimes for no greater ideal than personal profit. Shaw would be proud. The Bonnot Gang, aka the Auto Bandits, invented the get-away car. They also liked to break into expensive homes and murder the owners. Polidori transformed the lowly folklore vampyre into an aristocracy-feeding übermensch a century earlier, so I get why Feuillade resurrected the term. The superhuman Vampires are a deepening study in supervillainous ill will.

Technically Philipe Guérande, the "star reporter" investigating the gang, is the hero, but after debuting in the third episode, Musidora dominates. She's the Vampires' second in command, outliving each of the four Fantômas-wanna-be Grand Vampires. They all have their nefarious skill sets — disguise, poisons, paralysis glove, hypnotic eyes, even a retractable cannon fired from an apartment window — but none are as memorable as Musidora in Vep's black bodysuit. Feuillade opened *Fantômas* with a special effects dissolve displaying his villain's shape-shifting powers, and Vep has plenty of Mystique in her too, assuming the identities of her aristocratic victims seamlessly. She and her Vampires also push the limits of early twentieth-century technology, recording a millionaire's voice on a wax cylinder and playing it over a telephone to authenticate a forged check.

But they're not just thrill-seeking pranksters or second-guessing Raskolnikovs. Episode one opens with the report of a police inspector's decapitated body found in a swamp. Thirty minutes later, Philipe is opening a box with the missing head. Vep and her crew later dispatch a businessman with a hair pin through the back of his skull then shuck the body from a moving train. They murder a ballerina because she's rumored to be Philipe's fiancée. They also have a knack for lassoing nooses around people's necks and yanking them from balconies.

The image that most haunts me is the ball thrown by a baron for his niece — really the Grand Vampire and Vep in disguise. The Parisian aristocracy gathers for the baron's midnight "surprise" to find the windows boarded and gas flooding through the vents. Feuillade's camera is more stationary than many silent film directors', but he's a master of deep focus, staging a cascade of background and foreground action within a continuous frame. The gowned and tuxedoed guests flail and wilt across furniture and floors in a tableau of slaughter — followed by the silhouetted Vampires entering through a pair of backlit doors in the distant wall to plunder their jewels. I assumed they were all dead — the intertitle read "asphyxiate" — but when the police tear the planks from the windows the next morning, the guests miraculously revive.

Despite the mayhem, Feuillade seems to be rooting for Vep. When Philipe and his comic sidekick capture her, she poses like a damsel-in-distress. If you watch episode nine out of sequence, you would mistake her for the heroine valiantly struggling against her kidnappers. In fact, Vep, more than all the plundered jewels and bank accounts, is the serial's prize. The first and second Grand Vampires battle against the rival criminal Moreno not just for control of Paris but of Vep. Moreno falls for her, hypnotizes her into loving him, and next she's gunning down her former boss. When the captured Moreno is executed between episodes (I suspect the actor was called away on war duty), the next Grand Vampire, Venomous, proposes.

Philipe's wedding (Feuillade, apparently filming on the fly, introduces the new fiancée with equal haste) occurs between episodes, but the final, "The Terrible Wedding," features the Vampires in rambunctious celebration (I rewound the bodysuited dance duet twice). Again, if watched out of sequence, the gang is a fun-loving pack of pals — until Philipe and the police break in and gun them down. Some scramble for the balcony, but Philipe has sawed the floor so they plunge to the cement where they writhe and die. It's a surprisingly brutal ending. Only Vep escapes, sneaking to the basement where the heroes' captured brides are imprisoned. But Philipe has lowered a gun to the women, and his bride shoots Vep dead just before the heroes enter, embracing their wives before Vep's corpse. The End.

Feuillade may have been shooting for gritty realism, but the accumulative effect is moral surrealism. Love interests are tossed from the moving train of the plot without comment. Our sympathies flicker between villains and heroes, guided only by passing thrills. The film is beyond good and evil. It's a superman cinema completely alien to its later Hollywood cousin. Unless you consider *Silence of the Lambs* a superhero movie, which, according to Synder's definition, it is. Philipe and FBI agent Clarice Starling are dudes with serious problems, but Hannibal and Irma are the fascinating Gullivers we root for. Our love of supervillains is at least as strong as our love for superheroes. Of course it's hard to tell them apart.

So what tilts a Bruce Wayne toward the heroic when he's standing above Feuillade's flickering abyss? He could dedicate his supergenius to plaguing Gotham as an American Fantômas, but his inner übermensch wars on criminals instead. Why? His origin story offers one explanation. A child witnesses the murder of his parents and vows revenge. It's up there with radioactive spiders and Krypton exploding, but *Detective Comics*

ran six of Bruce's crime-crushing adventures before Bob Kane sketched his hero's supposed motivation. The origin story was an ad hoc rationalization retrofitted to the character's preexisting behavior. Batman was already Batman. So what's his real origin?

Legend has it Kane was planning to call him "Bird-Man" before scripter Bill Finger steered him toward "Bat-Man." After plagiarizing a Shadow novella for the first adventure, Finger plagiarized an even more obscure pulp for the origin story. The 1934 "The Bat" is credited to C. K. M. Scanlon, a likely pseudonym for superhero trail-blazer Johnston McCulley. You know Zorro, but you also know how The Bat chose his crime-fighting identity:

> He would not be able to appear in public unless he was carefully and cleverly disguised. . . . He must become a figure of sinister import.
> . . . A strange Nemesis that would eventually become a legendary terror to all of crimedon. . . . In the shadows above his head came a slithering, flapping sort of sound. As the creature hovered above the lamp for an instant it cast a huge shadow upon the cabin wall. "That's it!" exclaimed Clade aloud. "I'll call myself 'The Bat.'"

Five years later, Kane's Bruce Wayne sits alone contemplating disguises too: "Criminals are a superstitious cowardly lot. So my disguise must be able to strike terror into their hearts. I must be a creature of the night, black, terrible." Like McCulley's Clade, Bruce's needs are answered by a chance appearance: "As if in answer a huge bat flies in the open window!" It provides Bruce his needed inspiration: "That's it! It's an omen. I shall become a BAT!" He stands in full costume in the concluding frame: "And thus is born the weird figure of the dark . . . this avenger of evil, 'The Batman.'"

Will Murray was the first to identify Batman's debt to The Bat, but the story goes deeper. McCulley borrowed from an even older source. While Feuillade was defining supervillainy in France, D. W. Griffith was filming what he considered heroic American supermen, an adaptation of Dixon's *Clansman*. Griffith's 1915 *The Birth of a Nation* expands the masked men's origin story. Seeing his homeland under "Negro rule," future Klan leader Ben Cameron sits alone "in agony of soul over the degradation and ruin of his people." A group of children appear as if in answer. Two white children place a white sheet over their heads, and the black children are terrified by the ghostly sight. "The inspiration," declares the intertitle. Cameron stands, ready to act. "The result. The Ku Klux Klan." In the next frame sit three mounted Klansmen in full costume.

The sequence prefigures not only Batman's three-panel origin structure — hero alone, chance inspiration, first image of costumed persona — but also the "superstitious" rationalization for the disguise. Promotional posters also featured a Klansman on horseback, his cape fluttering and his Klan emblem centered on his chest. After *Action Comics* No. 1, these became standard motifs for superhero costumes.

Griffith's original title was the same as the novel, but after an early screening, he and Dixon expanded their vision to national proportions. A tale of southern vigilantism was now the rebirth story of a reunited Union. Fans agreed, literally galloping to premieres dressed as their favorite historical characters, those noble Night Hawks of Reconstruction. The Ku Klux Klan had died decades before, but since they had the robes, those cosplayers thought it would be fun to re-form the team, this time as a nationwide organization based on Dixon's fiction. Even their emblem was a Dixon invention; the nineteenth-century Klan never used a burning cross. The new KKK numbered in the millions and was praised as a much-needed crime-fighting force that succeeded where traditional law enforcement failed. The historian Richard K. Tucker sums it up:

> Mainline Protestant ministers often praised the Klan from their pulpits. Reformers welcomed it to vice-ridden communities to "clean up" things. Prohibitionists and the Anti-Saloon League supported it as a force against the Demon Rum. Most of all, millions saw it as a protection against the Pope of Rome, who, they believed, was threatening to "take over America."

Vice-ridden communities, plots against America, only one thing can save us — any of this sound familiar?

I seriously doubt Joe Shuster, a young Jewish artist from Cleveland, knowingly copied his Superman from pro-eugenic vigilantes, but the KKK had blurred into popular culture by the time he took up his pencil.

Bill Finger was only a year old when the silent *Birth of a Nation* premiered, but a sound version was re-released in 1930, when he and the other youngsters in the Batman creative team were middle-schoolers. McCulley was thirty-four at the time of the original release. Most likely McCulley borrowed from Griffith, and Finger borrowed from McCulley. However you sketch the lines of influence, the Klan darkens one of comic books' most defining heroes. Batman is the KKK in a cooler costume.

But the Klan had lost its fanbase by the 30s. Even Dixon opposed them as "unprincipled marauders" and "a menace to American democracy," condemning future superheroes too since "disguise is a dangerous weapon in the hands of many irresponsible and reckless people." Though masked heroes sold millions of magazines during the Depression, real-life vigilantes like the Black Legion were prosecuted as criminals. So Superman began his career as a vigilante-fighting vigilante, even foiling a lynching in *Superman* No. 1. He and the clan of imitations that followed him take some of their most defining characteristics from the KKK, while whiting-out the organization's villainous goals. As a result, Batman is a continuing contradiction too: a violent, law-breaking criminal fighting for law and order. The same as any superhero.

Despite his dark origin, Bruce Wayne's reign of terror on criminals includes no lynchings or burning crosses. He doesn't war on innocents either. The Joker, not Batman, is America's Fantômas. No other pop culture bad guy — Lex Luthor, Moriarty, the Wicked Witch of the West — is better known and more horrifically adored for his homicidal insanity or what Grant Morrison aptly dubs "super sanity." The Joker is one of our favorite nightmares.

But who dreamed it first?

Standard answers boil down to some combination of Kane and his assistants, Finger and backup artist Jerry Robinson. According to Kane though, Robinson "had absolutely nothing to do with it" because Robinson's contribution — the Joker playing card used in *Batman* No. 1 — was added after Kane and Finger thought up the character. But Robinson claimed "the concept was mine," including both the playing card and the "outline of the persona and what should happen in the first story." They're both wrong. The Joker was Finger's idea, and I know because he stole it.

Kane and Robinson agree that Finger handed Kane a photograph of Conrad Veidt from the 1928 film adaptation of Victor Hugo's *The Man Who Laughs*. A clown-faced ad for a Coney Island attraction has received some credit too. But Finger kept his primary source a secret. The Joker's first appearance in *Batman* No. 1 begins with a death threat: "Tonight at precisely twelve o'clock midnight I will kill Henry Claridge."

> Henry Claridge, frantic with fear, calls the police.
> CLARIDGE: "You've got to protect me!"
> POLICE CHIEF: "Don't worry, Mr. Claridge."
> Time drags on — seconds minutes then the fatal hour twelve o'clock.
> CLARIDGE: "I'm still alive! I'm not dead! I'm safe! I'm SAAAAGH! Aaghh!"
> The Joker has fulfilled his threat. Claridge is dead!! Slowly the facial muscles pull the dead man's mouth into a repellent ghastly grin. The sign of death from the Joker!
> CHIEF: "It's — it's horrible!"
> OFFICER: "Grotesque! The Joker brings death to his victims with a smile!"

The Joker repeats the pattern a page later: "At ten o'clock that fiend will kill Jay Wilde!"

> The toll of time — the fatal hour!
> BONG! BONG!
> WILDE: "Ten! It's going to happen now! The clock is ticking my life away!"
> A strangled scream — death!
> JOKER: "Are you so happy that you smile for joy, eh? I'm glad I have brought you so much cheer!"

My son was ten the first time he flipped through my *Batman Chronicles* reprint, half the age of my students who looked equally disturbed. It struck a nerve in 1940 too. Kane's DC editors rescued the Joker from a deserved death to keep him as a recurring character. They'd never seen anything like him. Which is surprising, since his first joke was published a quarter century earlier:

> Cocantin had just noticed that Favraux held in his hands a yellow envelope similar to the one that contained Judex's earlier message.
>
> The banker unsealed it. Scanning every word, he read it aloud:
>
> *"If before the stroke of ten tonight, you don't relinquish half of your ill-gotten fortune to the Public Assistance, it will be too late. You will be punished mercilessly."*
>
> And it was signed: JUDEX!
>
> "The joke continues," emphasized Cocantin with a humorous smile.
>
> "It has lasted for too long," scolded the banker while raising his eyebrows.
>
> "Don't be upset, Monsieur Favraux," implored Cocantin. "... This sinister joke will soon collapse due to my efforts.... I reassure you, Monsieur. I will look after you!"
>
> ... The monumental clock on one of the room's panels displayed two minutes before ten o'clock.... Instinctively, his eyes sought the clock. The hands had almost reached the time foretold by Judex.... Fear shook his mortal frame....
>
> The clock struck ten o'clock. Favraux's face contracted in a hideous convulsion.... As a frightful moan escaped his throat, he collapsed. He had been struck down!
>
> Judex had kept his word!
>
> In the commotion, guests ran to Favraux's side.... The facial features of the gilded banker were frozen in a grotesque grimace of superhuman fright.

Swap a few names — "the Joker" and "Judex," "Favraux" and "Claridge" or "Wilde," "Cocantin" and the Police Chief — and the scene is *Batman* No. 1. Except it was written in 1916 when Bill Finger was two. It's by playwright Arthur Bernède from his novelization of Louis Feuillade's *Judex*.

After the success of *Les Vampires*, Feuillade kept shooting with the same cast. The effect is further dizzying, since it's Musidora again, not the titular hero, in the opening scene. Despite the name change, the female Fantômas Vep is back plotting more impersonations and seducing Santanas, the second Grand Vampire — only now he's some banker named Favraux. Philipe has been demoted to the hero's extraneous brother, but his comic sidekick is front and center as a bumbling proto-Clousseau detective. It's like watching the latest Joss Whedon production, waiting to see which *Buffy* or *Firefly* or *Dollhouse* actor is going to wander in next. Despite hiring Bernède to give the script continuity, Feuillade repeats lots of his Vampire tricks — like throwing a sack over a good guy's head so when he switches bodies and escapes the bad guys murder one of their own. Sadly, when Musidora's body washes ashore in the final episode, she's not reborn in Feuillade's next serial, *The New Mission of Judex* — so maybe it's just as well those prints are lost.

Judex — aka "The Mysterious Shadow," often cited as an influence on the cloaked and slouch-hatted Shadow who in turn influenced Batman — is the hero, a self-appointed "judge" taking revenge on a corrupt banker. He, like Griffith's masked avengers touring theaters across the Atlantic, defines his own justice. It turns out the banker's not really dead, and his daughter is just the sort of damsel a heroic blackmailer could settle down with, but it's Judex still dictating the rules. He's Napoleon's latest heir, claiming the cinematic throne a century after the dictator lost his.

When Finger supplied his boss with the Veidt photo, he was filling in details for "the joker" of Bernède's text. It's possible Jerry Robinson drew his playing card independently — stranger coincidences happen. It's a greater leap to think Robinson handed it to Finger first, triggering Finger's memory of the "joke" in *Judex*. Either way, Bernède's contribution outweighs all others. Kane's drawing even echoes Judex's hat and white face of the 1916 *Le Petit Parisien* illustration. The magazine published installments timed with the theatrical release of each weekly chapter. I have no idea if Bill Finger saw the film, but a translation of the novelization was available since 1918.

Finger may also have seen the American *Fantômas* serial Edward Sedgwick directed for the Fox Film Corporation in 1920. No prints remain, but a press book suggests that the remake copied *Judex* too:

Fantomas plans to kidnap James D. Harrington, millionaire and well-known citizen; his purpose being merely to annoy the police. He sends word to Dixon of his plan and gives him the further information that the kidnapping will occur "On the Stroke of Nine" on a certain night.... On the night the kidnapping is to take place the police surround Harrington's home. Detectives sit by his side in his big drawing room. Yet "On the Stroke of Nine" the lights go out suddenly. When they are turned on again only a sneering note is found in the chair occupied by Harrington. Harrington has disappeared. Fantomas laughs at the police.

The laugh is less literal than Bernède's "grotesque smile," but the Batman episode does include the circle of police Kane later draws in *Detective Comics*.

According to Robinson, Finger was a voracious reader "who spent lots of time doing research." Robinson also called him his "cultural mentor," describing him as "extremely well read" and a "student of pulps and radio drama" as well as "Dumas and Shakespeare." Bernède and Feuillade, avid researchers themselves, read Alexander Dumas too. Judex's destruction of Favraux's ill-gotten fortune as well as imprisoning him until he acknowledges his wrongdoing — that's the Cliff Notes version of *The Count of Monte Cristo*, the fate suffered by one of the three men who falsely imprisoned Dantès before he assumed the guise of the vengeance-seeking Count. But neither Dumas nor Feuillade originated Bernède's joker scene. The silent picture includes little of the banker and the detective's dialogue (neither of the "joke" references), and when Favraux collapses on screen, Feuillade supplies no close-up. The "grotesque grimace" exists only in Bernède's text.

Bernède figures in Batman's origin too. When Kane needed an explanation for his hero's "lone battle against the evil forces of society," Bill Finger inserted a pair of murdered parents and a vow of vengeance. "I swear by the spirits of my parents," cries the kneeling Bruce Wayne, "to avenge their death by spending my life warring on criminals." The young Judex kneels too, before his father's body, as his surviving mother demands the same vow: "your father was murdered by a crook named Favraux. Swear before him that you will avenge his death."

The Joker and Batman are both Judex — a character who teeters between vengeance-warped villainy and damsel-rescuing do-goodery. Batman and the Joker are both self-appointed judges spliced from the same superhuman DNA. One we uphold as a paragon of unwavering morality, the other as anarchic psychopath. Those sound like polar opposites, but the distance is thinner than a dime.

⚡ ⚡ ⚡

I don't know if Patrick Drum read any Batman comics as a kid. He may be unaware how his Scorpion adventures duplicate the superhero formula, right down to its morally ambiguous core.

Bill Finger read lots of pulps, but they didn't make him pull on a hood and act out any heroically criminal fantasies. Anti-comics crusader Fredric Wertham accused Finger and his cohorts of making their impressionable readers take "sadistic joy in seeing other people punished over and over again while you yourself remain immune." Wertham called that a Superman complex, but pulp fans were suffering worse superhuman influences before comic books existed.

On May 21, 1924, Dickie Loeb and Babe Leopold rented a car, picked up Dickie's fourteen-year-old cousin Bobby from school, and murdered him with a chisel in the front seat. After stopping for sandwiches, they stripped the body, disfigured it with acid, and hid it in a drainage pipe under a railroad track. When they got home, they burned their blood-spotted clothes and mailed the parents a ransom note. It was the perfect crime.

Dickie was nineteen, Babe twenty, but both had already completed undergraduate degrees and were enrolled in law schools. They were also voracious readers. Clarence Darrow, their defense attorney, detailed Dickie's literary tastes: "detective stories," each one "a story of crime," ones the state legislature had wisely "forbidden boys to read" for fear they would "produce criminal tendencies." Dickie "devoured" them. "He read them day after day ... and almost nothing else."

Darrow didn't list any titles, but Dickie probably snuck stacks of *Detective Story Magazine* past his governess. The Street and Smith pulp doubled from a bimonthly to a weekly the year he turned twelve. McCulley published his first Zorro serial in it when Dickie was fourteen. McCulley was a favorite with fans. His gentleman criminal the Black Star wears a cape and hood with an emblem on the forehead. So does his Thunderbolt. Darrow said Dickie's pulps "all show how smart the detective is, and where the criminal himself falls down." But the detectives chasing the Man in Purple, the Picaroon, the Gray Ghost, the Scarlet Fox — they never catch their man. Those noble vigilantes remain safely outside the law. The proto-Batmen are also all young men born into wealth who disguise their secret lives. So Dickie, the son of a corporate vice president, learned to play detective, "shadowing people on the street," as he fantasized "being the head of a band of criminals." "Early in his life," said Darrow, Dickie "conceived the idea that there could be a perfect crime," one he could himself "plan and accomplish."

His friend Babe was an impressionable reader too. He'd started speaking at four months and earned genius-level IQ scores. Darrow called him "a boy obsessed of learning," but one without an "emotional life." He makes him sound like a renegade android, "an intellectual machine going without balance and without a governor." Where Dickie transgressed through pulp fiction, "Babe took to philosophy." Instead of McCulley, Nietzsche started "obsessing" Babe at sixteen. Darrow called the übermensch doctrine "a species of insanity," one "holding that the intelligent man is beyond good and evil, that the laws for good and the laws for evil do not apply to those who approach the superman." Babe summed up Nietzsche the same way in a letter to Dickie: "In formulating a superman he is, on account of certain superior qualities inherent in him, exempted from the ordinary laws which govern ordinary men." A member of "the master class," says Nietzsche himself, "may act to all of lower rank . . . as he pleases." That includes murdering a fourteen-year-old neighbor as one "might kill a spider or a fly."

So Babe enlisted Dickie as a fellow superman. And Dickie accepted Babe as a perfect partner in crime. The two genres have one formula point in common: their heroes are "above the law." When Siegel and

Shuster merged *Beyond Good and Evil* with *Detective Story Magazine* in 1938, they came up with *Action Comics* No. 1. Loeb and Leopold only got *Life Plus 99 Years*, the title of Babe's autobiography. Prosecutors wanted to hear a death sentence, but Darrow wrote a modern law classic for his closing argument. It brought the judge to tears. I wouldn't have executed Leopold and Loeb either. Like Raskolnikov, they eventually saw the error of their irrational ways. Maybe Patrick Drum's life sentence will have a similar effect. All supermen belong behind the bars of comic book panels.

William Jennings Bryan liked Darrow's closing argument too. He quoted excerpts during the Scopes "Monkey" trial the following year. Bryan was prosecuting John Scopes for teaching the theory of evolution in a Tennessee high school, and Darrow was defending him. Scopes, a gym teacher subbing in science, used George William Hunter's school board–approved *Civil Biology*, a standard textbook since 1914, and one that shocks my students. "If the stock of domesticated animals can be improved," writes Hunter, "it is not unfair to ask if the health and vigor of the future generations of men and women on the earth might not be improved by applying to them the laws of selection." After describing families of "parasites" who spread "disease, immorality, and crime," he argues:

> If such people were lower animals, we would probably kill them off
> to prevent them from spreading. Humanity will not allow this, but
> we do have the remedy of separating the sexes in asylums or other
> places and in various ways preventing intermarriage and the possi-
> bilities of perpetuating such a low and degenerate race.

This was one of Bryan's main objections to evolution, a term he used interchangeably with eugenics: "Its only program for man is scientific breeding, a system under which a few supposedly superior intellects, self-appointed, would direct the mating and the movements of the mass of mankind — an impossible system!" Bryan links eugenics to Nietzsche, as Darrow had the year before, saying Nietzsche believed "evolution was working toward the superman." The claim is arguable, but the superman was "a damnable philosophy" to Bryan, a "flower that blooms on the stalk of evolution." To a Christian like Bryan, the superman was the Antichrist.

"Would the State be blameless," he asked, "if it permitted the universities under its control to be turned into training schools for murderers? When you get back to the root of this question, you will find that the Legislature not only had a right to protect the students from the evolutionary hypothesis, but was in duty bound to do so."

Darrow declined to make a closing argument, preventing Bryan from making his before the judge too, so their final debate played out in newspapers. Either way, Darrow was talking from both ends of his übermensch. "Loeb knew nothing of evolution or Nietzsche," he told the Associated Press. "It is probable he never heard of either. But because Leopold had read Nietzsche, does that prove that this philosophy or education was responsible for the act of two crazy boys?"

Perhaps Darrow's hypocrisy is an illustration of a superman obeying only his own idiosyncratic laws. What does a superlawyer care about consistency? Scopes's guilt was never contested, and the court fined him $100, a penalty later overturned on a technicality. It's a lighter punishment than Drum's life without parole or Raskolnikov's exile in Siberia. The Joker regularly breaks out of Arkham Asylum for the Criminally Insane, and last I checked Hannibal, Fantômas, and Gyges are all still at large too.

I don't think anyone has arrested Batman recently either. Though comics creator Howard Chaykin would like to. "Batman, at its core," Chaykin told his *Special Edition: NYC* audience in 2014,

> is about a guy that had a bad day when he was eight, and we've been paying for it ever since. He's a guy who, with his billions of dollars, instead of investing in the public sector and private sector, uses all of his million dollars to buy bondage outfits and really cool things to beat the shit out of people that he doesn't know but knows are bad because that's the way they look. Like Jews in Germany.

If the Nazi crack is too much of a stretch for you, consider some of the other ambiguously amoral law-breakers adventuring before superheroes made it to comics. While Darrow was attacking/defending Nietzsche, the Mussolini-inspired "super-criminal" Blackshirt joined the merry band of 1920s pulp vigilantes. Adolf Hitler's *Mein Kampf* was ascending the übermensch best-seller list in 1925 too.

But Germany didn't meet the übermensch's American cousin till World War II. A columnist for S.S.'s weekly newspaper, *Das Schwarze Korps*, panned Siegel and Shuster's two-page Superman adventure in *Look* magazine in 1940:

> Jerry looked about the world and saw things happening in the distance, some of which alarmed him. He heard of Germany's reawakening, of Italy's revival, in short of a resurgence of the manly virtues of Rome and Greece. "That's fine," thought Jerry, and decided to import the idea of manly virtue and spread them among young Americans. Thus was born this "Superman."

Look wasn't a comic book. It vied with *Life* for adult buyers, but Superman was already big in 1940. Poland was dead, France was dead, and England was the next victim. But in the comic strip, suddenly Superman leaps across German and Russian armies to scoop up Hitler and Stalin to deliver them as criminals to the World Court. It's a whimsical act of superhuman morality that only bad guys could complain about:

> Well, we really ought to ignore these fantasies of Jerry Israel Siegel, but there is a catch.... He cries "Strength! Courage! Justice!" to the noble yearnings of American children. Instead of using the chance to encourage really useful virtues, he sows hate, suspicion, evil, laziness, and criminality in their young hearts.... Woe to the American youth, who must live in such a poisoned atmosphere and don't even notice the poison they swallow daily.

Americans are still swallowing massive doses of that superhero morality, only now Nazi Germany isn't left to complain.

The scholar Ben Saunders reads superheroes in spiritual terms, lauding Superman as a "moral agent who acts always out of his commitment to 'the good'"—a good that is "loosely defined," "constantly shifting," and yet somehow "absolute." I agree that sounds like a good thing, evidence of the character's "moral beauty," but in practical terms, it means superheroes enact the morality of the moment, championing cultural prejudices as absolute truths. So to that degree the comic book Superman is indistinguishable from the Nazi superman. Both are agents of "the good."

For *Superman: Birthright*, the first reimaging of Superman for the twenty-first century, Mark Waid looked back to Krypton, a "people of accomplishment and great deeds," "a race of adventurers and explorers eager to plant their banner to mark the victory of their survival." Superman fulfills himself "by *embracing* that heritage." Yes, he becomes a symbol of "selfless heroism," but only "*by acting in his own self-interest*." Waid identifies the paradox, but not its implications. Superman plants his banner on Earth and claims it as a noble explorer whose self-interests happen to resemble heroism to us. He could as easily fulfill his need for greatness through noble acts of homicide. What if he decided his superior heritage required him to euthanize our lesser race? Whether heroic or villainous, supersanity is inherently inhuman.

Waid also scripted *Kingdom Come*, an Elseworld in which the children of superheroes and the children of supervillains are indistinguishable. They're all überkinder. When they roughhouse, they don't care about the collateral damage of the human bystanders running from their rain of rubble. Some of them may have started out as Dudes with Supermuscles, but they're all Gullivers now. Their favorite philosopher is Glaucon: "a man is just, not willingly or because he thinks that justice is any good to him individually, but of necessity, for wherever anyone thinks that he can safely be unjust, there he is unjust."

When it comes to humans, I might disagree. But the superhumans of Raskolnikov's extraordinary philosophy are a hypothetical species. Their goodness is an illusion, and attempts to emulate it are delusional. In the multiverse of fiction, superheroes and their sibling supervillains are made of identical DNA, and their villainy and do-goodery are products of the same impulse. They are all aliens from the planet Fantômas, using feeble humanity to satisfy their superhuman needs.

The Scarlet Pimpernel, 1934.

No Heroics was a one-season nonwonder in 2008, but it beats the 2011 *Green Lantern* that Warner Bros. execs fantasized would replace their climaxing Harry Potter franchise. I watched it on the same couch with my then ten-year-old son. Three exposition-bloated minutes in he mumbled: "This isn't very good."

But the writers (seven names in the credits, never a good sign) got one thing right. When Lantern drops onto his love interest's balcony, she sees through his disguise in seconds. And when he finally gets his kiss at the end, she first asks:

"Hal, can you take off the mask?"

That's rule one in the Superhero Guide to Love & Sex: expose yourself. A superhero's most intimate act is unmasking. Jane Austen could tell you that. Her romance formula is the secret heart pumping through comic books. It's also why marriage is Superman's oldest kryptonite. The double-edged romance plot originates in the roots of the genre (Spring-Heeled Jack, Scarlet Pimpernel, Zorro). It branches during the 30s to the monkishly celibate and the superhumanly sterile (the Shadow, Doc Savage, Hugo Danner) and then to those earthier heroes with indulging sweethearts (the Spider, the radio Shadow, the Domino Lady). And it's still the core of twenty-first-century superhero romance now.

A timid newspaper reporter pines for his dream girl Lois. Not Lois Lane. Lois Amster. She attended Glenville High School with Jerry Siegel in the early 30s. He was a reporter for their school paper. They never talked, much less dated. Lois was popular. Jerry wasn't. She remembered him as some strange kid who used to stare at her.

Instead of asking Lois or anyone else on a date, Jerry dreamed up Superman alone in his bedroom. Supposedly the idea hit him one summer night between junior and senior years. Come morning he had pages and pages of script to hand to his pal Joe, another rising Glenville senior, who worked through the next day sketching.

They both loved Superman, but when they graduated a year later, their flame died. They had been rejected by every publisher they'd offered themselves to. Like a spurned lover, Joe burned his artwork in the

THE SUPERHERO GUIDE
TO LOVE & SEX

I sat by myself on our couch watching the British sitcom *No Heroics.*
the first episode, the superhero Hotness brings a groupie up to his bac
elor pad as he brags about his days back at Superhero Academy:

> "People from all over the world go there, you know, when their pow-
> ers come on."
>
> "Oh?" Vicky purrs, nuzzling closer on the couch. "And when i:
> that?"
>
> "Depends," Hotness answers, nervous as her hands begin to wan
> der. "Mostly around puberty."
>
> "Which makes me think there's a definite connection betweer
> — she leans in —"superpowers and *sex.*"
>
> "Indeed," he squeaks. "They should call them ... sexapowers?"

Or is he saying "sex 'em powers"? Maybe "sexerpowers"? The acce
tricky. They argue whether he has to wear his costume in bed ("It's
pinchy in the ball area") and whether her bondage fantasy is accu
("The Tourniquet doesn't really do knots; he's more an evil virus
of guy"). Vicky's right though, there's a definite connection, but
matters most is what's under the costume, the one she wants Hotn
leave on. His real name is Alex, but she doesn't care.

ultimate break-up gesture. Jerry tried wooing Buck Rogers artist Russell Keaton next, but after flirting with the material for a few months, Keaton jilted him too. Jerry and Joe reunited, but newspapers kept rejecting their comic strip about a superpowered loner trying to have fun on an unfriendly planet. Editors called him immature.

The problem wasn't Superman. It was Clark Kent. The name appears in the scripts Jerry mailed Keaton, but not the character, not the mild-mannered weakling who would come to define comic book duality. Without Clark, Superman is a god slumming with his worshippers. He needs a comically human alter ego to ground him. I'm guessing Jerry didn't read much Jane Austen in high school, which is a shame because Austen, the queen of literary courtships, could have solved his problems sooner. Superman didn't understand romance, and that's what Clark is all about.

We'll get to Austen's superhero ur-plot in a moment, but first a brief visit to her final, unfinished novel, *Sanditon*, to understand how the heartstrings of a Clark Kent character work. Austen was more or less on her deathbed at the time, which explains why she was writing about invalids at a beach resort, and, more sadly, why she never finished. But the fragment includes one of literature's first Clark Kents, the convalescent and hypochondriac Arthur Parker.

Charlotte, Austen's last heroine, "had considerable curiosity to see Mr. Arthur Parker; and having fancied him a very puny, delicate-looking young man, materially the smallest of a not very robust family, was astonished to find him quite as tall as his brother and a great deal stouter, broad made and lusty, and with no other look of an invalid than a sodden complexion." That's a casting call for Christopher Reeve. Arthur only receives one scene (Austen's pen slipped from her fingers on page 73), but it has all the hallmarks of a Kryptonian posing as a weakling.

His first line is an apology for hogging the seat by the fire. "We should not have had one at home," said he, "but the sea air is always damp. I am not afraid of anything so much as damp." Charlotte is fortunate never to know whether air is damp or dry, as it has always some property that is wholesome and invigorating.

"I like the air too, as well as anybody can," replies Arthur. "I am very fond of standing at an open window when there is no wind. But, unluckily, a damp air does not like me. It gives me the rheumatism." He is also, he confesses, "very nervous," an obscure nineteenth-century condition extinct by the time Siegel was writing, or Clark would have suffered it too. "To say the truth, nerves are the worst part of my complaints in my opinion."

Charlotte recommends exercise. "Oh, I am very fond of exercise myself," he replies, "and I mean to walk a great deal while I am here, if the weather is temperate. I shall be out every morning before breakfast and take several turns upon the Terrace, and you will often see me at Trafalgar House." But does Arthur really call a walk to Trafalgar House much exercise? "Not as to mere distance, but the hill is so steep! Walking up that hill, in the middle of the day, would throw me into such a perspiration! You would see me all in a bath by the time I got there! I am very subject to perspiration, and there cannot be a surer sign of nervousness."

Adding to sweat and humidity, Arthur reveals his most feared form of liquid kryptonite. "What!" said he. "Do you venture upon two dishes of strong green tea in one evening? What nerves you must have! Now, if I were to swallow only one such dish, what do you think its effect would be upon me?" Keep him awake perhaps all night? "Oh, if that were all!" he exclaims. "The use of my right side is entirely taken away for several hours!"

Is Arthur duping Charlotte the way Clark dupes Lois? Hard to say. It is clear, however, that the man is masking deeper appetites. Although he pretends, "A large dish of rather weak cocoa every evening agrees with me better than anything," Charlotte observes the drink "came forth in a very fine, dark-coloured stream," prompting his sisters' outrage. "Arthur's somewhat conscious reply of 'Tis rather stronger than it should be tonight,' convinced her that Arthur was by no means so fond of being starved as they could desire or as he felt proper himself." Arthur has a similar weakness for liberally buttered toast, "seizing an odd moment for adding a great dab just before it went into his mouth." Wine also does him surprising good. "The more wine I drink — in moderation — the better I am."

Charlotte, demonstrating the sleuthing skills of a girl reporter, notes "Mr. Arthur Parker's enjoyments in invalidism," suspecting "him of adopting that line of life principally for the indulgence of an indolent temper, and to be determined on having no disorders but such as called for warm rooms and good nourishment." Laurel Ann Nattress thinks the twenty-year-old has been "cosseted" (presumably by his doting sisters) "into believing himself to be of delicate health." That's the interpretation Bryan Singer adopted for his 2006 *Superman Returns*. The five-year-old Jason, the Man of Steel's love child from his 1980 hookup with Lois in *Superman II*, appears to be an asthmatic runt. Until he throws a piano at the thug menacing his mom.

Was little Jason just jerking everyone around? Hard to say. But his old man certainly was. The best scene from Quentin Tarantino *Kill Bill* is David Carradine's Superman monologue:

> When Superman wakes up in the morning, he's Superman. His alter ego is Clark Kent. What Kent wears — the glasses, the business suit — that's the costume Superman wears to blend in with us. Clark Kent is how Superman views us. And what are the characteristics of Clark Kent? He's weak . . . he's unsure of himself . . . he's a coward. Clark Kent is Superman's critique on the whole human race.

Jules Feiffer said it first in 1965: Clark "is Superman's opinion of the rest of us, a pointed caricature." Austen is caricaturing us too, our laziness and self-serving foibles, but being also a devoted lover of the marriage plot, would she have left poor Arthur to stew in his rather weak brew of humanity? Lois eventually pulls the glasses off Clark. I suspect Charlotte would have done the same for her tall, broad, and lusty invalid.

But Lois doesn't exist in Siegel's early Superman scripts. That's why Superman's alter ego is just a name, not a fumbling sap pining for his love interest. Superman is nothing without Clark, and Clark is nothing without Miss Lane. That's when Jane Austen swoops in and saves the day. When Siegel revived his spurned Superman scripts with a large dish of rather strong romance, he was importing tropes from Jane's home planet.

It's wildly unlikely Siegel read *Sanditon*. I theoretically read *Emma* in college, and I have an increasingly thin memory of *Northanger Abby* from grad school, but I only picked up *Pride and Prejudice* after my daughter selected it from her A. P. English summer reading list. Siegel was nearing Arthur's age when he graduated from Glenville and so was not taking any advanced placement courses, but he still knew Austen. *Pride and Prejudice* is the Big Bang event of the romance genre, and it reverberated its way into Siegel's head via one of Austen's imitators.

The Scarlet Pimpernel isn't the first dual-identity hero tale, but it was the most immediate inspiration for Zorro and dozens of other pulp do-gooders. Siegel was a dedicated fan and reviewed one of Orczy's many sequels in his school paper. That's how Arthur Parker makes it to Cleveland. It's unlikely Orczy read Austen's unfinished novel either, but Arthur is Austen's final variation on her well-established theme, one Orczy continued to pluck. Take away the mild-mannered Sir Percy and the mild-mannered Clark Kent vanishes too.

The Scarlet Pimpernel is a romance, one that replays Austen's *Pride and Prejudice* formula. It's told from the perspective of its female protagonist, Marguerite, who, like Austen's Elizabeth, is blind to the true character of the novel's hero. Elizabeth thinks Mr. Darcy is an arrogant jerk. Marguerite thinks Sir Percy is a cowardly fool. Or they do for the first halves of their adventures, because after a pivotal middle scene (Mr. Darcy proposes, Marguerite confesses), the second halves are spent revealing Darcy's and Percy's secret heroism. Austen uses the word "disguise," Orczy prefers "mask," but both metaphors are removed.

Those two versions of Mr. Darcy triangulating Elizabeth evolved into the robust Superman and the indolent Clark. I suspect a robust Arthur would have removed his indolent mask too, but Charlotte's unfinished tale never reaches that or any other closure. Siegel left the strings of his marriage plot dangling too. And that's where the serially jilted Clark departs from his Austenite predecessors.

While Austen's ur-Clark was a love-challenged invalid with a sexual appetite disguised under the well-mannered niceties of early romance, the first "Superman" was Don Juan. Actually, he was Don Juan reincarnated, but the original Don Juan was a kind of superman too: a rapist half-brother of the spirit-summoning Faust whom Goethe alchemized into a proto-übermensch.

Austen wrote in the first decades of the nineteenth century. The playwriting monk Tirso de Molina gave birth to Juan, aka *The Playboy of Seville*, two hundred years earlier, and Juan's reincarnation was born one hundred years after Austen. He began as a dare to George Bernard Shaw to write a Don Juan play "in the philosophic sense." Shaw took that to mean a story about a man "who, though gifted enough to be exceptionally capable of distinguishing between good and evil, follows his own instincts without regard to the common statute" and so "finds himself in mortal conflict with existing institutions."

Thus John Tanner of *Man and Superman*. He's a sexual revolutionist promoting out-of-wedlock reproduction on a national level. "One fact must be faced resolutely, in spite of the shrieks of the romantic," declares the pamphlet-writing eugenicist. "There is no evidence that the best citizens are the offspring of congenial marriages," but rather "good results may be obtained from parents who would be extremely unsuitable companions," and therefore "mating such couples must clearly not involve marrying them." But, like the Fausts and Don Juans before him, Tanner's final act is a descent into hell, and for him, that's Marriage. Although the institution is a hindrance to the production of a superman, he submits to the Life Force in the form of the formidable Ann Whitefield and renounces "the romantic possibilities of an unknown future, for the cares of a household and a family."

Austen readers applauded. So did superhero fans. All the early caped crusaders are wanton monogamists who long to retire to their marriage beds and have romping good sex. Look at Burrage's Spring-Heeled Jack again. While a young aristocrat adventures as a costumed highwayman to recover his stolen inheritance, his choice of hotels for headquarters "led to an adventure which introduced him to his future wife." Upon first seeing Lucy, "a strange but almost indescribable thrill passed through his whole body." Minutes later he's plunging into a river to save her. After "the supreme satisfaction of seeing the rich glowing tint of life return to her pallid cheeks," he declares, "But come, let me carry you to the hotel.

The sooner you get out of those wet things the better" (a pickup line even Don Juan couldn't pull off). As soon as that inheritance is secured, the two marry, and Burrage assures us "few mortals enjoyed so much earthly happiness."

We've already traced the romantic curves of *The Scarlet Pimpernel*, but take a closer peek through the bedroom keyhole: Orczy's estranged couple only consummate their marriage after Marguerite removes her husband's "mask of somnolent indifference" to reveal "a man madly, blindly, passionately in love." While his identity remained disguised, their "separate suites of apartments" were "well divided from each other by the whole width of the house." Once unmasked, Sir Percy gladly carries her half a league: "his arms, still vigorous in spite of fatigue and suffering, closed round Marguerite's poor, weary body . . . as she lay, quiet and happy." That's the orgasmic closure Austen's death denied Charlotte. Lois Lane was denied it too, at least for her first half-century of foreplay.

The trick with superhero sex is seeing how long you can keep your costume on. Without a false identity to be removed, would Percy have had as much vigor? Would Marguerite's body have felt quite so happy afterward? There's a lot of earthly happiness behind a superhero's costume, and even more in its removal. Striptease is the machine of every mystery plot — which is to say every plot. Readers crave that perfect pace of not-too-much, not-too-little, that keeps them peeling back pages, both wanting and not wanting to reach the last stitch of cloth, the mask.

Frank L. Packard's 1917 collection *The Adventures of Jimmie Dale* exposed one of the first pulp superheroines: the Tocsin, an almost supernaturally omniscient mastermind and mistress-of-disguise, who sends her gentleman thief on Robin Hood missions. Packard twists the marriage-unmasking plot into nearly explicit foreplay, focusing on the slow unveiling of the Tocsin's bodily identity. Jimmie, aka the Gray Seal, agrees "to link hands with this unseen, mysterious accomplice . . . with an eagerness that was insatiable." As "the bond between them" intensifies, the Tocsin reveals herself in tantalizing increments.

Her fragrant, handwritten letters are delivered at first through proxies, and then dropped by her gloved hand from a limousine window, and finally thrust into his in an anonymous crowd. She visits his home when he is absent and leaves her discarded glove and ring in his car while he dines alone. Her voice is a fading laugh from a speeding car, then a whisper on his telephone, and then a living presence in the dark of his own den speaking "from her own lips!" Jimmie, "mad with the wildest, most passionate exhilaration he had ever known," "reached out for her, and thrilling at the touch, swept her toward him," shouting, "Your face — I must see your face!" But she, "her breath coming sharply in little gasps," defers the climax, while stating the narrative contract: "some day, I promise you now, you shall have your reward."

That unmasking is fulfilled in the concluding novella of the twelve-story sequence. After "years of longing," Jimmie prepares to "see her for the first time face to face" with "no more barriers between them." But when "the supreme moment of his life" arrives and "at last they should be together," she is disguised as an elderly beggar. As "she was leading him into" her private room, the "half sob in [her voice] thrilled him with its promise," and the "blood was beating in hammer blows at his temples." Jimmie is "lost in mad ecstasy" and "a mighty sense of . . . virility" as he rains "kisses upon her face." "She did not struggle. The warm, rich lips were yielding to his. . . . She was his — his!"

That climax is accompanied by the revelation of her real name and life story, and the final, literal unmasking occurs when the thriller plot is completed and both of their crime-fighting alter egos are retired:

> The cape and hood had fallen from her, and with the hood had fallen the grey-streaked [wig] — and now as she smiled at him it was from a face that was very beautiful and very brave and very full of tenderness.
>
> And he held her there — and neither spoke.

The moment is postcoital in its intimacy, a mute echo of *Pride and Prejudice*'s equally silent climax: "Elizabeth was too much embarrassed to say a word" as her now fully unmasked Mr. Darcy declared his affection, though he says "but one word from you will silence me on this subject forever." The teasing Miss Austen denies us Elizabeth's response, lapsing into uncharacteristic paraphrase during the key dialogue, as if direct statements of love are finally just too intimate an intercourse to reveal.

Austen does give us twenty pages of falling action though, far more than Packard. Instead of sharing a cigarette, his now metaphorically naked lovers watch the abandoned Grey Seal sanctuary burn to the ground:

> The Sanctuary wall bulged farther outward, seemed to hang an instant hesitant in mid-air — and fell with a mighty crash.
>
> The Gray Seal was dead!

And with the turn of that final page, Jimmie is free to follow Shaw's Don Juan superman into the superhero marriage bed.

⚡ ⚡ ⚡

Several slang dictionaries list "jimmy" as a term for penis, but its etymological origins are vague. Both Ice-T and the Beastie Boys were rapping about their jimmies in 1988, but I don't know if Packard's readers saw the double meaning. I'm pretty sure Johnston McCulley did. He expanded the superhero eroticism two years later:

> The moment I donned cloak and mask ... my body straightened, new blood seemed to course through my veins, my voice grew strong and firm, fire came to me! And the moment I removed cloak and mask I was the languid Don Diego again.

That's my favorite passage from *The Mark of Zorro*. It's also the most thinly veiled descriptions of an erection I've ever read. For McCulley's hero, a mask is more than a prophylactic postponing intimacy. It's a fetish. It literally makes him hard. Without it, he's limp.

McCulley tells us Zorro is motivated by government persecution of monks and Natives, but he spends more time seducing his well-born wife:

> And suddenly she was awakened by a touch on her arm, and sat up quickly, and then would have screamed except that a hand was crushed against her lips to prevent her. Before her stood a man whose body was enveloped in a long cloak, and whose face was covered with a black mask so that she could see nothing of his features except his glittering eyes.

The indolent Don Diego bores Senorita Lolita, but Zorro's mask titillates her. Even its partial removal is a sexual act: "He grasped one of her hands, and before she guessed his intention, had bent forward, raised the bottom of his mask, and pressed his lips to its pink, moist palm."

The mask and the marriage bed were already wedded, but McCulley takes the striptease further. Zorro "tore off his mask" only after he gets Lolita to reveal "her true heart" and agree to "have offspring." Although Lolita "would rather have you Senor Zorro than the old Don Diego," she now loves "both of them." The seduction complete, Don Diego can retire both his mask and his "languid ways." People "will say marriage made a man of me!" That's the implied but endlessly postponed climax of the Lois-Clark-Superman love triangle too.

If this sounds quaintly old-fashioned, the same plot still turns today's superheroes. Alan Moore makes Don Diego's languid impotence explicit in *Watchmen*. Daniel Dreiberg can't keep an erection ("Oh Laurie, I'm so sorry, it isn't you, it's just . . .") until he's dressed as Nite Owl ("Did the costumes make it good?"). Or in the 2010 film *Kick-Ass* (a departure from Mark Millar and John Romita Jr.'s 2008 comic book), mild-mannered Dave can't get the girl. Why? Because she thinks he's gay. Fairbanks played the effeminate Don Diego to similar effect. Katie, however, thinks this new superhero Kick-Ass is pretty damn sexy. Where does Dave reveal himself to her? Her bedroom. What happens immediately afterward? The obvious. In fact, Katie can't keep her hands off Dave now, and next thing she's "totally fucking his brains out" in an alley. McCulley might have blushed at the R-rated sequence, but his Lolita had similar adventures in mind for her boy wonder. Like languid Don Diego, Dave and Dan need their masks to get the girl. In these tales of hypermasculinity, being impotent and being gay are the same thing. The more extreme the dual-identity contrast, the more traditionally manly the superhero appears.

The potent offspring of the Gray Seal and Zorro, all of them third-generation John Tanners and Scarlet Pimpernels, multiplied by the dozen in the 20s and 30s, reproducing the superhero's sexual narrative with them. Graham Montague Jeffries, writing under his own alter ego Bruce Graeme, duplicates the Gray Seal foreplay formula in his 1925 *Blackshirt*, placing another gentleman thief under the flirtatious but reforming

control of a mysterious woman. When she first calls to reveal her knowledge of Blackshirt's secret identity, hers is

> a voice which he would have had his Ideal Woman possess, for,
> like every other man, he sometimes dreamed of a mythical and
> absolutely impossible woman who was his conception of a perfect
> wife. He began to regret the intervening distance between the two
> receivers.

That distance is teasingly maintained until the last chapter, appropri-
ately titled "The Heart of Blackshirt," in which the united couple hide
together, listening to nearby ballroom music

> penetrating round the palms, sighing softly, crying of gipsy camps,
> of trickling water, of moonlight nights, of passion, and love of
> romance.
>
> Even into the hearts of these two the music entered so that they
> stirred at last, and Bobbie moved her head slightly, looking up at
> him.
>
> The movement intoxicated him. Gathering her still more closely
> to him, he bent his head and pressed his lips against hers. Hand in
> hand at last they opened the gates of paradise.

The apparent sexual metaphor refers to the subsequent verbal intercourse in which Bobbie reveals that she is Blackshirt's mysterious "Lady
of the 'Phone.'" After she unmasks herself and both are naked to each
other, "there was only silence, no sound of talking, for the two hidden
there had their lips sealed." The final phrase combines the imagery of a
kiss with the keeping of a secret, the intimacy of two dual-identity characters retiring from the adventure of their own courtship. Once again,
their new domesticity is a secret closed to us. Jane Austen would be
titillated.

⚡ ⚡ ⚡

So the mask is the wedding veil waiting to be stripped off. It's both a teasing fetish and a prophylactic against intimacy. It produces sexual tension
and virility despite, or perhaps by, postponing closure. Unmasking is the

climax that ends the story. After achieving narrative orgasm, most of the pre-Depression pulp crowd hung up their capes and retired into domestic oblivion.

Or tried to, until their readers and publishers and writers demanded sequels. But once you've put down the marriage plot, it's hard to get it up again. DC nixed Batwoman's proposal to her lesbian lover in 2013, not for fear of gay marriage controversy (Marvel's Northstar jumped that shark the year before), but because, DC copublisher Dick Didio explained, "Heroes shouldn't have happy personal lives. They are committed to . . . defending others at the sacrifice of their own personal interests." It's sweet that Didio imagines all marriages are happy marriages, but he was more concerned about the happiness of his writing staff. Marriage is death. Early superheroes invented a utility belt's worth of prophylactics to avoid it, and all of them are still in use:

1. Poker Night.

Yes, darling, we're married now, but I still have my manly pastimes. The Scarlet Pimpernel kept it up for decades. Ditto for Blackshirt. One problem though. With no romantic subplot, the hero is domesticated, all that manly excess bunched neatly into his briefs. For the Night Wind that means promising his new bride to stop breaking the arms of police officers who foolishly get in his way. By the second sequel, the speedster superman was barely using any of his mutant powers, and his series quietly petered away. Domestication has proven equally disastrous for contemporary heroes. The mid-90s *Lois & Clark: The New Adventures of Superman* enjoyed stellar ratings, right up to the wedding episode, after which viewership nose-dived and the show was canceled. Marriage is kryptonite. Orczy and Jeffries had to switch to other family members (sons and ancestors) to keep their plots up.

2. Dial M.

If the Mrs. is holding back your hero, kill her. Thanks so much, Louis Joseph Vance, for introducing this heartless trope in the first of your seven *Lone Wolf* sequels. Though his 1914 gentleman thief had happily settled down with the law enforcement agent who lovingly reformed him, Vance dispatches her between volumes, mentioning her death in passing chapter one dialogue. When Hollywood adapted Robert Ludlum's *Bourne Identity* sequel in 2004, they made sure we witnessed the girlfriend's death — though Ludlum, in chivalrous contrast, only has her kidnapped and, in the third novel, sends her off to relatives. Death is a grim choice, but one that acknowledges narrative logic. To marry, the superhero has to unmask and retire, and so ending that retirement also ends the marriage. Happily ever after is also a hard place to scrape up conflict. In 1973, when Marvel could no longer write around Spider-Man's eight years of romantic contentment, they shoved his girlfriend off a bridge. The Silver Age died with a SNAP! of Gwen Stacy's too-happy neck.

3. Groundhog Day.

Marriage? What marriage? Johnston McCulley is responsible for this first superhero reboot. When Douglas Fairbanks turned an obscure vigilante hero into an international icon, McCulley ignored the ending of his own novel. Zorro did not unmask, he did not retire, and he certainly didn't run off and get married. The solution remains annoyingly common. After two decades of marital bliss between Peter Parker and Mary Jane, Marvel signed a deal with Mephisto and rebooted Spider-Man in 2010. Like Zorro, Peter had also unmasked publicly, an event now erased from the minds of all onlookers (but not, alas, all readers). The comic book Lois and Clark, who married (like their short-lived TV counterparts) in 1996, suffered the same fate when DC rebooted their entire romantically challenged universe in 2011. The idea of the universe-wide do-over came from the writing staff's frustration with the Lane-Kent status quo and how its wholesome dullness prevented them from cooking up Superman flings. However you handle it, marriage is hell on a writer. Which is why the last solution is my favorite:

4. Perpetual Foreplay.

Packard ended his first Gray Seal collection with an implied bang. His proto-Batman waltzes off-stage with his superheroine girlfriend, unmasked nuptials and eugenic über-children to follow. When bad guys and good sales returned the hero to duty in 1919, the door to their bedroom slammed shut. Since the Gray Seal's adventures were motivated not by revenge or altruism but by superheroic lust for his bride-to-be,

Packard needed to stretch out their romance plot. His four sequels offer increasingly frustrating reasons why the lovers must defer their wedding climax.

Awkward as it sounds, Packard's approach became the strategy of choice among 30s pulp writers facing the titillating prospect of unlimited sequels. Starting in 1933, *The Spider* magazine published a novella every month for a decade. Wealthy socialite Richard Wentworth fights crime as a costumed vigilante while also courting (and yet putting off) fiancée Nita Van Sloan. Norvell Page, writing under the house name Grant Stockbridge, tells us Wentworth must "sacrifice his hopes of personal happiness" because "the *Spider* could never marry," could never "take on the responsibilities of wife and children" while continuing his crime-fighting mission. Fortunately, Nita, like the Gray Seal's would-be wife, is endlessly patient.

When Edward Hale Bierstadt adapted William Gibson's *The Shadow* for radio, he decided the lonely-hearted hero could use a fiancée too. The 1937 premier introduces Margo Lane sipping coffee in Lamont Cranston's private library, as she begs him to end his crime-fighting career. He'd promised he would five years ago when their courtship began, but Lamont, like Richard, feels "there is still so much to do" before he can settle down and unmask. "No, Margo," he explains, "no one must know, no one but you." Margo, the ever dutiful if ever jilted helpmate, agrees. But these women aren't dupes. They keep their own keys to their boyfriends' bat caves. Nita is the Spider's "best alley in the battle against crime," "the one woman in the world who knew his secrets." Lamont calls the good accomplished by the Shadow "our activities." Without Margo's legwork, half of his radio plots would stumble. But what other shared "activities" are these couples up to?

Page seems straightforward enough: "Greatly they loved." Nita and Richard (would you believe she calls him "Dick"?) share "pleasurable moments together," though of course "all too brief." How pleasurable? Page never pens a sex scene, but Nita has access to his bedroom when she leaves him notes while he's sleeping off a night of adventuring. As far as the Shadow, Alan Moore's original Nite Owl says it best in *Watchmen*: "I'd never been entirely sure what Lamont Cranston was up to with

Margo Lane, but I'd bet it wasn't near as innocent and wholesome as Clark Kent's relationship with her namesake Lois.'"

Since unmasking is the climax of superhero romance, these lovers already know each other in every sense. Their marriage plots never technically close, but readers knew what was happening between the covers. Sex and marriage were no longer wedded. This is why later comic book critics decided Batman and Robin were gay. Frederic Wertham noticed sidekicks play the same role as fiancées: "Like the girls in other stories, Robin is sometimes held captive by the villains and Batman has to give in or 'Robin gets killed.'" Bruce and his boy ward enjoy the same unmasked and therefore intimate relationship as the pulp couples who preceded them.

Despite the dynamic intimacy, Kane probably intended his duo to be celibate though, especially since celibacy became the biggest superpower of 30s heroes.

When Avon reissued Philip Wylie's 1930 novel *Gladiator*, they wanted to seduce a new romance market. Hugo, the bare-chested hero, gazes out from his paperback cover. Five women's heads — their eyes adoring, their smiles smitten — circle him. The header promises a lusty life of an uninhibited superman. The sales team wasn't lying: "He undressed her. He whispered halting, passionate phrases. He asked her if she was afraid and let himself be laughed away from his own conscience. Then he took her and loved her." After Hugo loses his virginity to Anna in high school, more sex follows with Iris in college: "She wore only a translucent kimono of pale-colored silk. She taught him a great many things that night."

The "superman" on the cover isn't a lie either. In addition to his apparently superhuman sexual prowess, Hugo can run "like an express train," jump "forty feet in the air," and is "like a man made out of iron." Jerry Siegel reviewed the novel in the second issue of his fanzine, months before drafting his first superman story. The similarities were obvious enough that Wylie later threatened to sue DC. There's no question of influence, but perhaps Wylie also recognized how Siegel had altered and in some ways improved his creation. By keeping Superman celibate, he stripped Hugo of his worst curse and turned a tragedy into a leotarded triumph.

Despite all that lusty lack of inhibition, Hugo is a loner. His sexual adventures only increase his isolation because his relationships inevitably fail. His fifth and final romance ends in screams of terror. One moment his boss's wife is telling him, "Sit closer to me then, Hugo," the next, "Don't touch me!" He killed a charging bull on the page between. Women, like all humans, are repulsed by his abnormal powers. Siegel solves Hugo's dating dilemma by giving his hero two identities — one human, one garishly superhuman — and removing him from the emotional battlefield of the romance plot. Siegel's Superman wants his isolation. Wylie's is tortured by it.

If I were Wylie, I'd be annoyed by Siegel's solution. Upending the marriage plot (Hugo dies alone on the final page) is Wylie's biggest contribution to superheroes, bigger even than that list of powers Siegel lifted. Before Hugo, a hero knew to be transformed by love. He unmasked, married, and retired, his adventures replaced by domestic tranquility (until the sequel). O. Henry was the first to reverse that plot expectation. His Jimmy Valentine abandoned his safe-cracking identity for the love of a smallville girl, but, like Hugo, his powers get in the way. He saves a child from suffocating in a bank vault but loses his love as a result.

Thwarted marriage was a twist ending in 1902. By 1930, matrimony was on its deathbed. Wylie killed it when he let Hugo romp freely across the sexual landscape. Hugo and Anna "loved each other violently and incessantly and with no other evil consequence than to invite the open 'humphs' of village gossips and to involve him in several serious talks with her father." Instead of marrying, the two grow exhausted and even bored with each other, and their "excesses," and are relieved when they separate. They had loved "too much."

So Wylie's tale of sexual awakening has a cautionary edge. Or it does if your mad scientist father drugged your pregnant mother's cordial with opiate in order to inject a hypodermic syringe of superserum into her swollen abdomen. Hugo's superheroic conception was a date rape. That was too much for comic Joe E. Brown when he starred in the 1938 adaptation of Wylie's novel. Appearing the August after *Action Comics* No. 1's

June cover date, the film version of Hugo receives his superman injection as a consenting adult. His happy ending means losing his powers (the serum wears off during — oh no! — a wrestling match with Man Mountain Dean) and winning the heart of a coed and an adopted son. If Iris still has that translucent kimono, she slips it on after the credits.

The shift away from marriage plot closure is partly an effect of serialization, a form that whittles Aristotle's three-part dramatic structure down to a quick opening and a never-ending middle. Serials don't end — they just get canceled. But chapter six also offers a cultural explanation for the superhero's anticlimax. Eugenics was in decline. In 1928, Frederick Griffith's DNA-revealing experiments pointed the study of heredity in a new and scientifically grounded direction. By 1935, the Rockefeller Foundation and the Carnegie Institute canceled all their eugenics funding. After the rise of fascism, the promise of a master race of ruling supermen overthrowing democracy no longer looked like such a great idea.

Superheroes had to stop reproducing too. Supercelibacy became part of the job description, the newest variation on the self-sacrificing curse of superhumanly blessed heroes. Take Doc Savage: "'Gosh! What Doc is passing up!' he ejaculated." So says Doc's buddy Monk after a kiss from Princess Monja. Monk just broke some bad news to the ravishing young Mayan gal: "There won't be any women in Doc's life. If there was, you'd be the one. Doc has come nearer falling for you than for any other girl. And some pippins have tried to snare Doc."

That's the premier issue of *Doc Savage Magazine*, March 1933, so the only crisp tart apple we've seen is the daughter of King Chaac, sovereign of a lost tribe of ancient Mayans conveniently hidden in the Central American jungles. They're the "highest class" Mayans too, none of those "low specimen half-breeds" Doc and the boys tangled with on the way down. Lester Dent, hacking out his weekly 60,000 words under the Street and Smith house name Kenneth Robeson, typed this description: "The exquisite fineness of her beauty was like the work of some masterly craftsman in gold." Which sounds like a perfect match for Savage, "a man sculpted in hard bronze," but the chisel-crossed nuptials are not to be.

A sentence after revealing how "the attractive Princess" is "greatly taken with the handsome Doc," Dent douses the romance. Doc "had long ago made up his mind that women were to play no part in his career. Anyway, he was not a nature to easily lend itself to domestication." But it's not an easy choice for the untamable Savage. This is self-sacrifice, not an arrested case of prepubescent indifference. He explains it better to the King (knowing the Princess is in earshot): "I would like to remain — always.... But there is the work to which my life and the lives of my friends are dedicated. We must carry on, regardless of personal desire."

Doc and his buddies fought shoulder to shoulder in Great War trenches and now get their excitement hopping around the globe punishing evildoers. It requires some serious testosterone bonding, so no girls in the clubhouse: "They were not interested in women, these supreme adventurers." Monk, by the way, stands for monkey, not a Catholic priest who takes a vow of celibacy and lives with men in a secluded fortress. Not that Dent wants readers to imagine these homosocial men are gay. Everyone but Doc openly ogles Monja, and he's asexual. His father "made" him (no mom involved) into a "superman" (Dent uses the word more than once) through mental and physical conditioning. To continue his education, he sneaks off to his "Fortress of Solitude" in the Arctic (this is before Superman took up residency) for "periods of concentration . . . long and intense." For all the male camaraderie, Savage is the ultimate loner. Even the boys don't know his Solitude's location.

That's the only secret Doc keeps from them. Which is why it's so easy for Dent to discard the romance plot. Doc Savage, unlike the legion of masked do-gooders his pulps fought shoulder to shoulder with in the newsstand trenches, doesn't have an alias and secret identity. Savage is his last name, and he has at least one doctorate. His first name is "Clark," but there's no costume for any Lois to peel off. No mask, no sexual tension for the reader, no sexual interest for the hero. It's not even a celibacy plot, which is just the marriage plot in drag. In *Doc Savage*, sex doesn't exist.

Street and Smith's first Depression-era blockbuster, *The Shadow Magazine*, employed a similar romance-busting strategy. The character began as a generic narrator for radio crime stories in 1930, but listeners fell for him and his iconic laugh. So the publisher used his voice for their romance stories too. That didn't last, but a year later his magazine, the first single-character pulp in over a decade, was outselling everything else. The Shadow keeps his identity a secret not only from the public, the police, and his network of dedicated agents, but readers too. No one (including, I suspect, the writer Gibson) has any idea who that guy slipping in and out of the shadows really is. We're led to believe he's wealthy socialite Lamont Cranston, but then Gibson yanks that mask away to reveal another. The Shadow was only pretending to be Lamont while the real Lamont was abroad!

In terms of a romance plot, changing your secret identity is the same as not having one — and so the Shadow can't have a love interest. Gibson draws from a reservoir of secret identity do-gooders, but he is the most influential writer to bar his masked superhero from dipping his toe in the dating pool. Before Margo Lane could sneak into the radio serial, Gibson first had to settle on Lamont as his hero's permanent alter ego. Lois pursuing Superman works because we're in on the joke. In *The Shadow*, it's the reader who's jilted each month. We keep reaching for that kimono-like cloak, but the Shadow always slips away before exposed.

Instead of the well-mannered niceties of a Jane Austen striptease, the superhero veered toward actual striptease. Though even for soft-core it was pretty tame stuff:

> A nightgown of sheerest, green silk was but scant concealment for her gorgeous figure. A chastely-rounded body and a slender waist served to accentuate the seductive softness of her hips and sloping contours of her slim thighs, while skin like the bloom on a peach glowed rosily in the reflected sunlight.

Or better still:

> With a feeling of naughtiness, she slipped into a pair of black-lace panties. Then, sheerest hose for her shapely legs, black velvet slippers for the dainty feet.

It's 1936 and we're flipping the pulp-grade pages of *Saucy Romantic Adventures*. Our heroine, a lady thief and another proto-Batman, is Ellen Patrick, aka the Domino Lady. She's going to punish those crooked politicians who murdered her father. Which apparently requires a great deal of bathing and napping and dressing and undressing, but no descriptions of genitalia, primary or secondary. The closest we get to a sex scene is:

"An hour later, Ellen left Raythorne's cabin."

Five stories appear in *Saucy*, and a sixth in the still milder *Mystery Adventure Magazine*. It's a short run, even by pulp standards, all credited to Lars Anderson, an untraceable pseudonym. Jim Steranko illustrated a collection of the original stories, plus a seventh of his own, "Aroused, the Domino Lady." Jim is saucier than Lars:

> Only the tops of Ellen's thighs were covered by the kimono. When she spun and kicked it was shockingly apparent that she wore no underwear and that her flesh was the color of pale alabaster in the secret slopes and valleys above her tanned legs.

"Domino," to be clear, is a description of Ellen's mask, the style sported by Robin and the Lone Ranger, not a variation on "dominatrix," the S&M term appropriated from Latin in the 60s. Ellen is no dominator. She's more likely to get herself into a compromising corner. Though, despite all that sloping and peach-blooming sensuality, she doesn't end up getting much.

The Domino Lady is one of the few Depression-era superheroines, debuting in 1936 with the Phantom, Ka-Zar, and the Green Hornet. Though not as abstinent as Doc Savage and Clark Kent, she has less in common with 30s mystery men who share their bat caves with "fiancées" or 40s comic book superheroes with their ambiguous "wards." Ellen is another loner. She likes foreplay, but always escapes before the climax. Where her male predecessors settled into their marriage plots, the Domino Lady, like Doc Savage, rejects happiness: "the amorous little adventuress had denied the love she craved with all her heart. To her affection and marriage were things to avoid, shun." Like Batman, Ellen's Daddy-avenging mission is all that gets her off.

It also helps not to have a recurring love interest. No Lois Lane is trying to peek under her mask and/or kimono every month. And no Margo Lane or Nita Van Sloan is cooking her breakfast. Ellen may spend an hour in Mr. Raythorne's cabin, but she climbs into her own bed alone at the end of her adventures. Raythone is just a one-story fling and so no threat to her secret identity. A month later the Domino Lady is saving another equally eligible bachelor from certain death, relieved afterward when the so-called detective remains clueless: "Ellen Patrick laughed throatily as she went to his open arms." Only the reader is in on the joke, because no one else sees her naked.

Her thrills, like the reader's, are vicarious. She specializes in stealing "compromising letters" from blackmailers, the plot engine of half her tales. The "indiscrete" content is never spoken, just Ellen's promise "that precious husband of yours will never find out." She likes secrets. She never reveals her own, and she never reveals any of the friends' she saves. It makes her an accessory after the fact, each adventure a retroactive ménage à trois. Plus there's the thrill of the adventure. In fact, forget Daddy. What really gets Ellen going is the danger, the threat of being caught and unmasked: "Her heart was thumping with the acceleration of the chase, the knowledge that here was new, exciting adventure in the making! It was her life, her greatest thrill of living!"

If unmasking is the deepest intimacy, a forced unmasking is rape. Anderson has Ellen flirt with that fantasized danger every issue. Her adversaries arouse rather than repel her. One blackmailer "was the type who could stir her soul to the depths and arouse the latent passions of her affectionate nature." When cornered for the first time in her career, her mask about to be torn away, "Ellen was thrilling as she had never thrilled before." If that orgasmic metaphor is too subtle for you: "Something totally primitive had awakened in her innermost being, she thrilled to the core!"

But these are fantasies under Ellen's control. Anderson's action sequences always turn on the Domino Lady's ability to remain "cool as a cucumber," "cool as winter breeze." Unlike Zorro's autoerotic costume, the Domino Lady protects Ellen from her own arousal: "hot blood in her veins turned to a gelid stream of ice as Ellen stared through the mask."

Virile men are her biggest threat, not as potential rapists but as lovers to whom she could surrender herself, give into the affection she's "starved" for. Ellen may love a "gaze penetrating to the very center of her being," but it's her own "hungry longings" she battles. The men are interchangeable, not the "compelling desire" she holds out against. Winning for the Domino Lady means no happy endings.

The fifth story concludes both her vengeance plot and her run in *Saucy*. Those dastardly politicians and their KKK brethren are brought to ruin for murdering her father. But a month later, Anderson reboots his daddy's girl in *Mystery Adventure*, and those vague and omnipresent villains are still at large. A superhero's mission is never ending. Or maybe the moral is: good girls don't unmask. It's a bizarrely sexualized version of the celibacy plot. In the end Ellen climbs into bed alone again, still anticipating the romance she defers, still only "vaguely cognizant of the emptiness of her lonely existence."

Though a soft-core superheroine never climaxes, the same can't be said of her readers. *Saucy* wasn't the only pulp magazine specializing in male voyeurism. According to a 1933 report in *Time*, Harry Donenfeld's line of "girlie" pulp magazines "consist of sleazy stories, drawings and 'art study' photographs of undressed females." This was four years before the DC cofounder released *Detective Comics* No. 1. Donenfeld was a dual-identity publisher. Children's market by day, soft-porn by night. This is the publishing world that produced the first comic book superhero.

Donenfeld launched his first magazine in 1929. *Juicy Tales*, retitled *Joy Stories*, was standard Depression-era soft-porn. PG-13 by contemporary standards, but titillating enough to keep Donenfeld in revenue. Three years later, he was buying out competitors and adding *Pep*, *Spicy Stories*, and *La Paree* to his harem. He favored *Spicy* and spent the next few years expanding the line: *Spicy Mysteries Stories*, *Spicy-Adventures Stories*, *Spicy Detective Stories*, *Spicy Western Stories*.

In addition to "art studies," Donenfeld's magazines included multipage comic strips of scantily clad heroines and, in the case of Margaret Sanger's *Birth Control Review*, illegally transported condoms (Sanger was also an aunt of Wonder Woman creator William Marston's polygamously bisexual lover, but that's another tale). Adolphe Barreaux's "Sally the Sleuth" and Max Plaisted's jungle adventurer "Diana Daw" premiered in 1934, the year future DC partner Maxwell Gaines released *Famous Funnies*, the first book of comic strip reprints in what would define the standard comic book format. The third *Spicy* strip, Watt Dell Lovett's "The Astounding Adventures of Olga Messmer, the Girl with the X-Ray Eyes," debuted in 1937, five months after *Detective Comics* and less than a year before *Action Comics*. Olga, who like Superman also sports superhuman strength, is the first superhuman heroine in comic strip form. She had a tendency to shred her clothes like the Incredible Hulk.

Were Superman creators Jerry Siegel and Joe Shuster fans of Olga? Hard to know, but according to comics historian Gerard Jones, the two young men from Cleveland pitched Superman as a soft-porn strip to one of Donenfeld's editors. *Super-Detective* (not all of his pulps were porn) would have been a better home for the future Man of Steel, but the boys probably had *Spicy Detective* in mind. Olga already had *Spicy Mystery* for herself. The editor said no, so it would be another twenty years before Joe, partly blind and fully broke, would debut in porn through a publisher below even Donenfeld's standards (the 1954 *Nights of Horror* was typeset on a basement typewriter). In the 30s Donenfeld was busy bankrupting his business partner and buying out Detective Comics, Inc. Comic books, like pulp porn, were just a way to steal a quick buck.

Donenfeld didn't hire Siegel and Shuster. They'd already worked their way onto the DC bankroll with one- and two-page strips of a non-*Spicy* variety. When *Action Comics* launched Superman, Donenfeld's pulp fiefdom transformed into a multimedia empire. Suddenly a children's market titan, Donenfeld dumped his soft-porns to protect DC's wholesome image. But it was a sleight-of-hand. The discontinued *Spicies* reappeared with Donenfeld's wife as one of the newly independent company's co-owners.

Not long before Donenfeld left publishing in the early 60s, one of his companies started distributing another promising magazine, *Playboy*. Its artists included Golden Age legend Jack Cole, best remembered for the thankfully nonpornographic Plastic Man. Donenfeld also started distributing a much less promising comic book line that would become DC's biggest rival: Marvel, a company boasting an equally pornographic history. Publisher Martin Goodman began more tamely than his future competitor, releasing his first magazine, *Western Supernovel Magazine*, in 1933 while Donenfeld was expanding *Spicy*. Goodman made up the distance in the 50s with his own line of men's adventure magazines that evolved into porn by the 60s and 70s. One included the comic strip "The Adventures of Pussycat," a spoof more lascivious than "Sally the Sleuth." Stan Lee reinvented the sometimes topless secret agent as *Stripperella* for Spike TV in 2003.

Did the pornographic underbelly of the comic book industry seep into its tales of unitarded superheroes? Probably. Some of today's comics would make Donenfeld blush. They haven't been targeted at children for decades. Wonder Woman's creator William Moulton Marston was a bondage-enthusiast, and more than one Phantom Lady of the 50s exploited that Amazonian allure. By the 90s, Wonder Woman's miniskirt would be reduced to a thong. Bill Everett's Sub-Mariner premiered in nothing but briefs in 1939, and Shuster's Superman is essentially as naked, his skintight shirt and leggings discernable only by color. These are bodies bulging to complete their striptease.

But whatever sexual messages superheroes of my 70s childhood were broadcasting from their gutters, they stirred not a drop of my prepubescent blood. I remember a teen neighbor flipping pages of a magazine in his driveway (Was it *Playboy*? Was it Goodman's *Stag*?). I thought it was a comic book. I probably asked, and got a laugh. Yeah, this is what Spider-Man looks like without his costume. This one is Daredevil. And see her? That's the Incredible Hulk. The last one tipped me off. Bruce Banner doesn't have a costume, he changes bodies, so that model couldn't be him. I probably wasn't as young as it sounds. Despite my years of superhero literacy, I was a newcomer to the genre of the undressed female. I preferred my comics. I didn't know their publishers and creators had other professional pursuits.

⚡ ⚡ ⚡

"Superman's powers weren't unique," writes Deborah Friedell, "but his schlumpy double identity was," because "it is the ordinary person, Clark Kent, who is the disguise."

The assertion is indirectly Brad Ricca's, whose biography *Super Boys* Friedell was reviewing, but I still have to raise my hand from the back row here and say, well, actually, no. Jerry Siegel can only claim uniqueness points if you ignore the range of earlier, disguise-reversing characters, including the Scarlet Pimpernel's 1934 film incarnation Siegel watched before his coincidental stroke of schlumpy inspiration.

The Harold Young adaptation is faithful to the original (the Baroness was one of the five screenwriters), except for point of view. Orczy, like Austen, prefers her heroine's perspective, so readers only know what Marguerite knows. Young's camera is more promiscuous and, like Shuster's panels, reveals the hero's transformation early. I've analyzed the novel with a half-dozen classes, and I still can't decide if Sir Percy's foppery is an act. The guy really does seem to love clothes, and he's still laughing that inane laugh at the end, even alone with his wife on his postcoital yacht. For that matter, Mr. Darcy *is* prideful. That wasn't an act he performed to trick Elizabeth; it was a weakness he had to balance with worthier strengths. For Austen, unmasking isn't a makeover; it's a deep transformation.

Young keeps things simple. Percy only acts the fool as a disguise. The film reached U.S. theaters in February 1935, shortly after Keaton returned Siegel's scripts, none of which included Lois Lane. Shuster's revised sketches would now feature the Clark/Superman duality that ever after defined the character. Like Leslie Howard playing the Scarlet Pimpernel, Superman is the true self, and Clark is just a pair of glasses. When Joe started sketching the newly conceived Lois, she looked like Marguerite actress Merle Oberon.

As long as Lois can't see through Clark's mask, she can't be united with Superman because the Austen-Orczy formula requires transformative suffering. Elizabeth and Marguerite recognize their mistakes in order to earn their closure. Austen says "humbled." Orczy says, "the elegant and fashionable [Marguerite], who had dazzled London society with her beauty, her wit and her extravagances, presented a very pathetic picture of tired-out, suffering womanhood." Unmasked hero and punished heroine may now live happily ever after.

Superman's serial form prevented such a happy ending. Or any ending. Lois is trapped in the first half of Elizabeth's and Marguerite's plotline. Instead of learning the truth with her, readers laugh at her mistakes from Shuster's omniscient angles. She's humbled, but she doesn't know it and so can't grow. After she confesses to Clark that she's in love with Superman, "Dazed — bewildered — crushed — Kent walks slowly off. . . . But once the door is shut behind him . . . he clutches his sides and doubles! Then shrieks with — LAUGHTER!"

A romantic obstacle invented to be overcome turned into a permanent joke on Lois Amster — I mean Lane. "From today's perspective," writes comics historian Les Daniels, "it's easy to denounce Lois as the misogynistic fantasy of a disappointed male." Very easy. Even Siegel admitted to creating the "big inside joke" after having "crushes on several attractive girls who either didn't know I existed or didn't care I existed." Because Lois thinks Clark is a languid "worm," she can never land her virile man of steel and complete her Austen arc. She's trapped in the maligning middle. So is Clark/Superman, but that's ideal for the superhero serial form of endlessly postponed closure. No climax means no retirement, no domestication — unlike Tarzan, the Gray Seal, Zorro, and Blackshirt, he stays hard forever. That's now what it meant to be supermasculine.

I like that Eric Berlatsky reads this ferociously heterosexual plot structure in homoerotic terms (Superman's idealized and all-but-nude body, Lois as a discarded pawn of male power), but Siegel did at least try to reach the second half of *Pride and Prejudice*. Perhaps as a result of having reached marital closure himself. It was two years into Superman, and he'd married the girl across the street, the one he used to stare at from his bedroom window as she walked home from Glenville High. She was eighteen. He was twenty-five. Like Zorro for the impotent Don Diego, Superman wooed her for him. The newspaper strip went into national syndication in early 1940. Jerry's hit was delivered right to her doorstep. They married a week after her graduation. Two months later, he submitted a script in which Superman reveals himself to Lois.

> LOIS: "Why didn't you ever tell me who you really are?"
> SUPERMAN: "Because if people were to learn my true identity, it would hamper me in my mission to save humanity."
> LOIS: "Your attitude of cowardliness as Clark Kent — it was just a screen to keep the world from learning who you really are! But there's one thing I must know: was your — er — affection for me, in your role as Clark Kent, also a pretense?"
> SUPERMAN: "THAT was the genuine article, Lois!"

The revelation completes the Austen formula. When Darcy tells Elizabeth, "You taught me a lesson, hard indeed at first, but most advantageous. By you I was properly humbled," the two can unite because now they are on the same plane. Superman comes to his "momentous decision" after Siegel introduces the superpower-stripping "K-Metal from Krypton," the only substance that can physically humble him.

DC rejected the story. Gerard Jones read the note an editor wrote in the margin of the script: "It is not a good idea to let others in on the secret." It would have run in *Action Comics* No. 20. Instead, Siegel brought back Superman's first arch-nemesis, the Ultra-Humanite, after his brain has been transplanted into the body of a gorgeous Hollywood starlet. I'm not sure how to read that transsexual plot twist, but Clark wouldn't reveal himself to Lois till No. 662, fifty years later. They married in 1996, the year Siegel died.

Siegel gave up Superman after he and Shuster sued DC for rights to their creation. They lost. Six months after the decision, Siegel's divorce came through. He was remarried a week later to Joanna Carter, the teen model who'd posed for Shuster's first Lois Lane sketch in 1935. She still looked nothing like Merle Oberon.

DC didn't miss Siegel. They had plenty of writers who could spin the Lois-Superman-Clark love triangle indefinitely. William Woolfork's 1949 "Lois Lane Loves Clark Kent" repeats the Doc Savage explanation for the never-ending marriage plot: "I've got to discourage Lois' affections! I can't marry her because it would interfere with Superman's freedom . . . and Superman must remain free to fight crime!"

He used dissociative identity disorder as a prophylactic, and soon multipersonality celibacy spread across the multiverse. William Marston had his Amazon trade places with an army nurse so she "can see the man I love," but Robert Kanigher's 1958 Wonder Woman is a reboot of the radio Shadow, with Steve Trevor as Margo Lane.

> STEVE: "When are you going to marry me? You know how I feel
>   about you."
> WW: "I do, Steve, but I can't marry you — until my services are
>   no longer needed to battle crime and injustice! Only then can I
>   think about myself."

Like the Scarlet Pimpernel's sleuthing wife or one of the Domino Lady's hunky hookups, Steve is Wonder Woman's most dangerous antagonist. When he tricks her into agreeing to marry, she has to escape: "What better place to conceal myself from Steve . . . than under his nose?" Enter Lt. Diana Prince, Col. Steve Trevor's new assistant. "And that's the story of Wonder Woman's dual identity!"

Twenty-first-century superheroes fly under the same rules of engagement. When DC turned their Death of Superman arc into the PG-13 cartoon *Superman: Doomsday* in 2007, Anne Heche voiced Lois's annoyance with Superman for keeping their (surprisingly sexual) relationship a secret. Not only does he limit their trysts to the Fortress of Solitude (the ultimate bachelor pad), but he's not confirmed his secret identity to her either. Heche's Lois can see through Clark's glasses, so she's not miffed because he's keeping her in the dark. She's hurt that her lover isn't committed to their relationship enough to expose his real self. It takes a scrape with the afterlife for the Man of Steel to come around. In the last scene, the postcoital Lois looks up from Superman's bedsheets to see Clark putting on his glasses. Intimacy at last.

Austin Grossman's novel *Soon I Will Be Invincible* plays by the same romance rules. The love-struck cyborg Fatale longs for her teammate Blackwolf:

> Our lips touch, and for a second it's everything I thought it would be. The metal in my jaw is awkward but somehow exciting, and he kisses back. I pull him down to me, get his weight against me. I'd forgotten what it was like to want something this much. He reaches up under my shirt, and the feeling is so good it makes me want to cry. Nobody but a surgeon has touched me there for a really, really long time.
>
> Then I make a mistake. I reach for the mask, and he catches my arm, ready to break it. His jaw sets, and I'm dealing with Blackwolf again.

Unmasking remains way more intimate than sex. It's another team member who eventually lands Blackwolf. The two "are making out in the rain like high school kids," and "Blackwolf's mask came off, showing the shock of white hair he usually keeps hidden." Even Fatale admits "it's just about the most romantic thing I've ever seen."

The mask means the same to gay superheroes. The hero of Perry Moore's *Hero* (2007 was a banner year for superhero sex) masturbates to online porn of wide-nippled Überman (the one page I mumbled over when reading aloud to my kids), but he doesn't find intimacy until he and the better half of his dynamic duo share identities. The novel's most touching (and gently erotic) scene takes place not in bed but during a picnic lunch in a public park:

> I . . . placed my hands on his face. . . . With one palm over his forehead and the other palm over his nose and mouth, I looked into those deep, dark pupils and saw the way he used to look at me when he was Dark Hero, when I didn't know. Goran took my hand off his mouth and held it. He raised it to his mouth, placed his warm lips in the middle of my palm and kissed it. . . . I reached my arms around Goran, pulled him in, and our lips met.

Zorro would approve. So would Austen. A happy ending still means getting your mask off.

Flash Gordon, "The Planet of Peril," 1936.

CHAPTER 8

BEST OF BOTH WORLDS

I first mentioned the census bureau checklist of superhero traits in the introduction. We've since penciled a lot of X's into a lot of boxes. It's an ever-mutating questionnaire, but here are some of the highlights. We beseeched the godmen of chapter one:

Are you an instrument of absolute good?

Have you ever been mistaken for Jesus Christ?

Can you throw more punches than Jesus?

Do you intervene because God is absent?

Does the universe have a way of making things work out for you?

Chapter two's revolutionaries answered these petitions:

Do you disrespect authority?

Do you know what's best for society?

Could you overthrow the government if you wanted to?

Have you ever outed yourself?

Do you liberate us by transcending the ordinary limits of human ability?

Chapter three's shadowy Parliamentarians passed more bills:

Has anyone ever called you a monster?

Do you have trouble controlling yourself?

Are your powers both a blessing and a curse?

Have you lost a part of your humanity to save humanity?

Are you a stitched together corpse of genre tropes?

Chapter four's Indians and cowboys circled another frontier:

    Do you love external threats?

    Do your friends and enemies know you by your symbol?

    Have you ever taken the law into your own hands?

    Are you stronger away from home?

    Do you have a shifting sense of self?

Chapter five's Darwinists leaped over these beastly questions:

    Are you the next great thing in evolution?

    Do you keep degenerates at bay?

    Do you keep your inner animal at bay?

    Does the thrill of adventure save you from boredom?

    Are you a superman who prevents the domination of other
        supermen?

Chapter six's philosophical villains and vigilantes pondered:

    Have you ever killed someone?

    Do you believe in absolute good but decide what absolute good is?

    Are you an extraordinary person trapped in a mediocre world?

    Does humanity give you purpose?

    Does that purpose include saving and/or killing them?

And chapter seven's lovelorn heroes flirted with these:

    Does your costume make you hard?

    Have you ever wished you could settle down and have a family?

    Does it feel like the world won't let you have a real relationship?

    Are children absolutely out of the question?

    Does it feel good to take off your mask?

Different characters check different answers, unless you're Superman. He scores a 35 out of 35 so far. He also gets a checkmark on my next question, the one "yes" I expect from every would-be citizen of the superhero multiverse:

    Are you a bastard?

Superheroes can be monstrous jerks, but I mean that more in the are-your-parents-married sense. If metaphorical Mom and Dad are wed, then baby can't be Super. In fact, Mom and Dad should be strangers, the more incongruously distant the better. Premarital counselors would declare them catastrophically incompatible, their oppositional orbits beyond even Venus and Mars. Your parents can have only one thing in common: you.

All superheroes are amalgams (Adam Strange is a space cowboy, Black Widow is a costumed secret agent, Hellboy is a superpowered occult detective), but they combine more than genres. A superhero is the merged offspring of two alien-to-each-other worlds, bridging an inconceivable gap between Us and not-Us. The character type is a half-human hybrid, an antimiscegenation crossbreed. Superheroes transgress just by existing. Most everything else on the checklist — costume, alias, superpowers, alter ego, mission — is an expression of that fundamental violation, an impossible, one-of-a-kind combination. Dad represents the ordinary, the human, the everyday, but your Mom half is "extra," "über," from "beyond." She's of a "super" realm defined by its distance from your earthly hometown.

For me, that's Penn Hills, the sprawling suburb of Pittsburgh where I lived in the same house, slept in the same bedroom for all my childhood and adolescence. Draw a dot in the middle of the carpet where I sat and flipped comics. That's the center of my multiverse, the metropole, ground zero. In my empire, all superheroes are half-Pennsylvanian. To locate their other half, you need a compass, the kind with a needle and pencil. Place the needle tip in the center of my rug and draw a circle. My world travels were measured by car odometer then, but you can make as wide a circle as you like. It doesn't matter. The scale of the map changes, but the circle is consistent.

"We" live inside the circle. "They" live outside. We call our side civilization. That Other side is an ever-changing species of wilderness dark with a thousand interchangeable names: Tibet, Mars, Mongo, Hades, Mordor, Skynet, Zombieland, Crime Alley, Kentucky. A nonsuperhero is one of us, born and bred here at home where he accomplishes his heroic deeds, battling nonsupervillains born and bred in our backyard too. But superheroes bridge the frontier. As Clare Pitkethly puts it: "the superhero straddles the boundary or an opposition and is simultaneously on one side and the other, incorporating both opposing sides." That also means their narratives run on an Us-Them engine. The Them is an alien other, something fundamentally different from Us and so fundamentally threatening. Since They are also more powerful than Us, we need a hero who is part-Them but who values his Us-half more and so employs his Them-powers to save Us.

Maybe he was born out there, or was born here but lived out there. Maybe while out there, They trained him in their Them ways. Maybe he only visited out there but returned Them-infected. Maybe he brought back a piece of Them — an object, a skill, a word, a way of thinking. Maybe someone else brought back a piece of Them and passed it to him here. Maybe one of Them traveled here to give it to him. Maybe his Them mentor gave it to him while he was out there. Maybe the loyalty of his Them sidekick is all the Them-ness he needs. Maybe he is one of Them but was adopted and raised by Us. Maybe he is in love with one of Us. Maybe he's a special one of Them who can see the superiority of Us values. One way or another, We reversed his Them programming.

The range of Their worlds is limited only by our metropolitan imaginations. I'll map out a few of my favorite regions: class, race, species, planet, substance. They're all variations of the same census bureau question: "What are you?" It's multiple choice, but with only two answers, A and not-A. Substance is the most fantastical: are you made of living or nonliving matter? When it comes to superhero astronomy, the universe has two planets: Earth and not-Earth. Same for species: human and not-human. There's a little more wiggle room along the race and class axes, but traditionally it's WASP and not-WASP. Whatever the dichotomy, if you're a superhero, you straddle the fence with a foot on each side. There are only two worlds, and superheroes embody them both.

To test the hypothesis, flip back to previous chapters and administer the two-world quiz to the oldest contestants. Chapter one offers a range of heavenly half-breeds, beginning with *Lascaux*'s bird-headed hybrid, Wounded Man. Golem and Talus are easy too, a man of mud and a man of yron, both fantastic amalgams of the living and nonliving. Merlin is an earth-born godman, a sorcerer "possessed of some spirit of God." Faust combines worlds too. By summoning Mephisto to his bedroom rug, he merges Earth with the not-Earth of hell.

The ur-vigilante Robin Hood's noble outlawness merges the two ends of the class spectrum: criminal commoner and law-protected nobleman. Chapter two's other aristocracy overthrowers are all reborn rulers of their own self-made order. The resulting Parliament of Monsters further marries the human and nonhuman of the Faustian underworld. Byron's protosuperman Manfred combines dual worlds twice over: his "garb and gait bespeak thee of high lineage," while his air is "Proud as a freeborn peasant's"; and his "mix'd essence" is "Half dust, half deity."

Chapter four's Indians and half-savage frontiersmen is an extended tour of the specifically American metaethnic border. The Darwin-driven fear of animal-men is metaethnic too, except that species of racial other migrated from the colonies to Metropolis when degenerates infested Crime Alley. The map scale shrunk, but it's the same borderland circling the castle keep. Chapter two's democratic mobs surround that aristo-cratic center too, revitalizing the pre-Revolutionary order by inoculating well-borns with peasant blood to breed commoner-kings like the cosmo-politan Napoleon — the amoral prototype of the hero-villain supermen of chapter six.

I'm not arguing all best-of-both-worlders are superheroes, though it's tempting. Doesn't Kevin Bacon crash-land in a smallville from the planet Chicago and free the teen underclass from Puritanical parents with his urban dance magic? Even setting aside strangers-who-come-to-town and their twins heroes-who-take-a-journey, there are plenty of other metaphorical world-blenders. Doesn't Jane Eyre defeat the Mad Woman in the Attic by using her Red Room powers of telepathy to merge with Rochester's sanity?

But comic book superheroes are the biggest hybrids. Superman is ob-vious, a space alien reared on Earth, but Batman is just as two-sided: his parents' murder bonded little Bruce to the dark animalism of the Go-tham underworld, giving birth to a crime-fighting half-animal. When the Fantastic Four crossed into cosmic-ray territory, they merged with extra-terrestrial radiation to be reborn as Cold War warriors. Duality is right there in the names: Spider-Man, Aquaman, Deathlok, the Human Torch. They're all mongrel über-children of fantastically incompatible parents.

It sounds like a tough balancing act, but the two halves are not equal.

It's not just, as Pitkethly notes, "the dynamic tension that results from the split" that makes a superhero — it's the stacking of the dichotomy into a hierarchy with one half always on top. Though superpowers sound powerful, it's the human side of the split-self who calls the shots. Jekyll commands Hyde. Clark is Superman's boy-scout heart. Marvel's radioactive heroes contain the fallout of atomic Armageddon. Even Wonder Woman and Sub-Mariner, alien others from nonhuman races, obey their humanizing impulse to defend their adopted society. We take a part of Them to use for Ourselves. In terms of travel, superheroes are tourists, importers, conquerors. They're ugly Americans, stuffing their pockets with magical loot.

For this final chapter, we'll walk the last of the one-way trade routes that lead to Krypton. I mentioned in chapter four that Poe fathered two superhero parents, detective fiction and science fiction, and those double helixes are still mutating into the new genre's DNA. It's the last decade, 1928 to 1938, before Superman explodes comic books into a multimillion dollar industry, so the tour bus is moving faster now. We'll begin in Earth's radioactive future, roam Mars's multiple superhero sites, punch our way through detective history, then sail around the West's colonial periphery aboard a Caribbean pirate ship bound for outer space. Expect a quick stop in Middle-earth. They're all other worlds that combine with ours to birth a multiverse of superheroes.

Science fiction is a maze of frontier lines. You can aim at one but end up tripping over another. Reed Richards wanted to be the "first man on Mars," but his Them weren't Martians, but Commies and their horde of missiles aimed at the United States. Soon the whole Marvel pantheon was glowing with the Otherly threat of nuclear war, protecting us from atomic fallout by absorbing it at the borderland of our imaginations. Radiation is an energy, not a substance — or a planet, race, species, or social class — but in the not-Us logic of sci-fi, it's all the same.

Radiation was a mother of superhero invention in the 50s too. Charlton Comics' Atomic Rabbit munched glow-in-the-dark carrots in 1955, before rechristened Atomic Bunny and then replaced by astronaut Captain Atom months before the Fantastic Four launched. Marvelman, the British knockoff of the canceled Captain Marvel, shouted "Kimota!" in 1954 — that's "atomic" backward, the magic word of an astrophysicist. Marvel was calling itself Atlas Comics when it revived the Golden Age Human Torch in 1953, newly atomic-powered by bomb tests in the Mojave Dessert. When Bill Finger revamped Superman in 1948, he fitted his home planet with a nuclear reactor. "Krypton," warns Jor-El, "is one gigantic atomic bomb!" I assume Finger had the horrors of Hiroshima and Nagasaki in mind, but Alvin Schwartz prophesied the build-up at Krypton's uranium core nine months before the United States dropped the dynamic duo Fat Man and Little Boy.

Superman's home wasn't the first alien world detonated by the atom. The "Lost Planet" of Mars, in Jack Williamson and Miles J. Breuer's 1929 short story "The Girl From Mars," is "destroyed by atomic energy released by intelligent entities." Those Martians blew themselves up. Though not before rocketing their offspring to earth — an idea that crash-landed in reader Jerry Siegel's teenaged head. We'll take a closer look at Mars in a moment, but my first atomic superhero prize goes to Philip Nowlan and *ARMAGEDDON — 2419 A.D.*, the 1928 novel that introduced the multiverse to Anthony Rogers, aka Buck Rogers.

Instead of destroying the world, Nowlan's atoms save ours by turning the owner of the American Radioactive Gas Corporation into a radioactive Rip Van Winkle. "It all resulted," explains Rogers, "from my interest in radioactive gases." Radiation was a roaring topic in the 20s. Cosmic rays had been around since 1912, when physicist Victor Franz Hess risked his life in a hot-air balloon to record them, but they weren't confirmed and named till 1927. Before that, physicists thought all radiation came not from the frontier of outer space but the underworld beneath the Earth's crust — which explains Rogers's origin story.

He was trapped in a cave-in while exploring "traces of carnotite" in an abandoned coal mine. By stepping into that underground realm, he, like the Fantastic Four, was flung across a radioactive border. "When I began my long sleep, man . . . had barely begun to speculate on the possibilities of harnessing sub-atomic forces." When he awoke, "the radioactive gas had kept me in a state of suspended animation for something like 500 years," "free from the ravages of katabolic processes."

Since he wakes in the same spot, Rogers, like H. G. Wells's 1895 Time Traveler, combined worlds by crossing a temporal instead of a geographic frontier. Both are equally fantastical. Superman originally time traveled here from Earth's future, a world Siegel later spun into space. James Cameron's reprogrammed-to-save-humanity Schwarzenegger cyborg hales from the future too. Pierre Boulle's novel *La Planète des Singes* began in a galaxy far far away, before *The Planet of the Apes* film franchise locked it into Earth's orbit. The future is a crowded superhero destination spot, and Philip Nowlan drove one of the first border-crossing tour busses.

Rogers's radioactive nap transforms his Pennsylvania homeland into an alien world and him into an alien visitor, one who hasn't devolved like his forest-dwelling countrymen. At "five feet eleven," he "was considerably above the average now, for the race had lost something in stature, it seemed, through the vicissitudes of five centuries. Most of the women were a bit below five feet, and the men only a trifle above this height." The time-traveling superman finds that his "20th Century muscles did have an advantage."

Underworld radiation bridges two centuries with a hero who champions them both. Rogers and his old-school know-how arrive at just the moment his ravaged nation needs him, during the "Second War of Independence" against not the British but those perilously yellow Mongolians who conquered America while he dozed. When he fell asleep China's Communist Party was struggling into power and Mongolia had been independent nation for over a decade, but Nowlan's "Hans" are too generic for such internal niceties. They're just not-Us.

It's still a popular plot. An invasion of fall-of-America shows have been broadcasting in recent years: *The Walking Dead, Falling Skies, Fringe, Revolution, Defiance, The 100*. But the trend is even older than the American Radioactive Gas Corporation. Rip Van Winkle's author, Washington Irving, imagined the United States conquered by inhabitants of the moon ("riding on hippogriffs — defended with impenetrable armor — armed with concentrated sunbeams, and provided with vast engines, to hurl enormous moonstones"). That was 1809, three decades after the First War of Independence. Irving was allegorizing the brutalization of Native tribes by Europeans, but over a century later, Philip Nowlan was more worried about his brutal nation losing its world stature. The same fear drives the zombies, six-legged aliens, and bald-headed futuremen infiltrating twenty-first-century TV.

America wants to be the multiverse's imperial center. We love to radiate Exceptionalism. The term was coined by America's arch-frenemy Joseph Stalin, just months after Rogers debuted. Stalin was trash-talking the notion that the United States was invulnerable to Marxist economic truths—a criticism soon supported by the stock market crash and the collapse of "the house of cards of American Exceptionalism." But recalling his homeland's roaring 1928, Buck laments: "The United States of America was the most powerful nation in the world, its political, financial, industrial and scientific influence being supreme; and in the arts also it was rapidly climbing into leadership."

Some of that cultural supremacy was provided by Buck himself. After *ARMAGEDDON—2419 A.D.* appeared in Hugo Gernsback's newly launched *Amazing Stories*, the first magazine devoted to the genre soon to be named science fiction, Nowlan teamed up with artist Dick Calkins for *Buck Rogers in the 25th Century*, the first sci-fi adventure strip in daily newspapers. Russell Keaton added a Sunday strip, and next Buck was leaping to radio and film. King Features needed a comic strip to compete, so instead of battling Mongolians in America, the first Buck knockoff, Alex Raymond's Flash Gordon, hopped to the planet Mongo, where he battled Fu Manchu knockoff Ming the Merciless.

Siegel would turn Mongo into Krypton, exploding it and its futuristic threat in the first panel of *Action Comics* No. 1. Later writers rescued a few Kryptonian survivors, most of whom, like Ming, view Clark's adopted planet as a place to plunder. Fortunately Superman is more "man" than "Super" when it comes to loyalty. He'll never let his adopted home become a Lost Planet.

⚡ ⚡ ⚡

Nowlan must have been *A Princess of Mars* fan, because John Carter, like Buck a decade and a half after him, inhales "some poisonous gas" inside a cave before being overcome by "dreaminess" and waking in another world. You know from chapter four that Mars was the Confederate superman's rebirth, one Burroughs midwifed through a mysterious opening "lost in dense shadows." That's the superhero birth canal.

Sci-fi writers Jack Williamson and Miles J. Breuer don't like to look at it. Their Martian daughter, Pandorina, enters Jerry Siegel's list of two-world predecessors through a metal cylinder. Her adoptive father pulls it from a meteorite's bloodless crater, not a C-section incision, certainly not a vagina. Like Burroughs, the authors of the first alien supergirl didn't understand much about the otherly world of women.

When "A Girl from Mars" landed in 1929, it was literally the first *Science Fiction* story. Hugo Gernsback, having just lost Buck Rogers's birth planet, *Amazing Stories*, was launching a new magazine, *Science Fiction*, with "A Girl from Mars" as a premier feature. Readers included high schooler Jerry, who corresponded with Williamson afterward. A few years later, Siegel's own alien child of a destroyed civilization would crash-land on earth to be reared by human foster parents too.

Breuer, a practicing physician when not penning pulp tales, should have been less queasy than his younger writing partner about pregnancy and childbirth. Pandorina is a test tube baby, conceived in and hatched from an incubator. They use the words "ovum," "sperm," and "fertilize," but not "uterus," "cervix" or "vulva." Siegel, even less comfortable with Martian canals, delivers his sanitized Clark swaddled in a cockpit. Both birth stories avoid the dense shadows of female anatomy. Pandorina is found by a recently widowed husband, Clark by an elderly couple long past child-bearing years. Instead of vaginas, we get funnel-shaped craters. Instead of intercourse, it's rocket ships and glass globes shot from interplanetary "guns."

Williamson and Breuer's narrator seems to love his adopted daughter well enough though, rearing her beside his own vagina-born son. He admires her "rare elflike beauty," her "soft, red bronze" hair, and her "astonishing aptitude," all "inheritance from a higher civilization." Like Clark, Pandorina passes from infancy to adulthood in less than a page. When I blink at my daughter — she was barely out of middle school when I started writing this book — I see the same blur. Next thing Pandorina's in love with her adoptive brother and glowing in the dark when "excited." My wife and I haven't been allowed to check on our daughter after bed for years, but I suspect she emits a similar "luminosity" behind her closed door. She's been dating a while too.

Perhaps all fathers eventually experience their daughters as alien. After eliminating female genitalia from Pandorina's birth, Williamson and Breuer's literary offspring has the audacity to grow her own. My father-tuned ears can hear the unspoken panic stirring under their narrator's scientifictionally calm prose. Who is this adult woman making herself breakfast in my kitchen before driving herself to high school? Where in the multiverse did those breasts come from? I'd like to think I've handled my paternal alienation better than Pandorina's dad. He sees her entire generation as Them-born monsters, especially when Martian men appear on the front porch demanding to wed his virgin daughter. They crash-landed here too, and the father is horrified as they battle over their would-be bride. Better they all die than allow Pandorina to discover her own uranium core on her wedding night. He lures her and the other planet-hoppers onto a heavy artillery range where they bloodlessly vanish in the smoke and dirt of an exploding shell. Deaths as sanitized as their births.

H. G. Wells also preferred his Martians "absolutely without sex, and therefore without any of the tumultuous emotions that arise from that difference among men." They bud from their parents like fresh-water polyps. And yet they probably "descended from beings not unlike ourselves." Instead of evolved asexuality, Siegel avoids opening Pandorina's box with a superhero sex-change operation. If Pandorina had lived, she could have been the first best-of-both-worlds superheroine: an alien reared on Earth a decade before her literary cousin Superman. If she'd married her brother, their hybrid superbabies could have protected us from Wells's Martians when they returned in 1938, four months after *Action Comics* No. 1's June cover date. That radio invasion was staged by Orson Welles, during one of his nights off from voicing *The Shadow*. His über-children crawl from craters and cylinders too. Wells's Martians stormed England, but Welles selected Grover's Mill, New Jersey, for their new birthplace, fifty miles from Camden, Pandorina's landing site, and sixty from Folsom, the smallville where one of her suitors crash-landed in a farmer's field like the alien invader Clark Kent.

Williamson and Breuer's "ultramundane man" isn't as catchy a name as Superman, but "the striking and powerful figure with his mighty, muscular limbs" was also set "apart from ordinary men" by his "inhuman" qualities. He just needed a loving Ma and Pa Kent to dedicate his alienness to protecting our world from other aliens.

Buck Rogers changed worlds by changing centuries, Pandorina by changing planets. But both Mars and twenty-fifth-century America orbit the metropole from the other side of the compass circle. Neither is a part of Us.

So where exactly is the boundary between Here and not-Here, and Now and not-Now? Washington Irving's Rip Van Winkle only napped twenty years, but that was enough to render him alien to post-Revolutionary America. What if the magic moonshine he drank sent him the other direction, to precolonial or dinosaur times? When exactly does the mundanely recent past become Exotically Distant?

Select a time period: the seventeenth century. And a different-than-Pennsylvania location: the Caribbean. Are those leaps enough to conjure a superhero into existence? Jamaica was a British colony then, one as alien to London as the seventeenth century is to 1930s Hollywood. The double leap is also why a pirate like Captain Blood is another best-of-both-worlds precursor to the armada of comic book crossbreeds sailing after him.

When I watched *Captain Blood* on my aunts' TV set as kid, I was confused when the pirate crew hoisted their Jolly Roger. It wasn't the standard skull and crossbones but a jawless one with two crossed but living arms with a sword in each fist. It was close, but imagine if Shuster had drawn Superman's "S" in Gothic calligraphy. Or if Batman swapped his chest emblem for a diagram of an actual bat. Such variations, though small, are enough to disguise the nearness of seemingly unrelated genre worlds, superheroes and pirates.

I didn't know the Captain was Errol Flynn in his breakout role. I didn't know the 1935 film was a remake of the 1924 *Captain Blood*. Fans grumbled about Andrew Garfield replacing Tobey Maguire's too-recent Spider-Man, or Sony rebooting *Fantastic Four* after a measly decade. But that's been standard Hollywood practice since the teens. When Flynn traded in his pirate hat for Robin Hood tights, they were still warm from Fairbanks, who'd torn them off Robert Grazer, who'd yanked them from Percy Stow.

Hollywood has always been a roving pirate ship. It plundered Captain Blood from Rafael Sabatini's 1922 novel. A decade had passed and swashbucklers were back with the box office booty 1934's *Treasure Island* shoveled in. So Warner Bros. dug Blood up for name recognition. Russell Thorndike jumped aboard too. He conscripted his 1915 Scarecrow (vicar by day, masked smuggler by night) and sent him sailing into his piratical backstory for a prequel novel. *Doctor Syn on the High Seas* floated five more books, plus a 1937 film and a Disney miniseries.

I missed Tom Hanks in *Captain Phillips*, but the inspired-by-real-events tale of low sea piracy adds to my bewilderment at the genre. I blinked in incongruous horror as my family rolled through Disney World's Pirates of the Caribbean, where jolly animatronic pirates endlessly chase buxom animatronic women in acts of slapstick rape. If we can romanticize seventeenth-century pirates into comic outlaws, will Buck Rogers's twenty-fifth-century Hollywood do the same for terrorists?

And yet that Jolly Roger — probably a corruption of the French "*joli rouge*," a warning that your attackers will kill you even if you surrender — is now a symbol of family fun. I used to wave it as I sat in the stands of Three Rivers Stadium cheering the Pittsburgh Pirates. It doesn't help that the KKK's Black Legion added those skulls and bones to their robes as they terrorized the port of Detroit in the mid-30s. They wanted to be heroes. Herman Landon's 1921 gentleman thief dubbed himself the

Benevolent Picaroon (Spanish for pirate), and Charles W. Tyler's Blue Jean Billy Race launched her modern pirate career in 1918, both harbored in Street and Smith's *Detective Story Magazine*.

Even Batman took a turn on the high seas. Chuck Dixon (no relation to Thomas I hope) and Enrique Alcatena rebooted him as Captain Leatherwing in a 1994 Elseworld. The pairing seems playfully discordant, but Wayne and Blood were already blood brothers. Ask them to fill out the 30s version of the superhero census questionnaire:

1. Do you have a penis?
2. Is it white?
3. Are you highly respected?
4. Ever been horribly wronged?
5. What's your catchy alias?
6. How comfortable are you working outside the law?
7. Got a nifty disguise?
8. What's your signature emblem?
9. Can you supervise one or more loyal assistants?
10. Can you fight?
11. Are you really all about the greater good?
12. Do you love thwarting that pesky government official who's always bugging you?
13. Are you into girls?

If that list isn't familiar, it should be. It's the original superhero formula, the one that came into full focus in the 30s:

> A (1) white (2) man of (3) high status is (4) wronged and so assumes an (5) alias as a (6) noble criminal with a (7) disguise and (8) emblem, and, with one or more (9) assistants, (10) fights for the (11) greater good while thwarting a (12) law enforcement antagonist and courting a (13) female love interest.

Batman answers yes to all thirteen plot points — if you count Commissioner Gordon, whom Bruce was clearly hoodwinking in his first issue. Bruce's forgotten fiancée, Julie, vanished along with writer Gardner Fox, but she was there in 1939 too. The rest is easy: Mr. Wayne is very wealthy and very white, was terribly wronged with the murder of his parents, goes vigilante in a bat-emblazoned leotard, while dodging police bullets and warring on criminals. Oh, and he picks up an underage sidekick and overage butler too.

Batman plundered that formula from an ocean of predecessors. Lots of rich, pissed-off white guys like to play dress-up, while stomping on bad guys, flicking off the government, and manhandling the ladies. Look at Captain Blood again. That's the title a noble physician assumes after he's unjustly convicted of treason, sold into slavery, and shipped to the colonies. He has a crew of not-quite-as-noble escaped convicts for assistants, as his emblematic Jolly Roger flaps like a cape. That naval commander in Jamaica keeps hounding him, but the commander's daughter is smitten anyway. And of course when the citizens of Port Royal are left undefended, it's Blood who rushes to their rescue.

Blood and Batman served aboard the 1930s Mystery Men, an overflowing ship of masked do-gooders captained by the Shadow with his pirate flag of a laugh, the original MWAHAHAHA. The crew even included "a Mystery-Man called Superman," as Siegel calls his hero in *Action Comics* No. 6. The 20s had roared with a dozen more, all high scorers on the lucky thirteen-point hero scale. The Gray Seal is only missing Bruce's murdered parents. The equally motiveless Zorro scores another twelve. Go back a decade farther and the Scarlet Pimpernel scores a thirteen while righting the wrongs of the French Revolution, while the thirteen-point Spring-Heeled Jack carves his "S" on his enemies' foreheads.

If pirates and gentlemen thieves don't look like superheroes, it's because their Jolly Rogers were stitched in a slightly different pattern than their later chest emblems. But the fabric is the same. There's just one ingredient missing: Superpowers. Bruce is awfully down-to-earth in the godlike company of most supermen. Blood and his shipmates are all flesh-and-blood too. But that's because Superman collides their piratical detective planet with the eugenically pseudoscientific world of science fiction. Poe mixed those ingredients in chapter three, and Siegel and Shuster completed the experiment.

Superman is an assistant-absorbing mutation of question nine. The Shadow employed a secret network of loyal sidekick operatives, Zorro had his galloping Avengers, Sir Percy his League of Scarlet Pimpernels. The KKK's only powers were in their numbers too. Even the superman Doc Savage led a team of skilled assistants. But after Superman, heroes didn't need to be team leaders anymore. Shower a pirate captain with cosmic rays, and he absorbs his crew of assistants, giving himself the strength of a dozen men. A superhero is a one-man man-o'-war. Most also gain their sci-fi powers by mutating question four into an experiment gone horribly wrong. Batman, Nathan Slaughter, and the Domino Lady suffer the deaths of loved ones, but the Marvel pantheon recovers from extraordinary accidents that transform them physically. Journalist Jim Rendon calls it posttraumatic growth and identifies superheroes as its poster children. That's why Austin Grossman sees "the larger theme of superhero life as trauma and recovery from trauma; the way superpowers arise in trauma to the body that one never quite gets over. The trauma impresses itself onto the body but also leads to a hyperfunctioning of the body."

Captain Blood, like Superman, only loses his home, but he still spells out superhero DNA. The Hulk's high status comes in the form of Dr. Banner's supergenius intellect. He's a formula white guy wronged by a gamma bomb and the Cold War that detonated it. With the help of his lone teen confidante, Rick Jones, he eludes the U.S. military while dating the general's daughter and committing violent acts of do-goodery. If he had an "H"-emblazoned cape, he'd score a thirteen. Spider-Man wronged himself but loses a point for unrespectable nerdiness. Convert "status" to "mutant giftedness," and you have an armada of X-Men. Even the convention-sinking Alan Moore is onboard with his wonder woman Promethea. Sure, her assistants are dead versions of herself, and her pesky law enforcement officer is Christianity, but she's a twelve, which goes to thirteen if you count her male incarnation. Hand the thirteen-point questionnaire to your favorite comic book character, and you'll see Captain Blood's formula flag is still sailing the superhero seas.

Blood is also another bastard, a world-crossed descendant of Robin Hood merging the mild-mannered planet of English nobility with the slavery and piracy of the so-called West Indies—a name as fictional as Flash Gordon's Mongo, where space piracy is a plot point too. If the good Doctor Blood had stayed home in Bridgewater tending the boxed geraniums on his windowsill, he would never have saved Port Royal from the nefarious French fleet. Instead, his travels transform him into another two-world hybrid, tying his emblematic flag to the backs of comic book superheroes.

⚡ ⚡ ⚡

Pirates are a violent species of antiheroes, one of a range of violent hero types populating the superhero spawning ground of the 20s and 30s. Dashiell Hammett's Sam Spade, the prototype of the hard-boiled detective, debuted in *Black Mask* magazine in 1929, two years after Conan Doyle published his last Sherlock Holmes story. Though both are descendants of Poe's ur-detective, C. Auguste Dupin, Hammett made sure Spade was no "erudite solver of riddles," but "a hard and shifty fellow, able to take care of himself in any situation, able to get the best of anybody."

The "D" in DC was already a major item on the superhero census questionnaire. *Detective Comics* No. 1 hit stands a hundred years after *Graham's Magazine* published "Murders in the Rue Morgue." But Batman, like Spade, combines Dupin's world of reclusive genius with the bare-knuckled descent of an adventurer into the dark continent of urban crime. Superheroes, while indebted to the classic detective model, are men of action, not armchairs. They pulverize a heavy dose of violence into the superhero mix of genre ingredients.

Superman clobbers a wife-beater in his first appearance, but the BBC's Benedict Cumberbatch never throws a punch—at least not in *Sherlock*. Cumberbatch's Khan throws plenty of punches in *Star Trek: Into Darkness*, but there he's a eugenically bred superman. Not that Holmes is a weakling. Dr. Watson reports the detective is "an expert singlestick player, boxer, and swordsman." But it took actors Robert Downey Jr.'s and Jonny Lee Miller's violently Americanized Holmeses to put those skills to practice.

Downey's *Sherlock Holmes* started life as the comic book producer Lionel Wigman penned instead of the usual spec script. Director Guy

Ritchie was thinking *Batman Begins*. The Marvel formula was pounding box offices by then, so Holmes's superpowered intellect would have to be "as much of a curse as it was a blessing." A young Holmes should have nixed the forty-something Downey, but who can say no to Iron Man? Especially when the director planned to restore all of Doyle's "intense action sequences." You know, like when Holmes sneaks aboard the bad guys' boat in "The Solution of a Remarkable Case":

> With a lightning-like movement he seized the hand which held the knife. Then, exerting all of his great strength, he bent the captain's wrist quickly backward. There was a snap like the breaking of a pipe-stem, and a yell of pain from the captain. Nick's left arm shot out and his fist landed with terrific force squarely on the fellow's nose.

Oh no, wait. That's not Sherlock. That's Nick Carter. And I'm not the only one getting them confused lately.

Nick Carter Detective Magazine, Street and Smith's pulp reboot of their once popular dime novel detective, returned to action in 1933. Sam Spade had something to do with it—though the influence runs in the opposite direction. Carter premiered as a thirteen-episode serial in *New York Weekly* in 1886, a year before *A Study in Scarlet* introduced Sherlock Holmes in England's *Beeton's Christmas Annual*. Carter was created by John R. Coryell and Ormond G. Smith, but Street and Smith hired Frederick Van Rensselaer Dey (remember him from the Night Wind?) to write over a thousand uncredited dime novels between 1891 and 1915 when *Nick Carter Weekly* changed to *Detective Story Magazine*.

Doyle wrote a mere four novels and fifty-six short stories, with the rare "action sequence" lasting a sentence: "He flew at me with a knife, and I had to grasp him twice, and got a cut over the knuckles, before I had the upper hand of him." A. O. Scott labels Holmes a "proto-superhero," one who's "never been much for physical violence," crediting the Downey incarnation for the innovation of making the detective "a brawling, head-butting, fist-in-the-gut, knee-in-the-groin action hero," what one commenter called "the precise opposite of Sherlock Holmes." The film opens with Downey in a bare-knuckled boxing match, displaying the skills

Doyle only hints at. Apparently Holmes once went three rounds with a prize-fighter who tells him: "Ah, you're one that has wasted your gifts, you have! You might have aimed high, if you had joined the fancy."

Nick Carter has the fancy: "He bounded forward and seized in an iron grasp the man whom he had just struck. Then, raising him from the floor as though he were a babe, the detective hurled him bodily, straight at the now advancing men." In addition to Holmes's sleuthing powers, Carter has a Valjean-level of superhuman strength, plus a temper — the secret ingredient missing from all those nonsuperheroic British incarnations. Miller's Holmes on CBS's *Elementary* doesn't hurl men like babes, but he has broken a finger or two sucker punching serial killers.

Sherlock is the last show my family watches as a family (okay, one of the last two), so I don't mind the BBC cauterizing the violent Nick Carter-ization of the character. Nick has mutated since the nineteenth century too: a 30s pulp run, a 40s radio show, a 60s book series. I have the anonymously written *Nick Carter: The Redolmo Affair* on my shelf. It's a musty James Bond knockoff I found in a vacation beach house and kept in exchange for whatever I was reading at the time. I can't bring myself to flip more than a few pages: "I streamrollered my shoulder into his gut and sent us both crashing to the deck. I got my hands on his throat and started squeezing. His fist was smashing down on my head, hammering into my skull."

In Nick's defense, Doyle considered Sherlock schlock too. He hurled him over a Swiss cliff so he could stop writing his best-selling stories — but the detective keeps bouncing back. So does Nick, if you count the genre of superstrong detectives who followed his 1933 pulp resurrection. He is part of that otherly world of violence that superheroes embody in order to keep our world so tranquil.

Unlike Errol Flynn, I'm no globe-trotting adventurer, but in 2011, seventy-four years after the 1937 publication of *The Hobbit*, my family moved to Middle-earth during my wife's Fulbright-funded sabbatical. Tolkien is a time-traveler like Philip Nowlan: "Most people have made this mistake of thinking Middle-earth is a particular kind of earth or is another planet of the science fiction sort but it's just an old fashioned word for this world we live in."

Old, in this case, is 6,000 years, so around the biblical Big Bang — but we're done touring those heavens. Our tour bus stopped in Rivendell and Hobbiton, and my family posed for a photo where Frodo and his friends tumbled down that hill before the Dark Riders almost caught them. Minas Tirith and Helm's Deep are gone, but we parked across the street from the industrial plant where they'd been built. It turned out Isengard is a public park. The base of Saruman's tower had been a blue screen draped in front of a children's swing set. When Aragorn's horse finds him washed ashore on a Rohan river bank, they had to angle out the power lines and suburban rooftops.

Still, Middle-earth, aka New Zealand, is a fantastic if not necessarily fantastical place. We did cross the international date line to get there, but that time leap falls short of the Exotically Distant. You could argue Martians, Mongolians, and pirates provide enough fantasy travel, but it was Tolkien's magic that transformed my thirteen-year-old daughter. If you hold the compass point at the center of her Virginia bedroom, New Zealand is the same as Mongo, Mars, and Krypton. Flash, John, and Clark became extraordinary by leaving their homes and adventuring far far away too.

That means leaving your old identity behind. My daughter was haunted by a third grade assignment in which classmates wrote descriptions of her: Quiet, Quiet, Quiet, Quiet. Actually, most misspelled it, "Quite," but the effect was the same. A spell that bound her. Until my mild-mannered daughter stepped off a plane in Wellington, New Zealand. When she walked into a sea of identically uniformed Wellington Girls College students, not one of them knew her. She could be anyone. It terrified her, no safety net of friends between her and the abyss, but she stirred up a spell of her own: The Audacious American Girl. She crossed out the word "quiet" and wrote "loud."

She took to the part like a pro, a better method actor than Sir Ian or Viggo Mortensen. Nobody could contradict her. Her laughter drowned them out. Meanwhile, New Zealand's directorial superhero Peter Jackson was at it again with *The Hobbit* in full production. We toured the outskirts of his Wellington studio, glimpsed the giant green wall where he was conjuring a new multiverse of impossibilities. He even flew into a benefit event dressed as the retro-superhero the Rocketeer, before unmasking and posing with his *Hobbit* cast. It made the front page of the Wellington paper, which I showed my kids over breakfasts of crumpets and muesli. I ignored the casting call for Elven extras, something I still half-regret. My wife loved me in that Legolas costume the tour-bus driver made me pose in.

But what would happen when Supergirl rocketed back home? All those old friends and their loving shards of kryptonite, would they unmask her and destroy the enchantment? John Carter and Flash Gordon are only supermen while visiting their alien planets. Instead of returning to his English homeland, Captain Blood remained in his transformative West Indies to become deputy-governor of Jamaica. Buck Rogers's radioactive nap was a one-way trip too — he couldn't return to mundane Pennsylvania.

Fortunately, Middle-earth magic works in Virginia too. It is, after all, Tolkien's subtitle: "There and Back Again." Bilbo returns to the Shire with bags of dwarvish gold, but he carries his real fortune inside himself. Of course my quiet daughter returned an audaciously loud fourteen-year-old. That's the superhero formula, born from British colonialism in the nineteenth century and crystallized in American imperialism in the early twentieth. England took possession of New Zealand in 1788, and the still-British dominion fuels the Gray Seal's adventures by temporarily stripping his superhero girlfriend of her family fortunes and motivating their war on crime. New Zealand began as a colonial extension of Australia, also the unexplained source for superstrength in Edgar Wallace's 1929 *Iron Grip*. My daughter returned from Down Under with a different kind of strength, but the metaphorical magic is the same across the multiverse. Travelers return transformed.

The colonial periphery is a merged blur to a citizen of Metropolis, so the superhuman tourist trade has a whole globe to plunder. Edward Said termed it Orientalism: "'the Orient,' Africa, India, Australia are places dominated by Europe, although populated by different species." Everything outside the compass circle is an undifferentiated smear.

Spring-Heeled Jack is an early example. "Fortunes could be made in India by any who had fair connection, plenty of pluck, and plenty of industry," and so Jack's father "managed to shake the 'pagado tree' to a pretty fair extent." When Jack bounds back to his homeland, he reclaims his English titles with the aid of his Indian tutor's "magical boot," which "savoured strongly of sorcery." When Zarathustra came down from the mountain in 1883, that mountain was in Asia too, since Nietzsche's superman prophet was a German translation of Zoroaster, founder of Zoroastrianism in the Iranian plateau, c. 6000 B.C.E. Baghdad's Sinbad leaped the metaethnic divide when Sir Richard Burton published his English translation, *The Book of One Thousand and One Nights*, in 1885. Aladdin shipped over with him, even though neither appears in the original text. The Robin-aged protagonist of Kipling's 1901 *Kim* is no superhero, but his mentor is another Shazam prototype, "a guru from Tibet" who needs an English boy to achieve his life quest; Kim in turn treats him "precisely as he would have investigated a new building or a strange festival in Lahore city. The lama was his trove, and he purposed to take possession."

Before transforming himself into Buck Rogers and Flash Gordon, Buster Crabbe made the leap to Hollywood via Tarzan's Africa. I prefer that other loinclothed Olympic swimmer, Johnny Weissmuller. I watched his black-and-white Tarzan on my aunts' TV too. I'm thankful my aunts didn't keep the horrifically racist fight scenes I doodled, all those blowdart-blowing savages gunned down by white hunters. MGM rebooted Africa because they had extra footage from *Trader Horn*, the first big budget film shot on location. The production team returned from Kenya with scene after scene of inaudible dialogue, a starlet infected with malaria, and the suitcases of crew members devoured by crocodiles and trampled by rhinos. They also had miles of jungle shots, way more than could fit into a single movie. *Trader Horn* came and went in 1931, but to capitalize on location footage they'd already paid for, MGM rolled out *Tarzan the Ape Man* the following year. It was a cheap hit that spawned five low-budget sequels that returned Burroughs's superman and Africa to the pop culture spotlight.

After Frank Chandler toured "the hidden places of the Far East" to discover "the secrets the ancient magicians knew," *Chandu the Magician* began his adventures on West Coast radio in 1931, moved to Hollywood for his 1932 film debut, expanded his radio magic to East Coast airwaves in 1933, and returned to Hollywood for a 1934 sequel in the body of Bella Lugosi, the actor who'd originally played his own arch-nemesis. After Lee Falk's comic strip do-gooder Mandrake the Magician picked up his powers in Tibet in 1934 too, Falk's 1936 Phantom found his dual identity in the India knockoff nation of "Bengalla," which magically wanders to Africa in later tales. Even the 1936 Domino Lady "had been on a tour of the Far East when news came to her of her father's murder," the event that transformed her from a carefree tourist to an avenging vigilante.

In 1937, both the radio and pulp Shadows revealed their imperial travels, the first in the mystic Orient, the later among the Xinca Indians in the Yucatan — next door to Doc Savage's and Hugo Danner's lost Mayan cities of gold and superpowers that modern science had only begun to re-create. Hollywood's *The Shadow Strikes* struck in 1937 too, as did *Secret Agent X-9*, who was accompanied by his trusty Filipino valet. The Spider preferred a "turbaned Hindu" for his servant, and Mandrake a fez-wearing African prince. The Green Hornet's Kato was Japanese until World War II, when he converted to Korean and then Filipino via the magic of Orientalism. California's original colonial superhero returned in *Zorro Rides Again* in 1937 too, and Will Eisner's bikinied Tarzan knockoff, Sheena, Queen of the Jungle, debuted as well.

Superhero tourism was booming long before *Action Comics*, and it kept booming. When DC rival Fox Publishing wanted a Superman knockoff, Eisner sent his Wonderman to Tibet, where turbaned gurus were still handing out magic loot. Wonderman couldn't survive the kryptonite of DC's court injunction, so for *Wonder Comics* No. 2 Eisner swapped the colored tights and briefs for a tuxedo and amulet-crested turban. Yarko the Great was one of a dozen superhero magicians materializing in Golden Age comics. Nine of them shopped at the same turban store — though Zanzibar the Magician got confused and grabbed a Turk-ish fez instead — and three stuffed Asian servants into their suitcases too. The tights-and-brief crowd sent another half-dozen new supermen east, three more to Tibet, with Egypt as a solid runner-up. Bill Everett's Amazing Man has the power of the Tibetan Council of Seven and can turn into "green mist," which must annoy the hell out of the Green Lama, another American lugging home bags of Asian superpowers.

Stan Lee listened to Chandu as a kid, so his Drs. Strange, Doom, and Droom would earn their degrees in Tibet too, where Drs. Silence, Van Helsing, and Hesselius interned in chapter four. Roy Thomas and Gil Kane's Iron Fist kept 30s imperialism thriving at Marvel into the 70s. Next door at Charlton, Peter Morisi's Thunderbolt returned from his Tibetan adventures with the standard package of superpowers. Since Alan Moore's *Watchmen* are rebooted Charlton characters, his Ozyman-dias not only "traveled on, through China and Tibet, gathering mar-tial wisdom" but was "transformed" by "a ball of hashish I was given in Tibet." Even the twenty-first-century Batman, as retooled in Christopher Nolan's *Batman Begins*, hops over to the Himalayas to learn his chops from another monkish mentor (never mind ninjas are Japanese). And you'll never guess where director Josh Trank sends his teen superhuman for the closing shot of *Chronicle* or where the last surviving mutants hide out in *X-Men: Days of Future Past*.

The 1930s is an Orientalist pit superheroes may never climb out of. The judge who shut down Wonderman saw no difference between Krypton and Tibet. Substitute Mars or Mongo or the seventeenth-century Carib-bean or twenty-fifth-century Pennsylvania or prehistoric Middle-earth and still nothing changes. They're all imaginary Them-worlds far far out-side their readers' bedrooms. When his guru instructs him to "go forth into the world," Wonderman returns to the United States. Real Tibetans were embroiled in diplomatic disputes with China over national auton-omy as conflict between successive regents built internally. Wonderman didn't care. He was back home and brimming with Far Eastern radiation.

Most comic book readers would have preferred Asia to remain outside their compass circles, but Japan's 1937 invasion of China caused international shock with the Rape of Nanking. The sinking of an American gunboat the following month deepened the threat of the United States joining wars in two hemispheres. Those once fantastically distant worlds were encroaching on American smallvilles, and so Metropolis needed an all-new protector — the ultimate culmination of every superheroic trope rotating in the collective imagination.

That same January, *Detective Comics* editor Vin Sullivan contracted a thirteen-page feature from two of his regular freelancers. He had a new title to fill. The other nine stories in *Action Comics* No. 1 are standard adventure fare — a reporter, a magician, an ocean explorer, all between one and eleven pages. Siegel and Shuster had spent five years amassing rejections, but as war fears spiked, Sullivan selected the incongruent fantasy of an alien superman, not as filler, but for his lead feature and debut cover.

Shuster's gutters are choppy, his panels cut and pasted from strips sized for newspaper layout. Siegel's plotlines are choppy too — origin story, death row rescue, wife-beater, Lois nabbed by mobsters, a crooked senator, war in South America. The "S" on Superman's chest is a shifting squiggle, his logic equally squiggly — why break into the governor's home to convince him to phone the penitentiary seconds before a wrongful execution instead of breaking into the penitentiary first? Superman's boots change color, his cape keeps vanishing, and why exactly do the wife-beater's shirtsleeves turn to rags after his knife breaks on Superman's skin? But at least the final panel proves true:

And so begins the startling adventures of the most sensational strip character of all time: Superman!
A physical marvel,
A mental wonder,
Superman is destined to reshape the destiny of the World!

Last I looked *Action Comics* No. 1 listed for $2,800,000. That's mint condition. Nicholas Cage sold his copy for $2.1 million in 2011. David

Gonzales unearthed a copy from the wall of a Minnesota garage he was renovating in 2013. Superman had been insulated for seventy-five years. "I brought my wife's auntie to see the house and she got excited, she said, 'oh, look, this is worth money.' I said, 'I know, don't touch it, don't touch it,' and she kept grabbing it and grabbing it. 'Just leave it alone!' Little pieces kept breaking off." That action downgraded his *Action* from a 3 to a 3.5 on an appraiser's 10-point scale, but Gonzales still pulled in $175,000 at auction. The dilapidated house had only gone for $10,100.

"Folks that dig up our civilization are going to learn more about us from our comic strips than by looking at ruins," said journalist Robert Quillen's comic strip alter ego Aunt Het. *Action Comics* No. 1 is one of our greatest ruins, a pulp-paper Sphinx rising from the quicksand of so many swirling hourglasses, its superman an artificial diamond pressed from centuries of revolution and evolution, of science fiction and fictional science, of righteous vigilantes and wrongful heroes, of racist mysticism and demonic do-goodery, of erotic celibacy and monkish striptease, of godly monsters and monstrous godmen, of borders crossed and crisscrossed by heroes and nations and genres, a still-spinning array of cowboys and aliens and alchemists and pirates and ghosts and robots and sorcerers, of every thrilling tale told since the genesis of cave paint and Big Bang mythologies.

And now you're ready to read it.

Sal Buscema and Klaus Janson, *The Defenders*, No. 15, 1974. ©MARVEL

MAGNETO'S GIFTSHOP

I started researching for this book in 1974. I was eight. I was sitting on my aunts' dining room floor with *The Defenders* No. 15, the first comic book I remember reading. It cost twenty cents. That copy isn't in my attic in a cardboard liquor box with the submint remains of my childhood, so I'm flipping pages of *Essential Defenders* Vol. 2 instead. My favorite panel features Magneto sitting in front of a stack of books. It may be the only image of a supervillain in nerdy repose. After escaping his prison at the Earth's core, Magneto explains:

> I reached what I thought was the surface — but swiftly reasoned was instead a long lost cavern — a cavern containing the ruptured remnants of a civilization that was ancient when homo sapiens were still living under rocks!... I found libraries — books written in a language that was surely never of this earth! For a time, I stayed in the cavern — deciphering the language — studying the books — until I discovered a secret so spectacular, I could not bear to keep it only to myself!

Magneto is soon seizing control of the world with the aid of his Ultimate Mutant, who instead shrinks him down to a crying infant at the end of the two-issue arc. The Ultimate Mutant also erases the memory of the events from the minds of men! Which sort of explains why no one goes looking for that secret library.

I started digging for it in 2008, after Shreya Durvasula asked me to create a superheroes course for her honors group. I discovered that other pop-culture archaeologists had been excavating for years ahead of me. Each tier of my descent unearthed more of their scholarship, until their names grew talismanic: Gary Hoppenstand, Richard Reynolds, Peter Coogan, Jess Nevins, Danny Fingeroth, Les Daniels, Will Murray. The book in Magneto's hands is propped on a stack of other books. Everything in this book is propped on other books too.

Superhero research isn't like the Chunnel connecting England and France. There are a thousand ways to access Magneto's cavern, some more idiosyncratic than others. I didn't break through until I noticed a resemblance between superheroes and the KKK — and then the whole floor collapsed and I was sprawling in the ruptured ruins of American culture. I kept reading. The 1920s Klan wasn't fighting Reconstruction — its brand of vigilantism was pro-eugenics — and eugenics, that was an extension of the scientific racism of colonialism — and fascism rose from the same impulses, with superheroes swirling in the same primordial gunk!

I started writing and, more slowly, publishing a sequence of essays tracing the superhero character type through the cultural evolution of colonialism, eugenics, the KKK, fascism, and gender politics. *Journal of Graphic Novels and Comics* published "The Ku Klux Klan and the Birth of the Superhero" (4.2. 2013); *PS: Political Science & Politics* published "The Imperial Superhero" (47.1. 2014); the *Journal of American Culture* published "The Well-born Superhero" (37.2. 2014); *ImageTexT* published "Zombies vs. Superheroes: *The Walking Dead* Resurrection of *The Fantastic Four* Gender Formulas" (7.4. Winter 2015); and "The Rise and Fall of Fascist Superpowers" is still winding its way through revise-and-resubmits. Together they are my Chunnel, my way of widening the work of those digging before me.

And now I've dragged you down here too. Behold my bookshelves! It's not everything. In fact, what follows is a kind of Works Not Cited, since works already named (Jim Holt's *Why Does the World Exist?* on the first page of chapter one, for instance) aren't necessarily repeated here (you can probably alphabetize "Holt, Jim" yourself). But I want to acknowledge the scholarly sources I used like shovels on the way down. Many of these names have since transformed into actual people, ones I chat with on COMIXSCHOLARS list-serve or in Noah Berlatsky's HoodedUtilitarian. com comment sections. Peter Coogan is now Pete, a name often swimming in my email inbox. He and Noah helped this manuscript evolve from the primordial blog goo that attracted the attention of my editor, Elisabeth Chretien. Her name does not appear below, but she used her many mutant powers to help shape-shift these pages (she also dressed as Mystique last Halloween). Lesley Wheeler has no superhero scholarship I can cite either, but she's seen me through each step of creation, critiquing everything from the first harebrained draft of that KKK essay to the thorniest midtransformations of this manuscript.

The tour of superhero prehistory is now officially over. You're free to browse the gift shop however you like, though I suggest you follow Magneto's lead and settle in for a good long stay. There are so many more spectacular secrets yet to be found.

BIBLIOGRAPHY

Amann, Peter H. "Vigilante Fascism: The Black Legion as an American Hybrid." *Comparative Studies in Society and History* 25.3 (July 1983): 490-524.

Anderson, Lars. *Domino Lady: The Complete Collection.* Somerset, N.J.: Vanguard, 2004.

Andrae, Thomas. "From Menace to Messiah: The History and Historicity of Superman." In *American Media and Mass Culture: Left Perspectives,* ed. Donald Lazere. Berkeley: U of California P, 1987.

"Are Comics Fascist?" *Time,* 22 October 1945. TIME.com.

Ashcroft, Bill. *Post-Colonial Transformation.* London: Routledge, 2001.

Babich, Babette. "Becoming and Purification: Empedocles, Zarathustra's Übermensch, and Lucian's Tyrant." *Articles and Chapters in Academic Book Collections.* Paper 61.

Benton, Mike. *Superhero Comics of the Golden Age: The Illustrated History.* Dallas: Taylor, 1992.

———. *Superhero Comics of the Silver Age: The Illustrated History.* Dallas: Taylor, 1991.

Berglund, Jeff. "Write, Right, White, Rite: Literacy, Imperialism, Race, and Cannibalism in Edgar Rice Burroughs' Tarzan of the Apes." *Studies in American Fiction* 27.1 (Spring 1999): 53-76.

Berlatsky, Eric. "Between Supermen: Homosociality, Misogyny, and Triangular Desire in the Earliest Superman Stories." March 2013. Comicsforum.org.

Bernède, Arthur, and Louis Feuillade. *Judex.* Trans. and adapted by Rick Lai. Tarzana, Calif.: Black Coat, 2012.

Berst, Charles A. "New Theatres for Old." In *The Cambridge Companion to George Bernard Shaw.* Cambridge: Cambridge UP, 1998.

Black, Edwin. *War against the Weak: Eugenics and America's Campaign to Create a Master Race.* New York: Four Wall Eight Windows, 2003.

Bloom, Harold. Introduction. In *George Bernard Shaw's Man and Superman.* New York: Chelsea, 1987.

———, ed. *George Bernard Shaw: New Edition.* New York: Bloom's Literary Criticism, 2011.

Blythe, Hal, and Charlie Sweet. "Superhero: The Six Step Progression." In *The Hero in Transition*. Bowling Green, Ohio: Popular, 1983.

Boehmer, Elleke. *Colonial and Postcolonial Literature: Migrant Metaphors*. 2nd ed. Oxford: Oxford UP, 2005.

Bolton, Andrew. *Superheroes: Fashion and Fantasy*. New Haven, Conn.: Yale UP, 2010.

Brown, Jeffrey A. *Black Superheroes, Milestone Comics, and Their Fans*. Jackson: UP of Mississippi, 2001.

Brown, Slater. "The Coming of Superman." *New Republic*, 2 September 1940, 301.

Buchanan, Allen. *Better Than Human: The Promise and Perils of Enhancing Ourselves*. Oxford: Oxford UP, 2011.

Burrage, Alfred S. *Spring-Heel'd Jack: The Terror of London. The Boy's Standard*. 18 July–August 1885. Project Gutenberg Australia.

Cheyfitz, Eric. *The Poetics of Imperialism: Translation and Colonization from The Tempest to Tarzan*. New York: Oxford UP, 1991.

Coogan, Peter. *Superhero: The Secret Origin of a Genre*. Austin, Tex.: Monkey Brain, 2006.

Coombes, Annie E., and Avtar Brah. "Introduction: The Conundrum of 'Mixing.'" In *Hybridity and Its Discontents: Politics, Science, Culture*. London: Routledge, 2000.

Cronin, Brian. "The Superhero Trademark FAQ." 28 March 2006. comicbookresources.com.

Cuddy, Lois A., and Claire M. Roche. *Evolution and Eugenics in American Literature and Culture, 1880-1940: Essays on Ideological Conflict and Complexity*. Lewisburg, Pa.: Bucknell UP, 2003.

Curtis, S. R. Preface. In *The Mark of Zorro*. New York: Tor, 1998.

Daniels, Les. *Marvel: Five Fabulous Decades of the World's Greatest Comics*. New York: Harry N. Abrams, 1991.

———. *Superman: The Complete History, The Life and Times of the Man of Steel*. San Francisco: Chronicle, 1998.

DeGraw, Sharon. *The Subject of Race in American Science Fiction*. New York: Routledge, 2007.

De Haven, Tom. *Our Hero: Superman on Earth*. New Haven, Conn.: Yale UP, 2010.

Dent, Lester. *The Man of Bronze. Doc Savage* 14. San Antonio, Tex.: Sanctum Productions, 2008.

Ditko, Steve. "Steve Ditko Explains His Creation Mr. A." 19 December 2013. poetv.com.

Dixon, Thomas, Jr. *The Clansman: An Historical Romance of the Ku Klux Klan.* 1905. Sioux Falls, SD: NuVision Publishing, 2005.

———. *The Leopard's Spots: A Romance of the White Man's Burden.* New York: Doubleday, 1902.

Doyle, Arthur Conan. *The Crime of the Congo.* New York: Doubleday, 1909.

Dubose, Mike S. "Holding Out for a Hero: Reaganism, Comic Book Vigilantes, and Captain America." *Journal of Popular Culture* 40.6 (2007): 915-935.

Eaton, Lance. "A Superhero for the Times: Superman's Fight against Oppression and Injustice in the 1930s." In *Ages of Heroes, Eras of Men.* Newcastle upon Tyne: Cambridge Scholars, 2013.

Eco, Umberto. "The Myth of Superman." In *Arguing Comics: Literary Masters on a Popular Medium*, ed. Jeet Heer and Kent Worcester. Jackson: UP of Mississippi, 2004.

Egoff, Sheila. "Precepts, Pleasures, and Portents: Changing Emphases in Children's Literature." In *Only Connect: Readings on Children's Literature.* Toronto: Oxford UP, 1980.

Eperjesi, John R. *The Imperialist Imaginary: Visions of Asia and the Pacific in American Culture.* Hanover, N.H.: Dartmouth CP, 2005.

"Everybody Has Telepathic Power, Dr. Carrel Says after Research." *New York Times*, 18 September 1935. ProQuest Historical Newspapers *The New York Times* (1881-2005).

Fanon, Frantz. *The Wretched of the Earth.* Trans. Constance Farrington. New York: Grove, 1963.

Feiffer, Jules. *The Great Comic Book Heroes.* 1965. Reprint, Seattle: Fantagraphics, 2003.

Fiedler, Leslie A. *Love and Death in the American Novel.* 1960. N.p.: Dalkey Archive, 2003.

Fingeroth, Danny. *Disguised as Clark Kent: Jews, Comics and the Creation of the Superhero.* New York: Continuum, 2007.

———. *Superman on the Couch: What Superheroes Really Tell Us about Ourselves and Our Society.* New York: Continuum, 2004.

Gabilliet, Jean-Paul. *Of Comics and Men: A Cultural History of American Comic Books.* Jackson: UP of Mississippi, 2009.

Galton, Francis. "Eugenics: Its Definition, Scope, and Aims." *American Journal of Sociology* 10.1 (July 1904). Galton.org.

Gibson, Walter B., and Edward Hale Bierstadt. "The Death House Rescue." *The Shadow.* Mutual Broadcasting System. 26 September 1937.

Gillispie, Michele K., and Randal L. Hall. Introduction. In *Thomas Dixon Jr. and the Birth of Modern America.* Baton Rouge: Louisiana State UP, 2006.

Glenn, Paul F. "Nietzsche's Napoleon: The Higher Man as Political Actor." *Review of Politics* 63.1 (Winter 2001): 129-158.

Graeme, Bruce. *Blackshirt*. London: T. Fisher Unwin, 1925.

Grant, Donald L. *The Way It Was in the South: The Black Experience in Georgia*. Athens: U of Georgia P, 2001.

Grant, Robert, and Joseph Katz. *Greatest Trials of the Twenties: The Watershed Decade in America's Courtrooms*. Rockville Centre, N.Y.: Sarpedon, 1998.

The Great Spy System, or, Nick Carter's Promise to the President. New Nick Carter Weekly, No. 563. New York: Street and Smith, 12 October 1907. Dime Novels and Penny Dreadfuls.

Green, Martin. *The Great American Adventure*. Boston: Beacon, 1984.

Hack, Brian. "Weakness Is a Crime: Captain America and the Eugenic Ideal in Early Twentieth Century America." In *Captain America and the Struggle of the Superhero*, Jefferson, N.C.: McFarland, 2009.

Hadju, David. *The Ten-Cent Plague: The Great Comic-Book Scare and How It Changed America*. New York: Farrar, Straus and Giroux, 2008.

Hall, Stuart. "Cultural Identity and Diaspora." In *Identity: Community, Culture, Difference*, ed. Jonathan Rutherford. London: Lawrence & Wishhard, 1990.

Hobsbawm, Eric. *Bandits*. 1969. Reprint, New York: Pantheon, 1981.

Hoffman, Hank. "Take That Klan Man." *New Haven Advocate*, 20 February 1997. The Museum of Black Superheroes.

Hoppenstand, Gary. Introduction. In Baroness Orczy, *The Scarlet Pimpernel*. New York: Signet, 2000.

———. "Introduction: The Missing Detective." In *The Dime Novel Detective*. Bowling Green, Ohio: Popular, 1982.

———. "Pulp Vigilante Heroes, the Moral Majority and the Apocalypse." In *The Hero in Transition*. Bowling Green, Ohio: Popular, 1983.

Hughes, Bob. Introduction. In *Superman in the Forties*. New York: DC, 2005.

Hunter, George William. *A Civic Biology Presented in Problems*. New York: American Book, 1914.

Jang, Keum-Hee. "Shaw and Galtonian Eugenics in Victorian Britain: Breeding Superman in Bernard Shaw's *Man and Superman*." *Journal of Modern British and American Drama* 20.3 (December 2007): 225-250.

"Jerry Siegel Attacks!" *Das schwarze Korps*. 25 April 1940. Trans. Randall Bytwerk. German Propaganda Archive. 30 April 2010.

Jones, Gerard. *Men of Tomorrow: Geeks, Gangsters and the Birth of the Superhero*. New York: Basic, 2004.

Joshi, S. T. Introduction. In *The Complete John Silence Stories*. Mineola, N.Y.: Dover, 1997.

Kaempffert, Waldemare. " "Genetic Principles." *New York Times*, 25 September 1932. ProQuest Historical Newspapers *The New York Times* (1881-2005).

———. "The Superman: Eugenics Sifted." *New York Times*, 27 May 1928. ProQuest Historical Newspapers *The New York Times* (1881-2005).

Kaplan, Arie. *From Krakow to Krypton: Jews and Comic Books*. Philadelphia: Jewish Publication Society of America, 2008.

Kaufman, Scott. "Noam Chomsky: Zombies Are the New Indians and Slaves in White America's Collective Nightmare." 14 February 2014. rawstory.com.

Keena, Justin. "Manfred and Overman: A Critical Comparison." Academia.edu.

Kerslake, Patricia. *Science Fiction and Empire*. Liverpool: Liverpool UP, 2007.

Kevles, Daniel J. *In the Name of Eugenics: Genetics and the Uses of Human Heredity*. Berkeley: U of California P, 1985.

Klock, Geoff. *How to Read Superhero Comics and Why*. New York: Continuum, 2002.

Kripal, Jeffrey J. *Mutants and Mystics: Science Fiction, Superhero Comics, and the Paranormal*. Chicago: U of Chicago P, 2011.

Kutzer, M. Daphne. *Empire's Children: Empire and Imperialism in Classic British Children's Books*. New York: Garland, 2000.

Legman, Gershon. From *Love and Death: A Study in Censorship*. 1949. In *Arguing Comics: Literary Masters on a Popular Medium*, ed. Jet Heer and Kent Worcester. Jackson: UP of Mississippi, 2004.

Lie, Nadia. "Free Trade in Images? Zorro as Cultural Signifier in the Contemporary Global/Local System." *Nepantla: Views from South* 2.3 (2001): 489-508.

Loomba, Ania. *Colonialism/Postcolonialism*. 2nd ed. London: Routledge, 2005.

Lott, Eric. "White Like Me: Racial Cross-Dressing and the Construction of America Whiteness." In *Cultures of United States Imperialism*, ed. Amy Kaplan and Donald E. Pease. Durham, N.C.: Duke UP, 1993.

Lupoff, Richard A. *Master of Adventure: The Worlds of Edgar Rice Burroughs*. Lincoln: U of Nebraska P, 2005.

Markstein, Donald D. *Don Markstein's Toonopedia*. August 2010. toonopedia .com. 20

Marston, William Moulton. "Why 100,000,000 Americans Read Comics." *American Scholar* 13.1 (Winter 1934-1944): 34-43.

Marvel Firsts: The 1960s. New York: Marvel Worldwide, 2011.

McCann, Sean. "Constructing Race Williams: The Klan and the Making of Hard-Boiled Crime Fiction." *American Quarterly* 49.4 (December 1997): 677-716.

McCloud, Scott. *Understanding Comics: The Invisible Art*. New York: Kitchen Sink, 1994.

McLaughlin, Jeff. *Stan Lee: Conversations*. Jackson: UP of Mississippi, 2007.

McLuhan, Marshall. From *The Mechanical Bride: Folklore of Industrial Man*. 1951. In *Arguing Comics: Literary Masters on a Popular Medium*, ed. Jet Heer and Kent Worcester. Jackson: UP of Mississippi, 2004.

Mein, Eric. "A Princess of Where? Burroughs's Imaginary Lack of Place." *West Virginia University Philological Papers* 53 (2006): 42-47.

Memmi, Albert. *The Colonizer and the Colonized*. 1957. Reprint, Boston: Beacon Press, 1991.

Mendel, Gregor. "Experiments on Plant Hybridization." 1865. Trans. William Bateson and Roger Blumberg. Electronic Scholarly Publishing Project, 1996.

Mills, Carl H. "Shaw's Superman: A Re-examination." In *Critical Essays on George Bernard Shaw*. New York: Macmillan, 1991.

Morlock, Frank. "France's Greatest Adventure Writer Dramatizes the Life of Napoleon — The Long Hot Summer of 1830." *Bulletin of the Napoleonic Society of America* 64 (Summer 1999).

"The Murder That Brought Down the Black Legion." *Detroit News*, 5 August 1997.

Murray, Will. "Intermission." *Doc Savage*. 14. San Antonio, Tex.: Sanctum Productions, 2008.

———. "The Shadowy Origins of Batman." *The Shadow*. 9. San Antonio, Tex.: Nostalgia Ventures, 2007.

Nevins, Jess. *Pulp and Adventure Heroes of the Pre-War Years*. reocities.com.

———. "Spring-Heeled Jack." In *Encyclopedia of Fantastic Victoriana*. Austin, Tex.: Monkey Brains, 2005.

Newton, Michael, and Judy Ann Newton. *The Ku Klux Klan: An Encyclopedia*. New York: Garland, 1991.

Nick Carter, Detective: The Solution of a Remarkable Case. Nick Carter Detective Library, No. 1. New York: Smith and Street, n.d.

Nordau, Max Simon. *Degeneration*. New York: Appleton, 1895.

North, Sterling. "The Antidote to Comics." *National Parent Teacher Magazine* (March 1941): 16-17.

Nyberg, Amy Kiste. *Seal of Approval: The History of the Comics Code*. Jackson: UP of Mississippi, 1998.

O'Herir, Andrew. "The Dark Knight Rises: Christopher Nolan's Evil Masterpiece." 18 July 2012. Salon.com.

Okudo, Akiyo Ito. "'A Nation Is Born': Thomas Dixon's Vision of White Nationhood and His Northern Supporters." *Journal of American Culture* 32.3 (September 2009): 214-231.

Page, Norvell. *The Spider: Robot Titans of Gotham*. Riverdale, N.Y.: Baen, 2007.

Palmer-Mehta, Valerie, and Kellie Hay. "A Superhero for Gays?: Gay Masculinity and Green Lantern." *Journal of American Culture* 28.4 (December 2005): 390-404.

Payne, Britton. "Superman v. Wonderman: Judge Hand's Side-By-Side Comparison for Superhero Infringement." brittonpayne.com/Marvel/Super manWonderman.

Pitkethly, Clare. "Straddling a Boundary: The Superhero and the Incorporation of Difference." In *What Is a Superhero?*, ed. Robin S. Rosenberg and Peter Coogan. Oxford: Oxford UP, 2013.

Proctor, William. "Regeneration and Rebirth: Anatomy of the Franchise Reboot." *Scope: An Online Journal of Film and Television Studies* 22 (February 2012).

Queenan, Joe. "Man of Steel: Does Hollywood Need Saving from Superheroes?" 11 June 2013. TheGuardian.com.

Raphael, Jordan, and Tom Spurgeon. *Stan Lee and the Rise and Fall of the American Comic Book*. Chicago: Chicago Review, 2003.

Reichstein, Andreas. "Batman — An American Mr. Hyde?" *Amerikastudien/ American Studies* 43.2 (1998): 329-350.

Reynolds, Richard. *Super Heroes: A Modern Mythology*. Jackson: UP of Mississippi, 1992.

Richard, Olive. "Don't Laugh at the Comics." *Family Circle*, 25 October 1940, 10–11, 22.

Rieder, John, *Colonialism and the Emergence of Science Fiction*. Middletown, Conn.: Wesleyan UP, 2008.

Reitz, Caroline. *Detecting the Nation: Fictions of Detection and the Imperial Venture*. Columbus: Ohio State UP, 2004.

Robbins, Trina. *The Great Women Superheroes*. Northampton, Mass.: Kitchen Sink, 1996.

Robinson, Jerry. Foreword. *The Shadow*. 9. Encinitas, Calif.: Nostalgia Ventures, 2007.

Rohmer, Sax. *The Mystery of Fu-Manchu*. 1913. Project Gutenberg.

Rowe, John Carlos. *Literary Culture and U.S. Imperialism*. Oxford: Oxford UP, 2000.

Royal, Derek Parker. "Foreword; Or Reading within the Gutter." In *Multicultural Comics*, ed. Frederick Luis Aldamas. Austin: U of Texas P, 2010.

Sadowski, Greg, ed. *Supermen! The First Wave of Comic Book Heroes 1936-1941*. Seattle: Fantagraphics, 2009.

Said, Edward W. *Culture and Imperialism*. New York: Knopf, 1993.

———. *Orientalism*. New York: Pantheon, 1978.

Saunders, Ben. *Do the Gods Wear Capes?* London: Bloomsbury, 2011.

Schell, Jonathan. "Invitation to a Degraded World." *Final Edition* 1.1 (2004): 4-9.

See, Fred G. "'Writing So as Not to Die': Edgar Rice Burroughs and the West beyond the West." *MELUS* 11.4 (Winter 1984): 59-72.

Shimeld, Thomas J. *Walter B. Gibson and the Shadow*. Jefferson, N.C.: McFarland, 2005.

Siegel, Jerry. "The Reign of the Superman." *Science Fiction: The Advance Guard of Civilization* 1.1 (January 1933): 4-14.

———. "The Victimization of Superman's Originators, Jerry Siegel and Joe Shuster." October 1975. Michael Catron's Home Page.

Siegel, Jerry, and Joe Shuster. "'Jerry and I Did a Comic Book Together. . .': Jerry Siegel and Joe Shuster Interviewed." *Nemo: The Classic Comics Library* 2 (August 1983). ohdannyboy.blogspot.com.

Silverman, Kenneth. *Houdini!!! The Career of Ehrich Weiss*. New York: Harper, 1996.

Simmers, George. "Is Blackshirt a Fascist?" 23 June 2008. Great War Fiction.

Singer, Marc. "'Black Skins' and White Masks: Comic Books and the Secret of Race." *African American Review* 36.1 (Spring 2002): 107-119.

Slide, Anthony. *American Racist: The Life and Films of Thomas Dixon*. Lexington: UP of Kentucky, 2004.

Smith, Jacob. "A Distinguished Burglar: The Cinematic Life of a Criminal Social Type." *Journal of Film and Video* 63.4 (Winter 2011): 35-43.

Southard, R. "Parents Must Control the Comics." *Saint Anthony Messenger: A National Catholic Family Magazine* (May 1944): 3-5.

Springhall, John. "Disseminating Impure Literature: The 'Penny Dreadful' Publishing Business since 1860." *Economic History Review* 47.3 (August 1994): 567-584.

Stilson, Charles B. *Polaris of the Snows: The Complete Trilogy*. Boston: Altus, 2003.

Stokes, Melvyn. *D. W. Griffith's The Birth of a Nation: A History of the Most Controversial Motion Picture of All Time*. Oxford: Oxford UP, 2008.

Stringer, Arthur. "The Cave of Despair." *The Iron Claw*. Episode XIX. *Atlanta Constitution Sunday Magazine*, 2 July 1916.

———. "The Triumph of the Laughing Mask." *The Iron Claw*. Episode XX. *Atlanta Constitution Sunday Magazine*, 9 July 1916.

Taliaferro, John. *Tarzan Forever: The Life of Edgar Rice Burroughs, Creator of Tarzan*. New York: Scribner, 1999.

Thomas-Lester, Avis. "A Senate Apology for History on Lynching." *Washington Post*, 14 June 2005.

Thorndike, Russell. *Doctor Syn: A Tale of the Romney Marsh*. New York: Doubleday, 1915.

Trexler, Jeff. "Superman's Hidden History: The Other 'First' Artist." 20 August 2006. Newsarama.com.

Tucker, Richard K. *The Dragon and the Cross: The Rise and Fall of the Ku Klux Klan in Middle America*. Hamden, Conn.: Archon, 1991.

Turner, Frederick Jackson. *The Frontier in American History*. 1920. Reprint, New York: Holt, 1958.

Vanardy, Varick. *Alias "The Night Wind."* N.p.: Borgo, 2007.

Vlamos, James Frank. "The Sad Case of the Funnies." *American Mercury* (April 1941): 411-416.

Waid, Mark. "The Real Truth about Superman: And the Rest of Us, Too." In *Superheroes and Philosophy: Truth, Justice, and the Socratic Way*. Chicago: Open Court, 2005.

Walker, Frances Amasa. "Restriction of Immigration." *Atlantic Magazine*, June 1896. TheAtlantic.com.

Walker, Jesse. "Hooded Progressivism: The Secret Reformist History of the Ku Klux Klan." 2 December 2005. reason.com.

Wallace, Jo-Ann. "De-scribing the Water Babies: 'The Child' in Post-colonial Theory." In *De-scribing Empire: Post-colonialism and Textuality*, ed. Chris Tiffin and Alan Lawson. London: Routledge, 1994.

Weiner, Robert. "'Okay, Axis, Here We Come!': Captain America and Superhero Teams from World War II and the Cold War." In *The Gospel According to Superheroes: Religion and Popular Culture*. New York: Peter Lang, 2005.

Weinstein, Simcha. *Up, Up and Oy Vey: How Jewish History, Culture, and Values Shaped the Comic Book Superhero*. Baltimore: Leviathan, 2006.

Wertham, Frederic. *Seduction of the Innocent*. New York: Rinehart, 1954.

White, G. Edward. *Justice Oliver Wendell Holmes: Law and the Inner Self*. Oxford: Oxford UP, 1993.

"The White Legion." *The Shadow*. 20 March 1938. Pulp Sunday.

Williamson, Joel. *Crucible of Race: Black-White Relations in the American South since Emancipation*. New York: Oxford UP, 1984.

Wolff, Tamsen. *Mendel's Theatre: Heredity, Eugenics, and Early Twentieth-Century American Drama*. Palgrave Studies in Theatre and Performance History. New York: Palgrave Macmillan, 2009.

Wright, Bradford W. *Comic Book Nation: The Transformation of Youth Culture in America*. Baltimore: Johns Hopkins UP, 2001.

Young, Robert J. C. *Colonial Desire: Hybridity in Theory, Culture and Race*. London: Routledge, 1995.

———. *Postcolonialism*. Oxford: Blackwell, 2001.

INDEX